CW01418361

Son of a Whore
A memoir

Herman Lategan

PENGUIN BOOKS

Son of a Whore

Published by Penguin Books
an imprint of Penguin Random House (Pty) Ltd
Company Reg. No. 1953/000441/07
The Estuaries No. 4, Oxbow Crescent, Century Avenue, Century City, Cape Town, 7441
www.penguinrandomhouse.co.za

Penguin
Random House
South Africa

First published 2023
Reprinted in 2023

3 5 7 9 10 8 6 4 2

Publication © Penguin Books 2023
Text © Herman Lategan 2023

Cover image © Herman Lategan

All rights reserved. No part of this publication may be reproduced,
stored in a retrieval system or transmitted, in any form or by any means,
electronic, mechanical, photocopying, recording or otherwise,
without the prior written permission of the copyright owners.

RESPECT CREATORS
SAY NO TO ILLEGAL COPYING

Making illegal copies of this publication, distributing them unlawfully
or sharing them on social media without the written permission of
the publisher may lead to civil claims or criminal complaints.

Protect the communities who are sustained by creativity.

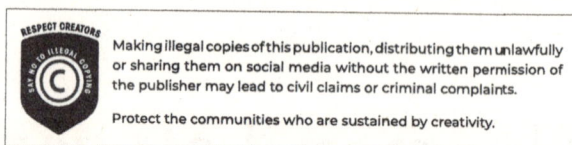

PUBLISHER: Marlene Fryer
MANAGING EDITOR: Ronel Richter-Herbert
PROOFREADER: Bronwen Maynier
COVER DESIGN: Sean Robertson
TEXT DESIGN: Ryan Africa
TYPESETTER: Monique van den Berg

Set in 11.5 pt on 15 pt Minion Pro

Printed by **novus print**, a division of Novus Holdings

MIX
Paper | Supporting
responsible forestry
FSC
www.fsc.org   FSC® C022948

ISBN 978 1 77639 124 0 (print)
ISBN 978 1 77639 125 7 (ePub)

To everybody, especially Graham Sonnenberg

Foreword

I didn't write this memoir in a linear mode, nor with a literary consciousness, but rather as a fireside chat around free-floating memories. Forensically, not all dates may be correct, but the facts are as I remember them. The names of people I mention are of those who've had an impact on my life, or who crossed my path, not an attempt at name-dropping. If there's a motive for this book, it's for readers to confront their vulnerabilities and tell their own untold stories. In South Africa, the potential harvest is rich.

'There are two cast-iron certainties in life:
You are born, and you die. The rest is improvisation.'
– **Marthinus Basson**

1

ONE OF MY FIRST MEMORIES is of my mother, Maria, cradling a dead white cat against her chest. She was crying. This cat, I learnt later, had been a present for me. We were supposed to grow up together. Something small, cute and alive, with which I could play.

A dog had bitten the cat. I was subjected to loss early in my life, something I would have to get used to. Surviving became a way of living. The white cat died, but in its place, my shadow, the black dog, was born. The one that follows me the whole time and has become my real, unloved companion.

I was conceived on a hot night in a boarding house in Kloof Street, Cape Town. It was February 1964, to be precise. The huge old place was called ABAC Apartments. Years later, I heard that it had also doubled as a bordello. It was at the bottom of the street, right opposite the Long Street Baths and the historic St Martini Evangelical Lutheran Church.

Oh, the sin, because this specific couple, who had met that night, was unmarried. It might have been the swinging sixties, but in South Africa, the morally two-faced and fundamentalist Dutch Reformed Church were the de facto leaders of the country.

The night was wild and rough. It was warm. Rumpy-pumpy was on the menu – and why not? My mother saw a handsome, olive-skinned man with an open face and black hair in a leather jacket. I know all these details because she often told them to me.

'His name is Sam Korck,' someone whispered in her ear.

'Is he Irish?' my mom asked. 'Mad about them: they're difficult, moody, wild, they drink too much, they're good writers.'

He was wearing tight jeans with a prominent knob. His face had a fuck-you expression. A good-looking man is everybody's man, goes the adage, but no, no, Maria didn't want to listen. The two drifted towards each other, chatted, smooched, soon found a room, and then made whoopie. Nine months later, on the fourth of November 1964, I popped out. They were both so young, only twenty-one. Your prefrontal cortex only stops developing at twenty-five.

I was born in Oranjezicht and delivered by an old-school doctor from Sea Point, Dr John Sonnenberg. As synchronicity would have it, this man would play a vital role later in my life.

At that time, my dad made a duck for it. Gone. Poof. Although they were great in the sack together, that was about it. They fought constantly. He drank and partied, lived fast, loved women. Like so many dads in South Africa, he just disappeared. My mom told me that before he left, she hit him over the head with a frying pan. He'd run out, jumped on his motorbike and sped off.

I don't know if she ever found out if he was indeed Irish. Later, when I looked at photographs of him, he looked like a person of colour. Not that I cared.

Years later, when someone told me that ABAC Apartments was a brothel, a refuge for hookers, scarlet women, I wondered: Could it be? Could it be that my mom, a naive eighteen-year-old girl from a farm in Namaqualand, had come to the big city and found it overwhelming?

When she stepped off that Bitterfontein train onto the platform at Cape Town Station, who fetched her? What did she do? She was a mere teenager, really, one who wanted to put the dusty platteland behind her. She had come for the twinkly lights and a fresh beginning, turning her back on the suffocating dust of a small life. But she might have found this new life hell. Who knows if customers paid her for sex? She never told me. It never crossed my mind. I do, however, have an inkling.

2

S OME OF MY EARLIEST MEMORIES are of a boarding house in Warren Street, Tamboerskloof. Specifically, the people. Footloose, unattached, all ages. Loners, strangers from all over the country, and from Britain. They all lived under the same roof and had to get to know one another. It was an old, double-storey house with a large lounge area. The kitchen was communal and was a jolly gathering space where everybody could meet, cook, drink wine and be merry.

As a baby, I remember clearly how a tall blonde woman with a beehive hairstyle, fashionable in those days, held onto a green Formica table, crying. Deep, out of her stomach. Other women stood around her, comforting her. I felt something sad was taking place. If someone was maudlin, I could feel it and would cry with them. They would pick me up, dry my tears and kiss my cheeks.

I felt loved by this motley bunch of oddballs; indeed, a village raised me. During the day, when my mom went to work, a few retired women looked after me. They loved it, and so did I. The only couple was Uncle Dougie and Aunty Esmé. They were frightfully kômmin, but in an endearing sort of way. Warmth and unpretentiousness oozed from them. I later found out they were Cockneys.

As I grew older, they reminded me of those suburban characters portrayed in black-and-white movies in the genre of British kitchen-sink dramas. It didn't matter that they weren't posh, I felt safe with them. Aunty Esmé reeked of rose water and rouge. She had large bosoms, which I would be pressed against while she sang me a lullaby. Uncle Dougie smelt of pipe tobacco.

For some or other reason, my mom and Aunty Esmé often had screaming matches. Afterwards, they would hug each other, cry and laugh, and all would be forgotten. They would go and sit down, pour tea and smoke cigarettes.

I realised at an early age that my mother was tempestuous. One moment she would be full of jokes and wisecracks, the next she would widen her eyes and throw a plate of food against the wall.

Oh, it was exciting to be surrounded by this cast of drama queens; never a dull moment, especially with my mother around.

Strangely enough, my first word was 'darra'. Ironic, as he wasn't even there.

3

MY CONSCIOUSNESS AND UNDERSTANDING OF the world gradually evolved. I remember warm days and the sound of crickets at night. Trips on those old busses, like the ones in London, where you embarked at the back and had to hold on to a pole. A conductor would clip your ticket.

One day, before I could really string a coherent sentence together, I was lying in my cot. A man came into the room. I was on my own. He opened my mother's wardrobe and stole her clothes; sneaked out with them. This man lived in the boarding house; I recognised him.

When she returned from work, she saw that the cupboard door was open. When she saw that her clothes were gone, she screamed and burst into tears. I knew who stole them, but I didn't have the language skills at that age to tell her. It frustrated me, as I knew exactly who it was.

Some days, my mother would sit on the corner of the bed with its green bedspread and cry. It would upset me; I would cry with her. I felt helpless, too young to understand or help, just this sorrow in my heart.

There were times when we were poor and my mom could only afford white bread and black coffee, no sugar. We would dunk the bread in the coffee, and she would turn it into a feast.

My mother loved lighting candles and playing records on our old gramophone. She loved Afrikaans and English music, and what she termed 'continental music' from Spain, Greece and Italy. Local black music wasn't freely available in white South Africa at that stage, but if it had been, she would certainly have embraced it. We listened to a duo called Groep Twee, who sang a cheesy but uplifting song, 'Die oukraalliedjie', Doris Day's 'Que Sera, Sera' and Shirley Bassey's 'Goldfinger'.

Also, Elvis Presley, Dean Martin, boeremusiek, Vicky Leandros and Nana Mouskouri. While we were eating and listening to music, my mother would say: 'Pretend you're on the farm, with Ouma. A farm with open fields. Fresh air, fireflies, stars, night sounds, a river that runs through vineyards.'

Then she would smack her lips as if the bread and coffee were exotic dishes fit for the best diners in the world. Food for gourmands. The intimate atmosphere by candlelight, with coffee, bread and music, embraced me as if in a cocoon.

My mother was theatrical and often read verses from the 1933 translation of the Afrikaans Bible. That specific version is dramatic, more like poetry, and you don't have to be a believer to feel the musicality and rhythm of each word.

Those readings were also conducted by candlelight to evoke memories of the farm. To entertain me, because I had no toys, she would hold her hands close to the candlelight, and the shadows they cast against the wall became a storyboard, a movie screen. She would imitate ostriches, elephants and other animals. Each animal had a story, and she would improvise as she went along. I would ask: 'And then? And then?'

My mother spoke with melancholy about her youth on the farm in Lutzville, on the arid West Coast of Namaqualand. My grandfather, Maans, died before I was born, but I do remember visits to an older woman who lived in a tiny house. She was my grandmother, Hansie, who would later play a crucial role in my life.

I remember seeing pumpkins on the zinc roof of this house. Eventually, my grandmother left the farm and moved into the nearby village. I remember the heat, loneliness, gravel roads, red sandstorms, but specifically the bleakness. A landscape stripped of its flesh, like bone. My grandmother always had a sad face.

4

ONE DAY THE NEWS CAME that the owner of the boarding house in Warren Street wanted to demolish it. We moved farther down the neighbourhood to Kloof Street, into another one. It was a large, old, double-storey Victorian building with the name Radyn, opposite a well-known café, Topolino. This café belonged to a brooding Greek and his Afrikaans wife, an imposing woman with large eyes and a quick temper.

There was a jukebox, and Formica tables where you could eat hamburgers and drink milkshakes. Much like those American diners, like an Edward Hopper painting with its subdued drama. On Friday nights, Topolino was packed with cocksure youngsters filled with testosterone and attitude. They came to dance, eat, play ping-pong and, hopefully, get laid.

Many of the teenage boys had motorbikes, polished to a shine, which they parked next to each other in perfect formation. These bikes were treated with respect, and if you had one, you attracted some of the best cherries or gooses, the slang words for pretty women back then. The chrome on these sex magnets gleamed under the streetlights – bright lights, bright nights.

Topolino enchanted me as a child. Was it the smell of decadence, Brylcreem, Old Spice and perfume? Women with sad red lips and low cleavages showing off a bit of breast. The boarding house was not a hangout or haven for nuns. I identified with the demi-monde from an early age.

Radyn consisted of bedsits in the British boarding-house style, where the bedroom and sitting room were one. Kloof Street could be described as bedsitter-land, a street filled with rented accommodation.

In the movie *The Lonely Passion of Judith Hearne*, Maggie Smith plays the eponymous role, a single, lonely woman who is emotionally and physically adrift in an uninhabited land. She lives in a rooming house with a disparate group of outcasts and eventually turns into a silent drinker: a drunk who drinks on their own.

Radyn was overflowing with pathos and people like Judith, but also strong people who had to overcome being different in a world that demanded conformity. There was much laughter, but also a quilt of many other emotions. The exterior of the building, with its huge garden and lonesome, tall palm tree, was somewhat rundown. The interior, however, was neat and old-world.

A ding-dong bell announced breakfast and dinner. Starched white table-cloths covered antique, dark-wood tables, the cutlery was polished, and tea and coffee were served in silver pots. The serviettes folded in the shape of swans were a camp touch.

Morning conversation was muted, as most people had a babelaas or were simply not looking forward to another dreary day in a boring job. That's if you had a job, as some people were retired or simply unemployable. Yet everyone seemed to have some form of income, such as the remittance men. These were gay men from Britain who had embarrassed their families and been paid by their relatives to go away, often to South Africa, where they would be out of sight.

Breakfast consisted of bacon, eggs, Vienna sausages, white toast, butter, marmalade, and coffee or tea served with hot milk. The dining room really came alive at night when some of the guests pitched up already tipsy. Dinner ranged from fish and chips to steak-and-kidney pie, bangers and mash and shepherd's pie. Real bôrdinghuis kos. Sunday lunch was a big occasion: a carvery with assorted meats and vegetables.

Apart from the vibe over lunch on Sundays, the dining room during the day was quiet, mysterious, deserted, tidy. A room waiting for company. A place where one could sit and weep quietly, should the fancy take you.

The rooms were spacious, and there were heavy green curtains that hung right to the floor, which were dark-brown Cape teak and smelt of Cobra lavender floor polish. I remember copper-coloured chandeliers, white-painted pressed ceilings and a long, fan-like, sweeping staircase as featured in the musical *Hello, Dolly!* Dark-wood panels adorned the bottom part of the walls, while the top section was painted bright red.

On Saturday nights, there would be huge parties where a woman of a certain age, who wore too much make-up, played the piano. My mother told me it was because she couldn't see well, so she just slapped on the rouge, mascara, eyeliner, lipstick and green eyeshadow willy-nilly. Her many brace-lets tinkled as she pounded the keys. As the booze kicked in, she would throw her head back and sing raucous English pub songs, with the rest of the crowd joining in, all pissed and smoking. One of her favourite songs was from the musical *Oliver!* She would belt out: 'Oom-pah-pah! Oom-pah-pah! / That's how it goes / Oom-pah-pah! Oom-pah-pah! /Ev'ryone knows.'

During the day, those people who weren't working looked after me. Some of them were, how would one say it, *filles de joie*, women who worked at night, but there were also retired people who loved looking after a young child.

One woman, a retired teacher, didn't waste time on niceties; she taught me the basics of reading and writing, and loved telling tall stories. She had a large library but no friends. That was how I spent my days, with people from all layers of life. And how charming they all were. To be exposed to such an assortment of characters was a blessing and one I have appreciated my whole life. They expanded my horizons, as even in those early years I was attracted to odd people, mavericks, free-thinkers and counterculturists. This is where the seed was planted.

My mother loved all people, but she most enjoyed the company of strong, single women and gay men. They were always visiting in the evenings and would dance to records, or just skinder and chat.

The one guy's name was Jewels; he was from Switzerland. He was a printer who worked as a typesetter in Long Street and smoked long, purple cigarettes with silver-coloured filters. They were always neatly stacked in a silver cigarette case. Before he started telling a story, he would say in a posh English accent: 'Aaaaaaaactuallyyyyy, what I'm about to tell you might just shock you to the core of your existence.' He had a passion for so-called coloured men and often brought them along. Nobody complained; it was that sort of place.

There was another wonderful man, called Lady Peterson, who was, in fact, a boerseun who had left his family farm to start a new life in Cape Town. He invented a whole new identity for himself and lived in Radyn. Lady Peterson never spoke about her past, but we suspected that she had money because she never worked. In the mornings she slept in because she had been out clubbing the previous evening.

The one club, near the harbour, was called the Catacombs. The bouncer there, Billy Monk, took photographs of people dancing or passed out, and became famous as a photographer after his death. He was shot over a mattress, I think. His photographs became an invaluable peek into Cape Town's nightlife in the sixties, specifically the Catacombs, as it was racially mixed during the height of apartheid.

Here, Lady Peterson picked up sailors from all over the world. A well-known actress from that era, who shall remain anonymous as her family are frightfully posh people, claimed she could speak six languages, all picked up during pillow-talk with sailors. And she could too, as she translated quite a few plays into Afrikaans and English from other languages.

I was too young to really understand the horrors of apartheid, but I hear the police left the Catacombs alone, as they, too, merrily partook in the forbidden fruit across all colour lines.

Lady Peterson wore beautiful dresses with quality jewels. Her make-up was always impeccable. Sometimes a sexy hunk would emerge from her bedroom. One day, they carried someone on a stretcher, covered in a blanket, out of her room. My mother called me aside and told me that one of Lady Peterson's lovers had taken his own life after they'd had a fight.

I didn't understand the concept of death – the white cat had been a foretaste, but that was it. Lady Peterson didn't come out of her room for a long time. 'She's mourning,' my mother said.

5

O NE DAY, JEWELS DIDN'T PITCH up at the boarding house. My mom wondered what was going on, because she and some of their mutual friends were going to Camps Bay, to lie on the beach and swim. This is what they enjoyed doing.

We went down to Gardenia, a block of flats near the bottom end of Kloof Street. Once we arrived there, we knocked on Jewels's door, but there was no answer. My mom got hold of the caretaker and asked if there might be a ladder. He fetched one and we put it up against the wall, all the way to Jewels's window. The caretaker climbed up to the window, but he was too big to fit through it. There was no front-door key.

Everybody looked at me, obviously because I was smaller than the adults. I climbed the ladder – it was thrilling – and forced myself through the small windowframe. I saw Jewels lying in the room, mouth open and motionless. I ran to the front door and opened it.

The caretaker and my mom ran in. They tried to shake Jewels to get life back into him, but it seemed he was finished, gone. Then they found that he had a faint pulse. They phoned the ambulance, and once again someone was carried out on a stretcher, different place but same thing. They rushed Jewels to hospital. A few days later, he was discharged.

For his homecoming, my mom organised an evening by candlelight. She played a scratched record of Nana Mouskouri singing love songs and prepared his favourite dish, tomato bredie. It was also my best-loved dish. To this day, when I smell it, I think of my mother, Maria.

Jewels arrived and the two of them danced, smoked cigarettes and drank Capenheimer Perlé. He was his old self; when I look back, those were good times. I was content living with my mother, with all her wacky friends, and with life in the boarding house.

Maria's work at the Cape Provincial Administration Library Services in Green Point paid a measly salary. She had a junior position. Often there was no money, but we survived somehow. You had to pay for the meals at Radyn. My father, I heard later, never paid maintenance. Such a typical South African story. He was a young skirt-chaser who only thought about his own needs.

At Radyn also, my mom would sit on the corner of the bed, crying. This usually meant that there was no more money, that she was broke. Or that she was missing the farm, pining after the old days. Or that her heart had been shattered. Again.

My mom's girlfriends were mostly single mothers. It was the era of the Afrikaner's urbanisation. Young white men and women streamed into the cities from the platteland, in search of a new life, to study or to find jobs that offered new opportunities.

So-called coloured women also trekked to the cities. They spoke Afrikaans and were eager to escape the hardships of the onderdorp, which was like a township. Because of white affirmative action and second-rate education, they ended up working in kitchens and boarding houses, or as cleaners in white people's houses.

My mother formed close bonds with these coloured people from rural areas. They talked about droughts, berg winds, boyfriends, nights when you could see all the stars. She also befriended the kitchen staff and cleaners in the boarding house.

It all seemed so natural; I had no clue that it wasn't allowed. One friend, Lorraine September, always started crying when my mother put Doris Day's *Christmas Album* on the gramophone. Why it moved her so bitterly to tears I didn't know, but I was naughty. When I saw her coming down the corridor, I would quickly put the record on the turntable. 'Jou vabond (rascal)!' she would exclaim while running down the hallway, wiping away her tears.

One day a doctor diagnosed Lorraine with lung cancer. My mother tended to her until she died. The hearse took her away. The people of Radyn were gutted, my mother sobbed with grief. Lorraine's family came all the way from Pacaltsdorp, a suburb of George, to fetch her from the morgue. Every night, for a long time, my mother would light a candle for her.

6

NOTHER OF MARIA'S FRIENDS WHO played a significant role in my life was Griet van Biljon. Griet insisted that I should not call her 'tannie'. She died in her eighties, while I was writing this book. She had a son my age, Ivan. Griet was originally from Bloemfontein and drove a light-blue Volkswagen Beetle. The four of us often drove in this tiny car over Kloof Nek Road to swim at Camps Bay, which was like a little village in those days, with a café and a chemist. People looked down on it, as it was too windy. There was a huge white horse that roamed the area with his pal Nellie, the donkey, from 1932 to 1967.

Ivan and I would sit in the back of the car in those hollow spaces that served as luggage compartments. We would press our noses against the back window and pull faces at the people driving behind us. Inside, the car had painted metal surfaces and a blue dashboard, with rotating vent windows.

Once at the beach, we would lie under our umbrellas and watch the sky-blue sea for hours. The water was icy, and we had red lilos. One day, on this beach, I overheard my mother say that the Dutch Reformed Church didn't want to baptise me because I was illegitimate. They wanted her to stand up in church and confess her sin, but she refused; this was an ongoing saga that went on for years.

Although she wasn't a devout Christian, Maria read her Bible and wanted me to be baptised. Why, I don't know. Perhaps it was the remnants of the platteland that made her think that way. It was as if her heart was on the farm but her body in Cape Town. The Dutch Reformed Church had a strange emotional hold on Afrikaners.

To acknowledge her so-called sin in a packed church was out of the question. 'Hulle moere,' she said. She'll never set foot there again. She said they'd called me a son of a whore. It was a huge slap in her face. How can it be a sin to have a child? How could a church, one she grew up in, treat her in such a hard-hearted manner?

When I overheard this, a strange feeling overcame me. I knew that I was different, unwanted, by a church. I was bad. It was a feeling, like so many others, that would follow me my entire life. Someone suggested we approach St Mary's Cathedral opposite Parliament. Although Catholic, they were a progressive church.

I was only five, but the memory stuck. We went with my mother's older friend, Iris Basson, who was known as Ma Basson. She drove a maroon and grey Wolseley 16/60, posh, with a shiny wooden dashboard and red leather seats. The car was like a ship for a little boy; it was huge and rocked as if on an ocean. Ma Basson smoked non-stop; the car's ashtray was always over-flowing. She was a drinker, a euphemism for a lush. Ma Basson was always hosting parties, where she would drink brandy and Coke.

She wore a hairnet and rouge on her cheeks. She smelt of talcum powder.

One sunny day, we climbed the Catholic church's steps. The inside was dramatic, with the statues, candles and high ceiling. I suspect that Ma Basson was Catholic and had arranged the whole occasion. On entering, we had to cross our hearts. I can't remember any more, except that a priest spoke in a funny language and sprinkled water on my forehead.

On the backseat of Ma Basson's car, I sat and thought: 'I'm the child of a whore. My mother's church rejected us.'

7

ONE DAY AN UNCLE OF mine, Ross, decided to fly me to Pretoria. He was a pilot with the old South African Airways (SAA) and married to my mother's sister, Helna. Helna, though, insisted on being called Helena. Helena considered herself a cosmopolitan woman, one who specifically loved Germany and the rest of Europe. In her mind, we were more European than African. Through her husband, the pilot, she could travel regularly. He was a tall, thin man who spoke 'scary' Afrikaans, like a dominee.

Ross and Helena were typical of many of their tribe during the seventies: *nouveau riche*, entitled and flashy. That said, it was kind of him to fly a five-year-old to where they lived in Kempton Park. I was afraid to travel alone, as this was the first time my mother and I would be apart. She and her motley bunch of screwball friends were my world. My familiar inner circle and I were to be torn apart.

Once again, our old and trusted friend, Ma Basson, took us to the airport in her car. We arrived and a kind airhostess took me by the hand. I cried as I left my mom behind. The hostess led me to a huge flying machine with loud engines. We walked up the stairs and she seated me right in front, near the flight attendants' workstation.

She and her colleagues kept an eye on me and exclaimed over my thick black hair and green eyes. When I looked behind me, I saw a long corridor. In my imagination, I was certain there was a huge hole at the back of the aeroplane that would suck me out if I didn't sit still. I held onto the armrests of the seat and closed my eyes. That big hole behind me would push me into space and I would fall down to earth and die on impact. I would never see my mother again, ever.

I kept my thoughts of horror to myself. Once we were high up in the sky, the nice airhostess came to fetch me and took me into the cockpit. There I saw my uncle at the control wheel, which in my mind looked far too small for a big, surging plane. The terror … what if it broke off in his hands?

Two other men in uniform sat with him, tampering with switches while red lights flashed ominously. Everything looked new and modern, far removed from old boarding houses and hippies. I looked through the windscreen, down, down, to the earth. It was a pretty sight. The landing went smoothly.

I drove with my uncle in his car to their house, where my aunt opened the door to greet us. There was always something cold about her, like a mannequin with a blonde wig and a frozen half-smile. I remember how long she took to groom herself before she and Ross went out. She was always teasing her hair, mostly in front of a large mirror, taking ages to shape herself into a Barbie doll.

My cousin, Cecilia, was my age and kept me company. It was before TV. The days were bland, and we didn't have much to do. I missed the lively atmosphere of the boarding house. The suburban scene, with a family, felt strange and uncomfortable. Ross was strict at night when it came to dinnertime. I had to eat the last grain of rice on my plate. The conversation was hardly colourful or convivial, not as vibrant as those with my mother and her friends – even if we had to eat white bread dipped into black instant coffee, with no sugar.

They meant well, but I missed home; the visit was just too cheerless. Ross, however, did teach me how to tie my shoelaces.

8

BACK IN CAPE TOWN, MY mom and Griet fetched me in the light-blue Beetle. I felt happy. I climbed into the back of the car, into the little cave.

At the boarding house, everybody was glad to see me. Lady Peterson even wore a new dress. 'She especially dressed like Sophia Loren. She's a famous Italian actress,' my mother explained. Ooh, it was great to be back. I'd hardly put my suitcase down before we were all bundled into Ma Basson's ship. It was payday and we were going to La Perla in Sea Point, where we could sit outside.

Sea Point made us happy. The shades of blue, the white foam on the waves and the golden sun created an air of abandon. My memories of sitting outside on La Perla's balcony are vivid. But La Perla wasn't the only source of happiness. My mother befriended a woman, Maraai Masoet, who lived in District Six. Maraai worked in the kitchen of our boarding house, and they got on well.

'Lekker like a Christmas cracker,' Maraai used to say. She often came and sat in our room, and she and my mother would chat about recipes. Later, we started going to District Six to visit the Masoets. They were a small family with a son my age, George, and Maraai's husband, Noor. Golden times, as the neighbourhood had a lively atmosphere. Children played in the streets, elderly people sat on their stoeps, and the smell of food hung in the air. Spices, fish and bredies.

The front doors of the houses were always open, so you could see right into people's homes. It was here that I overheard the word 'moffie' for the first time. The gay men and drag queens were always friendly and coquettish. I'm always amazed that young people throw around the words 'gender-fluid' and 'non-binary' as if they are new concepts. You should have seen District Six, Kloof Street, the nightclubs in Cape Town and Sea Point. And that was in the 1960s.

One moffie often came to visit Maraai, and he fascinated me. Hoosain, my mother and Maraai could talk for hours about tomato bredie, smoorsnoek, carrot and pea stew, and afval. They would drink Glen Tea and smoke Rothmans cigarettes. My mother's third language was swearing; it was part of the lingua franca of Namaqualand, and she brought it with her to Cape Town.

I recall walking past places like the British Bioscope, the Rose & Crown Hotel, Hanover and Tennant streets. Gradually, our visits became fewer. The authorities were knocking down homes and businesses. Again, I was too small to understand what was going on. My mother was seething about this.

Towards the end, she became more despondent with each visit. The rubble increased and there were fewer and fewer people around. The laughter with Maraai in her house stopped.

9

ONE SATURDAY MORNING, MY MOM woke me and said that we were going to go to The Market in town. She brought me a cup of coffee and stroked my hair. The Market was a psychedelic hippie hangout where you could buy incense, bangles and long, printed dresses. The people who used to frequent The Market had calm expressions on their faces … Durban Poison, of course. My mother confirmed that they smoked dagga. She didn't mind the dagga, or people smoking it, but it made her scared, as if someone was peeping at her from behind a curtain.

That morning, the women in the shop were very friendly to me. 'Oh, look at his eyes,' the one swooned. 'And his hair,' another chirped. Those were my strongest features, it seemed. 'Is he Greek?' a tall, thin woman asked. 'No,' my mom answered. 'It's a touch of Namaqualand genes and Irish blood.' Sure. 'Oh, how exotic,' the long, thin woman said.

It was a warm morning, one that I'll never forget. My mother looked beautiful. I felt safe and loved. We went back to the boarding house and sat down in our room. 'Herman, you are going to school next year. I am desperately poor. You saw that I didn't buy anything at The Market. It's bad. Your dad doesn't contribute anything, no money. Nothing. I had to plan. We'll see how it works out. We can't just live on coffee and bread.

'I can't afford the meals at the boarding house. They charge extra for those; not much, but if you earn as little as I do, it's a battle. I'm sending you to a place in Durbanville, near a school.

'I don't have to pay, it's like a boarding school, but it's an orphanage. These are desperate times. While you are there, I will try my best to get a better job, one that pays more.'

I wasn't sure what it all meant. I'd never heard of Durbanville. So, I just sat there with my missing tooth, bushy black hair and red cheeks. That November, I turned six.

In January, my mother packed my small suitcase for me. My tiny pyjamas with the duck pattern, all my clothes, beautifully packed, firmly, in my suitcase. She closed it decisively. For a moment, we sat in silence. Ma Basson, always dependable, came. In her boat.

We drove and drove. I saw places flash by that I'd never seen before.

At the back, staring through the window, I began wondering about my new life. A new life that would leave permanent psychological scars, but I was unaware of that as I sat and waited for the short and wonderful life I'd had to end.

We drove through big gates and the car stopped. We got out. A woman came to the car, shook my hand and introduced herself as Tannie Prins. Then my mother kissed me. Ma Basson was close to tears. I went and sat on a bench under a tree with Tannie Prins. She held my hand. This scene would repeat itself in my memory over many years. To this day, in fact.

I watched as my mother and Ma Basson drove away. My mother turned around, looked at me and waved. They left through the big gates.

A black hole sucked me in. I was outside my body, adrift in space. The vision of the open gates paralysed me. Tannie Prins squeezed my hand again. I wanted to talk, but I had no words. They flew away, through the gates, with my mother, Maria.

10

THE REST IS VAGUE. I can remember my room. It was a single room, tidy, white tiles, one bed. The evenings were the worst. I was scared. Lonely. I can hardly remember the other children but was well aware of a teenager with a leg affected by polio. At night, I could hear him walk in his leg brace. I thought he was coming to my room to harm me.

The first day of school was awful. There was a huge Dutch Reformed Church that you had to pass, down some stairs and then to the school. The church was a mountain and had an ominous feel. Little interested me at school. I missed my mom and longed for all the people at the boarding house. I blocked out the world and stopped talking altogether.

On Friday evenings, they showed movies. Everybody around me laughed, but we were the throwaway people. The nothing people.

Tannie Prins became worried about this mute, silent boy. After a while, she asked me if I would join her for a weekend visit to her parents. We drove there in silence. I have a hazy memory of her parents and the house, but what does stand out is that there was a dog that had given birth to a litter. I walked towards these tiny animals and stroked them. At that moment, I started talking. Words came back to me. I cannot remember what I said. But I thawed and started feeling like a person again and not like an empty shell, or a thing from outer space.

Years later, when Tannie Prins (as I still call her) and I met again, she told me that that weekend was also a tipping point for her parents. They couldn't understand why she wanted to work in an orphanage. The stigma attached to children's homes was enormous. But after they saw me transform from a wordless child to one who could talk and even laugh again, they changed their minds. They noticed her kind interaction with a small child and realised that her work had value. She gave love to children who felt unloved.

Although the orphanage was a haven, and even if they looked after us and took us on outings, served us meals and tried to create some warmth, I wanted my mother. It was a yearning that traumatised me to such an extent that, in later years in therapy, my psychologist diagnosed that little discarded boy as my primal wound.

The fallout was permanent: bad self-image, vicious outbursts of anger, sharp tongue, inferiority complex, imposter syndrome, endless feelings of melancholy and a fear of rejection. I learnt through years of psychoanalysis to manage these emotions, but they've never left me.

Even if you achieve success, you feel hollow. Every day, I feel as if something terrible is going to happen; even more horrific, that nobody will be there to catch me when I fall. There is a label for that feeling of ennui and cynicism, for that void: it's called Peggy Lee syndrome. Peggy Lee sang the song 'Is That All There Is?' Even if you succeed in something, you feel, 'Is that all there is?' It is a dreadful condition, but you soldier on. Naturally, there are highlights, tight and important friendships, a life fully lived, but the barrenness remains. I often feel invisible, even to myself.

My mother phoned once a week. I found the short conversations with her more depressing than uplifting because I knew the call would end. Her voice would be gone. I would be alone again. We could not say goodbye. Instead, we would say ta-ta to each other, up to twenty times. One of us had to put the phone down first. She didn't want to, neither did I.

'Okay, bye, okay bye, okay bye …' On and on and on. Then poof. Gone.

Certain weekends she could visit, but they weren't many. She did not have transport and was dependent on friends. Sometimes she would let me know that she was coming, then I would stand on my bed to peer through the window into the car park to see if I could spot her. If I saw her, I would run outside, and she would wait for me. I would run into her arms. She would pick me up and swing me around and we would both cry. She usually packed coffee, biscuits and sandwiches in a little picnic basket.

Later on, I would stand on the bed every Sunday and stare into the car park. Staring at nothing. On the Sundays when she didn't come, the pain was unbearable.

One day, I saved one of my mother's sandwiches. At school we were given buttered white bread with red strawberry jam for lunch. To this day, I cannot stomach that jam. So, I thought that I would treat myself to a special sandwich one day and hid it in my cupboard. I took it to school in my suitcase and went onto the playground at break. When I bit into it, I found that I had kept it too long; it was covered in mould. I spat it out and cried; grief overwhelmed me.

11

A FTER A YEAR IN THE orphanage, my mother came to fetch me. Yet again, she arrived in Ma Basson's elegant Wolseley. Over the years, Ma Basson had crept into my heart, with her rouge, fake eyelashes, red lipstick and alcohol breath. I should have been ecstatic, but instead I felt insecure. What did the future hold? What if my mother abandoned me again? I felt a bit like a stray cat that had found a new home but wasn't all that confident that it would be permanent.

My mom now lived in a block of flats called Gardenia near the bottom end of Kloof Street. She had never mentioned that she had moved. It was the same block in which Jewels lived and where we had saved him from his attempted suicide. Today, it's an ugly office block.

I didn't live there for long before my mother told me that I would be moving in with her cousin, Oom Braam Lategan, his wife, Tannie Tina, and their five children. My mom was saving up for a move to Sea Point and waiting for a promotion. In those days, Sea Point was an affordable suburb, so it wasn't as if she had delusions of grandeur.

I'd attend Jan van Riebeeck Primary School and be much closer to her. Again, I felt a pang of injury. Am I in the way? It was so nice to be back with my mom. I pined for the days when life was sunny.

My Oom Braam, as I called him, was a tall beanpole of a man with a deep voice and a firm stare. And he was grand. His body language oozed authority. He drove a long, black Mercedes-Benz, like many of the politicians and Dutch Reformed Church dominees of the time.

At that stage he was an important state prosecutor, known for his role in the infamous Ronald Cohen court case. Cohen was a rich and influential socialite and grandee who was prosecuted for the murder of his twenty-five-year-old wife, Susan. She was killed in their swish Constantia home on the night of 5 April 1970.

The state claimed Cohen had killed her with an ornament in a moment of rage, but he denied it and said he couldn't remember anything: how her blood had stained his shirt, or why the 'intruders' had neither stolen anything nor sexually assaulted Susan.

The case was high profile and received an enormous amount of press coverage, which made Oom Braam famous. Because of Oom Braam's thorough interrogation of Cohen, the judge sent him to jail. I, of course, was unaware of this. My world centred around my feelings of bereavement and heartache, memories of a time when I'd felt cherished. Oom Braam would progress to become Attorney-General and, later, a judge.

Once I was an adult, I heard that his judicial appointment had been controversial, as it was of a political nature. Oom Braam was a Broederbonder with the right connections. Soon, he would become known as the hanging judge. If you appeared in front of him for murder or rape, you were going to hang.

The psychotherapist Juliana Coetzer once told me that she sat in on a court case in the early eighties, where a man appeared on a charge of rape. The sweat poured off the accused's face, as if a bucket of water was being poured over his head. Oom Braam gave him the death sentence and said: 'You will hang until you die.' All colour drained from the man's face.

A paramour of Oom Braam's, an advocate whom he was seeing on the side, walked into the courtroom while he was delivering the judgment. He still had the temerity, in the face of death, to look at her and say to a packed courtroom: 'I see we are in good company.'

Oom Braam was married to a politically well-connected woman, whom I called Tannie Tina. Her maiden name was Loots and her brother was the Speaker of the House of Assembly, Jannie Loots. Boere-aristocracy, farmers from Prieska and hardened Nationalists. Tannie Tina's connections were vital to Oom Braam's rise to the top. It also helped that congregants could see him as an ouderling (elder) in the Groote Kerk in Adderley Street on Sundays. It was a church supported by all the important people: politicians, wealthy businessmen and noted professionals.

I remember going there, and it stank of patriarchy, testosterone, cheap perfume, overdressed women and sombre, moustachioed men wearing black suits, often with big, black-framed glasses. Nobody smiled. Black people were not allowed in the church; no wonder they called it 'the National Party at prayer'.

Like Darth Vader in his black robe, the dominee would ascend the stairs of the imposing pulpit, designed by Anton Anreith. The sculpted podium consists of two lions on whose shoulders the lectern rests. The dominee would lift his arms operatically, the congregation would rise, he would bellow out a prayer and then everybody would sit down again.

The poor organist, pale like tinned asparagus, would hit the keys with fervour, while the brainwashed simpletons would stand up again to sing as if at a funeral. Nobody could keep a note. Once, a baby started crying. The saccharine-sounding dominee said in Afrikaans: 'Don't worry, Mevrou, there's nothing as sweet as the sound of a baby.' I thought, 'Fuck that, what is a baby doing in a church?'

Oom Braam made the whole family attend this church every Sunday.

This part of the Lategan clan was rich and lived in a huge house on the slopes of Table Mountain. Right at the top of Oranjezicht, in Rugby Road. The rooms were huge, with views of the mountain, sea and city ... and beyond. At the back, there was a play area that went right up against the steep mountain. I could swing, which I often did, while singing made-up songs of how I missed my mother. In summer, you could smell the hot, heaving mountain and the pine trees, and huge red locusts came flying out of nowhere and landed on the lawn.

Of course, there was a swimming pool, a trampoline, a wall to bounce tennis balls against and a large braai area. Next to the braai was a snooker table, which Oom Braam often used to prepare the wild buck he hunted in the Karoo.

Oom Braam had a nice side; at night, he would read fairy tales to us. After school we could read children's books and listen to records with stories for kids. Once, Oom Braam took me to a rugby match. It was raining, so we sat in the car. In silence. When Tannie Tina and I drove, that, too, was in awkward stillness.

My life with a family was now in full swing. From an only child to an orphan, to a stepchild and stepbrother. It was overwhelming. The pomp, the display of wealth, the grandness of it all.

Oom Braam dropped us at school in his big black car, right at the gate. I found it embarrassing. That was his morning duty; Tannie Tina collected us in the afternoons. If she couldn't, there was a bus that stopped right in front of the school and drove us up the steep hill. It stopped a few metres outside the front gate of the house.

Oom Braam was full of contradictions. One day I used the words 'milk boy', as this is what I'd heard the other kids at school say. He reprimanded me and said I should say 'milkman'. When I was older, I often wondered what the subplot was. Was he truly aware of the demeaning tone of referring to a man as a boy, or was he concerned about how grammatically correct it should sound?

Oom Braam and Tannie Tina held formal dinners around a huge table in their dining room, heavy with distress. The atmosphere was as tight as a straitjacket.

I had a lisp, so Tannie Tina sent me for elocution lessons to a remarkable actress, Babs Laker, who was the head of the Academy for Dramatic Art, also situated in Kloof Street. This woman would have a huge influence on me later in my life.

Even as a little boy she taught me about poetry and prose, which I had to read out loud. I had to 'project'. Then she had a bag, filled with objects, such as a bunch of keys. I had to close my eyes and feel in the bag and describe what I felt.

I was drawn to her, as she reminded me of my mom and her wayward friends. Babs was spontaneous, strong, clever, dramatic. She would play Leonard Cohen records; I remember 'So Long, Marianne'. Then she would burn incense and get a faraway look in her eyes, which would fill with tears. I was only seven, how wonderful ... She asked me to really *feel* the music.

Babs became more like a substitute mom to me, as I hardly saw my own mother. In retrospect, I suppose the Lategans asked her to keep a low profile so that I could bond with the family.

The relationship between me and Tannie Tina started to turn frosty. Trouble was brewing. I was outspoken, I swore. What did one expect? Boarding houses full of foul-mouthed troublemakers had been part of my formative years. Oom Braam would give me a hiding with a sjambok for cussing. Supporting apartheid was hunky-dory, just don't swear.

Their oldest son, also Braam, often bullied me. For no reason. He would hit me hard on my shoulder and I would fall down in pain. But I had a good relationship with two of the children: Henk, the youngest son, with whom I shared a room, and An-Sophie, who always had empathy for everybody. The two of us are still in touch.

The tension between me and Tannie Tina led to psychological problems. I started wetting the bed. Once, we went on vacation in the huge black Mercedes to visit Tannie Tina's family on their farm in Prieska. The farm was called Blyvooruitsig, please. It was a whole road trip, and how all the kids fitted in on the backseat was a miracle. The smallest one sat in front, under Tannie Tina's legs, with four of us in the back. Our first stop was a farm in the then Orange Free State. A tall, thin man came to greet us. His name was Oom Blackie.

We stayed overnight, and the next day we hit the long, hot road to Prieska, then Pretoria, and later the Kruger National Park. All very exciting but let me mention that I peed in my bed that night in the Orange Free State. Cruella de Vil lost it and scolded and humiliated me like nobody had ever done before.

Later, I would discover that Oom Blackie had been the first state president of the Republic of South Africa, CR Swart. I don't think many people can claim that they peed in a bed belonging to a state president. Take a bow, thank you. Rumour has it that when he was young, Oom Blackie acted in silent films in Hollywood. How different that must have been to the endless flat fields of the Orange Free State.

So, Tannie Tina declared war on me. She was chilly and openly hated me. She would criticise the way I walked, as I have flat feet. I was also too fat. She often stared at me with disdain. Back in Cape Town, metaphorical underground seismic shifts started between me and Cruella. You could hear the faint rumblings.

Sundays at the lunch table were a stately affair with plenty of traditional boerekos: huge plates of fluffy white rice, pumpkin fritters covered in a sweet syrup, crushed green beans, roast potatoes, peas, glazed carrots, game, roast leg of lamb, chicken, pork and lamb gravy, followed by koeksisters and a baked Malva pudding with loads of custard.

Cruella kept the conversation stilted and polite; you spoke softly, never answered back, knew your place. You could hear the cutlery click-clack, click-clack on the plates. No robust laughter or joking; so unlike the boarding houses, and even the orphanage. Cruella insisted that we chew our food thirty-two times, and she watched us as we took each bite. She targeted me and, with the voice of a foghorn, would cut me to shreds. Click-clack, click-clack, the silver cutlery against the expensive plates and a cuckoo clock that cooed every thirty minutes. It was like a scene from a horror movie – think Bette Davis and Joan Crawford in *What Ever Happened to Baby Jane?*

One Sunday after church, Tannie Tina asked me – as she often did – what the dominee had said during the service. This, of course, was setting me up to fail, as I never paid attention. I was an evil little urchin; the flat-footed, fat, blasphemous devil's son. But she couldn't catch me out. That day, her voice was as glacier-like as the Arctic Circle. Her eyes, murderous. I felt hot lava boiling within me and an anger that knew no bounds.

The cuckoo clock broke the silence, and then it was quiet again. I stared at her, took a deep breath and said: 'He said, "Jou ma se pap poes!"'

A lull. A look. A moment. Time. Stood. Still. The children stared at their food. Braam asked me to leave the table.

That was the Sunday.

On the Monday, Cruella asked me in a friendly tone if I would like to go for a drive. I could sit in the back of the car and pretend that she was my personal chauffeur. I mistrusted her; she was churlish and hated me. She drove straight to Gardenia, my mother's apartment block in Kloof Street, where she stopped the car and sat, not moving, engine running.

My mother came out, opened the boot and removed my luggage. The heartless way Tannie Tina did this remains with me to this day and will forever after. Before she drove off, her last words, which she spat at my mother and me, were: 'One day this child *will* end up in the gutter!'

Then she put her foot on the pedal and sped off. We never spoke again. Years later, I saw a photograph of her when she was elderly and sickly. She was bedridden and had Alzheimer's. Her daughter, An-Sophie, was with her, holding her hand.

I looked at how vulnerable she seemed and, at that moment, decided to forgive her. I let my resentment go, but her remark about the gutter haunted me for decades and still plagues me. Who knows, one day she could be proven right.

12

Back with my mom, what followed were some of the happiest years of my life. Shortly after Tannie Tina's aggressive departure, a gentler and kinder era was ushered in. We moved to Sea Point, which had always been my mother's dream. Like the siblings in Anton Chekhov's play *Three Sisters*, for whom Moscow symbolised the unattainable in life, my mom longed for Sea Point. Now it was possible; she had found her Moscow.

But some of my last memories of Kloof Street, a road that would feature prominently throughout my life, were quite dark. One day, while I was standing outside in the sun, waiting for my mom, an unknown man walked up to me. He spoke nicely and asked me to join him on a visit to a friend of his. I thought nothing of it and went along. At the bottom end of Kloof Street, right opposite the place where I was conceived, is a block of flats called Overbeek. He walked ahead of me up the stairs.

There was a corridor and an open door from which some voices were audible. The man sat down on the stairs and said I should walk past the open door so that his friend could see me. So, I walked past the door and made eye contact with one of the men. I thought it was just some silly game and walked back to the man sitting on the staircase. He asked me to sit next to him, which I did. I was wearing a pair of shorts and a T-shirt.

He then put his hands down my pants, moved his fingers into my underpants and started playing with my genitals. It meant nothing to me; I was too young. It felt like he was tickling me, yet something didn't feel right. So, I jumped up and ran back to Gardenia, our block of flats.

Then there was the time my cousin Tersia came to visit us, also at Gardenia. She was the daughter of my mother's brother, Cobus, who was an alcoholic, poet, artist, bullshit artist and esoteric philosopher. Tersia came to visit, big excitement, because it was the summer of 1972; it was hot, I was eight and I was looking forward to taking her to the Long Street Baths. To walk from Gardenia to the baths took three minutes.

We arrived there and jumped into the pool. The smell of chlorine, the laughter of teenagers and children reverberating to and from the ceiling... When we got ready to leave, a man asked us if we needed a lift home.

Outside the tar was hot, we were barefoot, and it sounded like a good idea. We got into his car, and he sped off, right past our block of flats. He kept driving, up Kloof Street, then turned into Kloof Nek and raced like a maniac up the mountain. He then turned into The Glen, a picnic spot in a wooded area between Cape Town and Camps Bay. The man stopped under one of the trees. I was sitting in the back. He turned to Tersia, then about ten, and started kissing her. When he pushed his hands under her dress, I hit him on his head from behind and screamed at Tersia to jump out.

We started running up the hill to the road, but we were young and directionless (on many levels, also later in life). We were confused: should we run up the road, or down the road? We ran up the road and started crying; we were lost. Luckily, the man had disappeared.

All that we could do was run down Kloof Nek's steep road, sobbing and terrified. A while later, after much trauma, our surroundings started to look familiar. We ran into Kloof Street and finally found our block of flats.

Years later, I wondered what sort of people do this to children. They move silently among us; they are people you wouldn't expect to be evil. But there they are, lurking, salivating. Our streets were not as safe as people claim when they hanker after the good old days of apartheid – just ask me.

My mother was furious when we told her our story, and after she was attacked in the flat by an intruder one night, she started looking for a place in Sea Point; it was the tipping point.

Before we moved, I was sitting on the staircase in Gardenia one day, as I often did. Thinking. A woman walked up the stairs and stood in front of me. She was pretty, with long blonde hair, wearing a tight red dress. She opened her mouth and said: 'Hello beautiful little boy.' It was a man's voice. It gave me a fright, I don't know why. My mother had a wide circle of cross-dressing or trans friends. I don't know why I had such a strange reaction. I ran up the steps to our flat, but when I turned around, I saw the sadness on her face. To this day, I will never forget how hurt she looked.

One day a homeless man, whom we called a bergie, knocked on our door. Did my mom have some small change and bread? I burst into tears. I couldn't understand why this man was hungry; what was going on? That day my mother gave me some good advice, but I didn't listen. 'My child, you are sensitive. It's a good thing; it's a terrible thing. It can break you. You must be able to wear the world's burdens lightly on your shoulders.'

A bit cheesy, but if only I had listened. And if only she had listened to her own advice.

13

THE BLOCK OF FLATS IN Sea Point was called Lido Court, which sounded very grand, and it was rent-controlled. The building is still there, right opposite the Sea Point Pavilion. Lady Peterson lived in the flat facing us. My mom, Maria, was in the prime of her young life. She wore huge sunglasses, flowing dresses and bikinis to the beach. She had a big personality and a quirky sense of humour.

We had a cockatiel named Polly; not a very original name, nevertheless. We loved the little bird, even though it made a terrible noise. One day she flew away. Later, I spotted Polly with the pigeons in the little park opposite Lido Court. The bird looked happy and free. I decided to let her be.

To get to school, I took the bus to town, then walked up Long and Kloof streets. Long Street had many bookshops, and there was a famous butchery, called Morris Butchery, known for its droëwors. One of Cape Town's first delicatessens was also there, and its owner had the most eccentric habit. Once a year he would display his false teeth, with a 'for sale' sign, in the window, as he would buy a new pair every year. The old false teeth usually sold on the same day.

Long Street: antique shops, a specialist bottle store, second-hand clothing shops, a record shop, rooms to rent in places like the Blue Lodge and Carnival Court, usually occupied by hookers. Flats with balconies, where people would sit and smoke dagga. It really was a labyrinth of gaiety, the perfect street for a young boy to navigate on his way to school; every shop was a place to peep into.

At school, the Lategans from Oranjezicht ignored me, and I suspected that Cruella de Vil had instructed them to look right through me. I wasn't bothered, as I was happy to be with my mother and her friends.

After school I would walk down Long Street again, with some of my buddies, and into St George's Street, where I would catch a bus outside Clicks to Sea Point. I remember clearly how I could smell the sea once we drove through Green Point, then Three Anchor Bay, into Sea Point. Summertime, and a cool breeze would blow through my hair. I would change into my swimming costume, pop over to the pavilion and swim in the salty water. One wonderful thing about the orphanage, they gave us swimming lessons, so I could swim by the age of six.

The boarding houses, too, had been helpful. The retired teacher thought that no time should be wasted, and she'd taught me to read and write at five, even though it was on a basic level. My speech therapist, Babs Laker, introduced me to Leonard Cohen and the world of drama; what more could a little boy have asked for? That was all thanks to the posh Lategans. It sounds cheesy, but from each experience, a new lesson.

My mother and her entourage of friends would meet up under umbrellas at the pavilion. They would lie on the green lawn, and in the background the waves would break, spouting white foam onto the edges of the lawn. Often, someone would bring a picnic along. Everyone in our crowd read the newspapers on Sundays and discussed everything from Anneline Kriel to politics. My days were honey, sweet and thick.

There was lots of laughter. At home, my mother would say she simply couldn't believe that black and so-called coloured people weren't allowed to swim at the pavilion. On the farm where she grew up, everybody swam together in the Olifants River.

I became aware that the domestic workers stayed in little rooms behind many of the blocks of flats. They wore pink uniforms and pushed white children around in prams. One day I asked a woman, Doortjie, who lived in one of these rooms, where her children were, as I saw a photo of kids on her bedside table.

Her room smelt of paraffin, as she used a Primus stove. She had no electricity, only candles. She said her children were in Lavender Hill. On the Cape Flats. Some weekends she could visit them, but the madam often needed her to work then. Again, I was too young to grasp the horror of the situation. She was looking after the madam's children, but her elderly parents had to look after hers.

Years later, JM Coetzee wrote about this situation in his novel *Life and Times of Michael K*. On reading the book, I felt all too familiar with it. Michael's mother lived in the fictitious Côte d'Azur apartments in Sea Point as a house cleaner for a property owner, her room the size of a coffin.

While writing this part of my memoir, I started corresponding with the activist and ambassador accredited to the Republic of Benin and Togo, Ruby

Marks. It was synchronicity that connected us, as her memories touched on mine.

She spoke about a visit to Sea Point: 'I moved into an Airbnb in Sea Point, right opposite the place where the old benches stand that black people were forbidden to sit on. And every night when I took my long walk from Sea Point to Maiden's Cove, I would pass all the black domestic workers pushing prams carrying happy white babies. They didn't look happy, mostly just sullen and resentful.

'I wonder how many white babies were raised upon the rage of black nannies who earned a pittance, and who were allowed – if they were lucky – perhaps two weeks of leave to spend with their own children?

'Do we have white and black children in therapy because of that part of their childhood history? Now the benches allow everyone to sit and take a load off, but when I was growing up within the shadows of the small servant's room in Sea Point, my mother was not allowed to take a seat.

'And when we would have our little picnics consisting of mixed fruit jam on brown "government" bread, we would have to sit on the sharp rocks or on the sand. I pass all these benches that tell their own stories of exclusion and marginalisation, and I notice that you can now put a dedication plaque on the benches.

'But I only see white names. I think I would like to have a bench dedicated to my mother, and all domestic workers who were not allowed to sit down and rest in the country of their birth. Who instead had to continue to walk and walk and walk and walk.

'I hope that when I do have a bench dedicated to my mother and all domestic workers for their pain and sacrifice, I hope something in the spirit of all of those who have since passed on will somehow settle, now that they have been acknowledged.'

Just as this correspondence with Ruby took place, synchronicity reared its head again. Lizzie Andries, a domestic worker from Sea Point, whom I'd met through the white family for whom she worked, died. We'd known each other for decades. I wrote about her passing on Facebook: 'Lizzie Andries died last night. She had cancer and was in her early seventies. Like many so-called "coloured" women, she came to Cape Town, from just outside Oudtshoorn, about fifty years ago. That was the time when young women came from the platteland to seek a new life in the city. Lizzie was a domestic worker in Sea Point for most of that time. She was a tough old bird, thin, took no nonsense. Some would even say she was rude, but it was just her mode of survival. She conquered alcoholism, abusive men, stopped drinking and went to church.

'I met her and got to know her through the Sonnenberg family and once interviewed her about her life in Sea Point for an article. Her face was mapped with a life that forked in many directions. Lizzie was like hundreds of "coloured" women in Sea Point, who are and were the backbone behind many households. Women like Lizzie raised many families in this area, the often-unseen role models who, in another time and era, would have led different lives.

'This is also a tribute, with Lizzie's death, to all those domestic workers in Sea Point who quietly just got on with it, but your voices are not unheard. I will keep writing and talking about women like Lizzie; they will not be erased from their stories, which must be told. They should also tell their own stories (it's not for me to hijack their private narratives), maybe one day in a book. *Goed gaan Lizzie, geseënd is jy.* We must be careful not to romanticise domestic workers' lives; I'm certain it's not what they would have chosen. Also, I'm not the "hero" in telling her story – she is.'

But back to the past. One Saturday I asked Doortjie if she would come with me to the OK Bazaars in Adderley Street. It was a huge supermarket with escalators and a tearoom, The Tempting Tray, where you could drink coffee and eat toasted sandwiches.

A voice announced the day's specials over an intercom. Whoever did this took the job very seriously – the specials were announced in spectacular fashion, as if an aeroplane was about to take off.

My mom liked to sleep in on Saturdays, but there was a young Scottish girl, Lena Zavaroni, who was touring South Africa and would perform live at the OK. I knew Doortjie also liked her music, as she often listened to Lena's famous song, 'Ma! (He's Making Eyes at Me)', on her small transistor radio.

We took an early bus into town, but then something happened that I will never forget. I wanted to sit next to Doortjie, but I couldn't. It was a double-decker, so she had to sit upstairs. I called after her, but she just shook her head. The white people in the bus turned their heads and looked at me with scorn. I felt as if I had done something terrible. The look in Doortjie's eyes said it all.

There was already a crowd when we arrived at the OK Bazaars. Lena entered from behind a black curtain and walked down a catwalk. When she sang her hit song, the crowd went wild, as did Doortjie and I.

Going to a department store in those days was such fun: a carnival atmosphere, a happening, a place to drink coffee, have a toasted sandwich on white bread, even have your hair done, and there was also a photographer in the vicinity. A lot of stuff to do; it could take a whole morning.

Back then, from the nineteen-forties to the seventies, there were pavement photographers in and around the OK Bazaars in Adderley Street, which was an unusual concept if you think about it today. You'd be walking down the street and the next thing a photographer would take a snapshot of you. He'd hand you a card and you could collect the picture two days later at the Movie Snaps Studio on the Parade.

One such photograrpher took a picture of me and Doortjie that day, where she was holding my hand. I had it for years, but it disappeared during a move. Once I had a similar photo of my dad in a safari suit, his black hair gelled with Brylcreem, socks that went all the way to his knees, Grasshoppers shoes and a comb tucked into his left sock. It's also missing.

The Parade, where you would fetch your photo, was then a lively market, with fruit, vegetables, snoek, spices, fabrics, hats, buttons, ties and hot dogs with Vienna sausages, or French polony sandwiches, for sale. Three to four 'street priests' would stand at various spots and caution you that the flames of hell were already licking your buttocks. They would stand there for hours, in the heat and rain, and shout out their message. As a little boy, they fascinated me, because how did their voices not pack up? Did they go for lessons to yell like that, and how did it happen that they were preaching on the Parade?

On our way back to Sea Point, Doortjie and I had to sit apart again. Over fifty years later and I still can't forget Doortjie's shiny bright eyes when we got onto the bus.

Back in Sea Point, I told my mother about the outing, and she regretted not coming along.

But our days in Sea Point just got better. In the evenings, my mom would cook bredies from recipes Maraai had given her when she still lived in District Six. People were in and out of our flat; it was always busy. My mom kept candles on the balcony, which reminded her of the farm. The soundtrack of that era was Nana Mouskouri, Vicky Leandros, Tom Jones, Simon & Garfunkel and Miriam Makeba.

My mom also had a passion for fondues. On fondue evenings, there would be dancing. The women still had a touch of hippie about them: long brown or psychedelic dresses, mascara, green eyeshadow, large fake black eyelashes, purple lipstick. Men often popped in, but the group of close friends quickly kicked them out of the circle if they discovered they were cheating on one of the women. Relationships came and went.

Maria knew all the restaurants in Sea Point and befriended the owners. Before the Victoria & Alfred Waterfront existed, Sea Point was like a tiny Manhattan by the sea. The suburb was not known only for the ocean and its magnificent views over Table Bay, but also for its many restaurants and venues where you could dine and dance.

I accompanied my mother to these places. We would pop in at Caponero during the day, where she knew the owners, and drink coffee, and they would tell us about the previous night's events. Caponero was so popular, there would be a queue of people outside waiting to get in. Hundreds of bottles hung from the ceiling, and the smell of pizza, garlic and seafood was always present, even when the restaurant was closed. Seafood was abundant and cheap, with large crayfish and perlemoen featuring on most menus.

If the manager or staff said the fish was fresh, they meant it, as the catch of the day still had a metaphorical pulse by the time it arrived at the restaurant. Oysters were cheap, and there were tanks in which the oysters and crayfish were kept alive.

Another much-loved Sea Point trattoria was the Pizzeria Napoletana, which opened its doors in 1957. It closed after Covid, in 2021, and a part of the suburb's institutional memory was lost that day. The news that it had closed saddened me, as I remembered distinctly how often I went there as a child with my mom and her friends.

Sloppy Sam sold Greek food, as did Ari Souvlaki, then in a tiny building on Main Road. When the actor Telly Savalas (of *Kojak* fame) came to Cape Town, he dined at these places. Ari openly had a relationship with a so-called coloured woman, which was illegal under apartheid's Immorality Act. They didn't give a toss though, and nobody took any notice. Ari's girlfriend could be seen driving around Sea Point in his gold-tinted Mercedes-Benz, looking fancy and glamorous.

The music in these Greek spots was loud, and as soon as the alcohol started flowing, the excitement would become unbearable; the customers would start smashing large white plates to smithereens and dance in a circle to the Greek music; you could hear them when you walked down the street. The next morning, the owners and staff would sweep the shards off the pavement.

There was also a popular decor and bric-à-brac boutique called La Maree, which was run by a glamorous couple, Chang van Dyk and Martie Vorster. Martie was loud and swore like a trooper; Chang was a gentle presence with a dry sense of humour – they were a hilarious double act. Too overpowering for most.

La Maree sold expensive items like chandeliers, crystal glasses and crystal balls, as well as Fabergé eggs, door handles, furniture ... all completely over the top. The shop also imported furniture from Spain. I don't know why Spain was so big then, but the 'Spanish look' extended even to architecture, as was evident in all the Spanish-style houses that sprung up all over the place.

If you had money in the mid-seventies and early eighties, you bought from La Maree. Chang and Martie were like celebrities. If you told someone in Sea Point, 'I bumped into Chang and Martie,' you were revered. Even better: if people visited you and you said, 'These wine glasses are from La Maree, you know,' an admiration-filled silence would follow. 'La Maree,' they'd whisper, and gently touch the item with a faraway look in their eyes, as if they were staring out to sea.

I was about ten when I saw a crystal ball in La Maree. I asked a random woman: 'Tell me, can you see the future in this ball?' I can't remember what she said, but I stared into that ball and only saw my own face reflected back. A bit disappointing.

Chang and Martie were invited to many opening nights and soirees. Martie had big hair, which she teased into a beehive, and she loved wearing brightly coloured silk caftans in red, yellow or green. Chang was always dressed in an expensive, bespoke suit, of course.

With all these characters and iconic restaurants, Sea Point was the place to be. I was lucky to have a mother who had a good relationship with every-body, from homeless people right up to cabinet ministers, although one of the latter would later change the course of our entire lives.

14

O NE DAY MY MOM'S FRIEND Stella Branca arrived with big news. Stella was another who demanded that I not call her 'tannie'. She was the editor of well-known Afrikaans children's publications such as *Bollie* and *Tina*, as well as an author and translator of books. A strong woman, who had to raise her children on her own.

She was also a friend of the poet Ingrid Jonker, who took her own life one turbulent night in Three Anchor Bay. When Stella told her friends how badly certain of the country's biggest writers had treated Ingrid, they lit cigarettes and seethed. Others claimed that, in fact, Ingrid knew exactly what she was doing. Differing opinions caused intense discussions.

Once Stella was attacked by a man, after which she started karate lessons. She excelled at karate and later made documentaries for women on how to defend themselves when attacked. Stella loved granadilla lollipops and road trips through Namaqualand. She moonlighted as a hostess, in a long evening dress, at the Top Hat restaurant on the Foreshore.

On this occasion, Stella brought tidings of a ship's captain she'd met. He was from a French warship, christened the *Jeanne d'Arc*, which was moored in Cape Town harbour. It was a huge ship staffed by sexy sailors and would be in the harbour for quite a while to undergo repair work.

'Oh, how gorgeous!' a chorus of young women sang. Vicky Leandros was singing 'When Bouzoukis Played' in the background, and although a Greek song, it was close enough to France to add to the heady atmosphere. Even Julio Iglesias would have done.

Stella was tall and sexy, with full lips and a good, strong physique. 'I'm in love,' she declared. A few days ago, she and the captain had gone for a picnic on the slopes of Table Mountain, where he'd kissed her.

'Some of the sailors and officers would love to meet my friends,' Stella told the women. Excitement was running high. My mom suggested that they introduce the sailors to boerekos and other local foods, like Durban curry, potjiekos, smoorsnoek, game and Malay dishes from the Bo-Kaap. The men could bring wine, so long as it wasn't Capenheimer, one of the cheapest Perlé wines on the market.

Dawn Swart, who worked as a receptionist for Dr John Sonnenberg in Sea Point, had a large flat. She was a woman with *savoir faire* and a certain campness and would host the gathering. Stella would speak to the captain; he would decide whom to bring along.

The night of the party arrived. Us children had to entertain ourselves in Lido Court, where we played games and then wrecked the place. A fight broke out, someone knocked over a vase, general mayhem ensued. A neighbour came round and knocked on the door, screaming; we ignored her.

The next morning, when I woke up, the place still looked like a ruin. Maria was fast asleep. It was summer, Saturday morning, and I was restless. The pavilion was calling. I ran barefoot with my costume and towel to the swimming pool. I went and stood next to the railing and looked out across the sea. It felt like I had a place to hang my hat.

The people from the boarding houses stayed in touch and came to visit us. While I was standing there, I thought of the couple we knew from the boarding house in Warren Street: Aunty Esmé and Uncle Dougie, as I called them. They had been married for years, and were working-class in the way they spoke and dressed and in their demeanour. So what? They were always welcoming, like a bowl of hot soup in winter.

They also had five children, so eventually they moved into a small house. One night I had to sleep over at their place; I can't remember why. I had to share a bed with their sixteen-year-old son. I was about nine. In the middle of the night, I could feel him rubbing me between my legs while he made movements with his other arm. I turned around and fell asleep, too tired to be concerned.

'Did he touch you last night?' his sister asked me the next morning. I didn't know what to answer. 'He always does it,' she said. With whom, I couldn't figure out, but in hindsight, why did they allow him to share a bed with me?

Years later, I bumped into him on the Foreshore. He was working as a projectionist at the Broadway cinema. He looked a tad sheepish, but I remember how impressed I was with his job. I was addicted to films and movies. If I became a projectionist, I could see all the new movies for free. My heart was set on becoming one.

One day, long before this per-chance meeting, this guy's entire family arrived in Sea Point in their green Morris Minor station wagon. They invited us to the Locomotive Hotel in Salt River, where we would have a pub lunch. If food was served, the hotels allowed kids to enter.

All the children were bundled into the back of the car, while my mom sat with Aunty Esmé and Uncle Dougie in the front. Aunty Esmé always wore heavy make-up, just like Ma Basson, with false eyelashes, loads of mascara and watermelon-red lipstick. She also wore dresses that were far too short. Uncle Dougie looked like Sid James from the *Carry On* movies and loved laughing out loud at his own jokes.

At the Locomotive Hotel, the mood was merry. The pub was huge, with snooker tables and a jukebox. The clients were mostly railway workers from the Salt River Junction. They had no inhibitions, were loud and always cracking jokes. They also smoked a lot.

After that first visit, we often went there with the whole gang. The songs on the jukebox were mostly Tom Jones, the Carpenters and Johnny Nash. One Sunday, when we were paying another visit, a couple whom I often spotted there was playing their usual Elvis Presley song, 'Can't Help Falling in Love'. They would close-dance slowly, going round and round, unaware of the people around them. After this song, they would always take their seats at the same table, light cigarettes, and she would gently wipe away a tear.

'Why is she crying?' I asked my mom that day.

'About life, my darling, and love.'

'But why does it make her cry?'

'Because love is a dangerous game, and so is life.'

15

I WAS STILL LOOKING OUT TO sea, thinking about the Locomotive Hotel, when I heard someone call my name. It was my mom and her happy retinue of friends who had come for a tan and a swim. The women were all in bikinis, carrying colourful umbrellas and picnic baskets. Among the group was Leon, son of Dawn, who was blond and older than me. He sang, or crooned, well, and the teenage girls swooned over him.

Leon told us that he was going to sing 'Never Ending Song of Love' at the Van Riebeeck cinema in town, where a whole host of people would perform. You had to be under eighteen to enter. He said we should all come along.

In the background at the Sea Point Pavilion, loser-types of disillusioned men sang sad songs, accompanied by wailing banjos. They sang Country and Western songs as if the lyrics had been written just for them. Sometimes a blonde woman, who had seen too much sun and too much life, would accompany one of them. The performers all had lined faces; their eyes looked like raisins. Alcoholics singing for a dime.

On the other hand, the orchestra that also performed there would play boisterous songs from musicals. Sometimes an elderly woman in a bikini would stand on her own and sing Vera Lynn's 'We'll Meet Again': 'Let's say goodbye with a smile, dear / Just for a while, dear, we must part.'

A cafeteria sold ice creams, sweets, chips, pies and cooldrinks. A queue would form outside, and when the sun was really hot, your bare feet would burn on the tar. Then you jumped from one foot to the other until you'd bought your snacks. Run, run to the green grass. Sit down under the umbrella. Cool down. Finish your ice cream. Sprint to the pool, jump in at the deep end.

Once a year, there would be a Mrs Sea Point pageant. Twenty women would walk up and down, turn to the crowd and blow kisses. They were all white women, of course; in hindsight, I realise in what a bubble we lived.

My mom and her friends started talking about the previous night, which they'd enjoyed with the sexy officers from the *Jeanne d'Arc*. Later, the captain would invite them for dinner on the warship, which by that stage had been splashed all over the front pages of the local newspapers. The ship was famous. It would be in the docks for three months. So, my mom and her posse enjoyed three months of the high life and bundles of merriment.

They attended a dinner dance on the ship and would eventually visit every restaurant in Cape Town, from the Harlequin in Parow right through to the Dragon Inn in Mouille Point, and beyond. The beyond included La Perla in Sea Point and boerekos in Stellenbosch.

For fine dining, there was also the Ritz Plaza Hotel with its revolving restaurant on the twenty-second floor, complete with pianist, sweeping staircases and flambé desserts. A seventies' time capsule for decades to follow.

Female hairstyles evolved from beehives to 'big hair': fluffed, puffed, the larger the better, teased out and sprayed with Lecca. White men had to be tanned, with open-neck shirts, hairy chests and a gold chain. The French, however, had a continental look, whatever that meant. I overheard my mother using the word.

Maria and her friends learnt quite a few French words during this time, obviously during pillow-talk. Suddenly, it was all *merci, au revoir* and *bonjour*. They would say these words while pouting their lips like dancers at the Moulin Rouge.

Some of the women started wearing chartreuse-green lipstick, and even yellow. The longer the *Jeanne d'Arc* was anchored, the bolder they became. This ship was a welcome respite from the world of John Vorster, the Broederbond and the Dutch Reformed Church. The Rooi, Roomse and Swart gevare.

When the ship left, many hearts were broken, but it was Stella who suffered most, in dignified silence. Everybody knew that the captain was the love of her life. Years later, when I wrote about her love affair, she was furious and wrote to me that I'd portrayed her as a dockside dolly. At that stage Stella had moved to America, to live with her daughter. She stopped replying to my emails. It was hard for me because she was a huge figure from my childhood. She never spoke to me again.

When Stella died at eighty-nine, her daughter sent me a photograph via WhatsApp. While she was rummaging through some of her mother's clothing and possessions, she discovered something – a ribbon with the words 'Jeanne d'Arc' on it.

The Dragon Inn in Mouille Point was one of Cape Town's first Chinese restaurants, and the cognoscenti labelled it one of *the* places to be seen. Locals, however, called Mouille Point the Cinderella Suburb. People hated the wind. The Doll House, right opposite the Dragon Inn, was a drive-in restaurant where you could sit in your car and order milkshakes, slaptjips and hamburgers. It was one of the few attractions in the area. Of course, there was the little Blue Train for children, which is still there today (one of the few remaining trains still running in South Africa).

At the Doll House, they attached a tray to your car window, and you had to be careful that the seagulls didn't swoop down and steal your food. There were far more seagulls around then than there are today. For the Dragon Inn, you dressed up. It was an occasion. The highlight for me as a child were the fortune cookies, served with Chinese tea, after dessert. Inside were hidden messages like 'The early bird gets the worm, but the second mouse gets the cheese.' Or: 'The fortune you seek is in another cookie.' How true.

I think I might have missed another restaurant in the Cinderella Suburb, the Harbour Tavern? And the Bay Hotel, where on Sunday nights you could go for curry and rice for twenty cents.

Some people who lived in Mouille Point lived in cheap but sensible blocks of flats, but the elderly and 'lower-middle-class' white families lived in small houses. It was apartheid, but the Chinese restaurant's owners also lived there. In those days, the government classified Chinese people as so-called people of colour, but Japanese people were considered white. Try to get your head around that. But I digress.

The lighthouse's foghorn was much louder then than it is today – you could hear it all the way to Oranjezicht and Milnerton. On Sunday evenings, an elderly man would sit in his lounge, on his own, and people who walked past his house could see and hear him playing his violin. I would often walk or cycle there just to listen to him.

On rainy days, when the rain was gentler than it is today (we call it a motreën in Afrikaans – a 'soft rain', as gentle as a moth touching you), it was quite an atmospheric experience. The sea, the rain, an old man playing a violin through a blurry window … what a mood.

Today, the suburb is packed with restaurants and high-rise flats; goodbye, Cinderella, hello, Princess. Damn, on a rainy day, I'm sure I can still hear a violin playing somewhere in the background.

16

THE DAY OF THE SINGING competition at the Van Riebeeck cinema in Riebeek Street arrived. It was a Saturday morning. Leon was ready. This gala event took place just before the end of the school year. A concierge wearing white gloves, a hat and a shiny suit welcomed you at the entrance and kept an eye on the rowdy crowd. He just gave you one look, and you knew you had to behave. Ushers, often chewing and popping bubble-gum, showed you to your seat.

Years later, one of the ushers, Sedick 'Boeta' Diekie Tassiem, would pop up at the Labia Theatre in the same outfit, although his suits varied in colour from purple and red to yellow, like those lipsticks my mom and her friends wore. Poor Sedick died in his early seventies from a Covid-related illness.

At the Van Riebeeck, the ushers used torches to show you to your seat. A man of advanced years would carry a tray (in Afrikaans, 'n penskafee) in front of him, held steady by a rope of sorts around his neck. He was immensely popular with the youngsters, as he was the conveyor of sweets and, therefore, happiness.

On the day of Leon's performance, the usual Laurel and Hardy movie was shown first, but there was no second show. Instead, ten teenagers would sing and try their best to win over the audience. After each song the crowd would applaud, and the performance that elicited the loudest applause would win. Prizes were at stake: money, sweets, yo-yos, dingbats, free movie tickets.

We accompanied Dawn and her new husband, Dick Swart, who was a primary-school principal. He was a stern, friendly, good-looking man who drove a large Triumph 2000. In the back, on the red leather seats, sat Leon, his younger brother Dino, and me. Dick always had to drive around the old Green Point traffic circle a few times, much to our delight. The car would tilt to the right, and we'd shriek all the way to the cinema.

Dawn asked us to be as loud as possible when it was Leon's turn to sing 'Never Ending Song of Love'. On arrival, the tension and excitement felt unbearable. The action was going to start. After the movie, one singer after another came on stage. People whistled, stamped their feet, jumped up, screamed.

Leon was the last singer to perform. By that stage, the guy who'd performed before him was a certain winner. This guy's voice had already broken, and when he sang 'It's Not Unusual' by Tom Jones, he sounded and even looked like a young Tom dressed in his white catsuit.

We silently knew what was coming – disappointment. But when Leon walked onto the stage with his blond tuft of hair and a certain swagger, the teenage girls gasped. Two in front of us held onto each other, as if they might faint. Leon was handsome, well-built and resembled a young Jon Voight in *Midnight Cowboy*. He started singing, moved his hips, shook his head, shiny hair all over the place, and flirted outrageously with his female fans: winking, blowing kisses, even clutching his groin.

When he finished, he bowed. The entire cinema stood up and Leon received a standing ovation that lasted for ten minutes. One girl was sobbing uncontrollably. Leon was the winner. Dawn also cried, mascara running down her face. The young women threw themselves at Leon and begged him for his autograph.

After that, with his looks and new-found fame, Leon never had a shortage of girlfriends. To celebrate, we all went to the Spur; the day was light and full of rock 'n' roll.

Because Leon was a star.

17

MY MOTHER ARRIVED HOME ONE day and told me that she was in love. 'Again,' I thought. The *Jeanne d'Arc* was hardly over the horizon and here she goes. The man's name was Fritz; his surname escapes me. He was an Austrian and was passionate about mom. As an immigrant, he was still waiting for his work visa.

At the time, white people could easily become South African citizens, as the National Party depended on their votes. Fritz was like a puppy in my mom's hands. She could do whatever she wanted. Fritz took her out to every restaurant imaginable in and around Cape Town. The one they liked the most was the Austrian Innsbruck Inn, at the bottom end of Sea Point, right at the circle.

It had a sweeping staircase, perfect for dramatic entrances, and at the bottom of the stairs a man sat and played the accordion and sang Austrian songs. The waiters spoke German and the main course was a fondue with expensive cheeses, complete with copper pots, fresh rolls and other Austrian dishes. I loved going there, as it felt so cosmopolitan. The bright lights of Sea Point, so glorious for a young boy.

During this time, members of the Jewish community often came to visit Maria. I heard them talk glowingly about communism during their late-night discussions. In hindsight, it became clear to me that my mother engaged with a wide spectrum of people about what was going on in the country. Not bad for a boeremeisie from Namaqualand.

My mom often took me to the Labia Theatre and The Space, where she sometimes had to smuggle me in because I was too young for certain productions. The National Party hated The Space, if not for the foul language, then the content of the productions, or because black people performed on stage.

Maria also introduced me to the works of various poets, from Breyten Breytenbach to Sylvia Plath. I sometimes had no idea what she was reading to me, but it was thrilling, because it all took place by candlelight.

18

RITZ WAS SO IN LOVE with my mother, he took her to the Victoria
Falls, where they partied and had a great time. On their return, I had
to look at photographs of her in front of the falls, of her holding a fish,
of her tossing the poor thing back into the water, of her posing in front of
the hotel with large Jackie O sunglasses.

There were hardly any photos of Fritz, but it was clear that he was smit-
ten. This, however, did not keep them from having huge fights, with Maria
kicking him out, slamming the door and telling him to fuck off right out
of her life. Shortly afterwards, he would be back: humble, desperate, shame-
faced. Atonement and forgiveness would follow, and nobody spoke about
it again.

Fritz drove a yellow Volkswagen Kombi kitted out like a camper van.
There was a sofa in the back, and a gas stove, a fridge and a bed. The roof
could lift and let in air, the back door could slide wide open – it was so hip.
A little house on wheels; I loved it. We drove all over Cape Town, specifically to the German Club in town, which was hidden behind high walls and
a block of flats. Once you were inside, it was always one helluva party, with
oompah bands, accordions, guitars, trumpets, drums and flugelhorns.

The men laughed loudly and had red faces, like watermelons, and the
female waitresses smoked and had ponytails. Not your stereotypical vision
of sour and strict Germans. Fritz opened another world to us.

But he was a complicated man. One day he invited my friend Ivan and
me to come along with him in his camper van; we'd park next to the sea,
and he'd cook something. We stopped on the road to Llandudno, right next
to the ocean.

It was a lovely afternoon, not too hot, the sun slowly setting, a salty breeze.
Fritz made bacon and eggs. Ivan and I were sitting on the sofa being silly and
laughing at our own jokes. Suddenly, Fritz erupted like lava from a volcano,
and he threw all the food into the sea. He was white with fury. He sped home
to Sea Point, demanded that we get out, and off he went, into the distance.
He thought that we were laughing at him.

He was gone for two days. When I told this story to my mother, she just rolled her eyes, lit a candle and put on a Shirley Bassey record.

Little did we know what other drama was awaiting us.

Fritz arrived with the news that he wanted to open an Austrian restaurant and delicatessen in Three Anchor Bay, on the left corner as you entered Sea Point, opposite the library. It had to be the best restaurant in Sea Point, and he would import all the furniture and decor directly from Austria. He had a posse of friends, some top chefs from his *heimat*, in Cape Town. Its name would be Café Wien.

Soon, they started installing the fittings, and large, ornate, dark-wood furniture arrived, as well as a grand piano. I walked past Café Wien every now and then to witness this new venue gradually unfolding on the corner of Glengariff and Main roads.

I also attended the opening night, dressed up in traditional lederhosen, which are basically leather shorts with H-shaped braces. It was a horrible outfit and I felt like a fool. My mother played hostess and the crème de la crème of Sea Point's gourmands and socialites filled the place.

Lady Peterson dressed like Marlene Dietrich and stood at the piano, singing war songs in a raspy voice. Café Wien became an enormous success. Twice a week, in the evening, my mother would play hostess and walk people to their tables, making them feel comfortable.

She loved it. Life had never been so good; we were happy, and everything was beautiful.

19

ONE DAY FRITZ ARRIVED AT the flat with a sad face. He told us that, when he'd applied for his work visa, he'd had to fill in which religion he belonged to. He'd written down that he was an atheist. In the meantime, he had met my mother, opened a restaurant and invested money in the country. It was all part of his plan to settle in South Africa, a place he loved.

Now there was a problem with his lack of religion. Dr Connie Mulder, one of the apartheid regime's most dangerous apparatchiks and a fervent supporter of the Dutch Reformed Church, was then the Minister of Home Affairs. Immigration rules and criteria for citizenship fell under him. He was adamant that he would not allow any atheist immigrants to become South African, even if they were highly qualified or here to boost the numbers of the white population.

The power of the Dutch Reformed Church was immense. This Church of God could brainwash cabinet ministers and convince its congregation to support apartheid. It also advocated homophobia, and metaphorically condemned women to the kitchen. Patriarchy flourished. Some Afrikaans women even called their husbands 'pappa'; these men sat at the head of the table when dinner was served.

John Vorster had a brother called Koot, who was a dominee. A large, angry man, he was the editor of *Die Kerkbode* in the early seventies. *Die Kerkbode* was the mouthpiece of the NG Kerk, and whatever appeared in its pages was law.

In the early seventies, the Dutch Reformed Church synod held a congress to discuss permissiveness and moral decline in South Africa. The synod advocated the implementation of a series of Sunday rules, based on the official Church's viewpoint. No swimming would be allowed on Sundays, no wearing of informal clothes in public, no buying or receiving of any of the Sunday newspapers, and no social visits.

In those days, therefore, atheism was the equivalent of communism, which meant you were here to overthrow the government. Fritz looked tense, my mother was sombre, the atmosphere in the flat was dark.

Fritz went to talk to people at the Department of Home Affairs. One Sunday, I had to put on a suit, as we were off to church. It was a purple suit; I felt so shy. My mom wore a hat, her Jackie O sunglasses and understated make-up, while Fritz was in a black suit. We got into the yellow Kombi and drove to the Cape Peninsula Reformed Church in Kloof Street, which was in a tiny building next to the Dutch Reformed Church's community hall and offices.

As we arrived, I remember a group of photographers descending on us while Fritz parked the Kombi. We got out and the cameras clicked away. The photographers even followed us to the entrance of the church.

After the service, we walked back to the Kombi while people stared at us, then drove back to Sea Point. What a curious experience … I had no clue what was going on, but the aftermath was even worse. The government decided Fritz was persona non grata and he had to leave the country.

I saw him and my mother in tears in the kitchen. She held a *Cape Argus* in her hands, and on the front page there was a huge picture of Fritz. The article was about his atheism and that the National Party would have nothing to do with it. Fritz had to go. The Nats were deporting him, with the full support of the Dutch Reformed Church.

This inhumane decision would change the course of our lives. One man, the demon-like Dr Connie Mulder, with one signature, started a series of Kafkaesque nightmares that would haunt us forever.

Fritz begged my mother to come to Austria; I could come along too. But she didn't want to, as she loved South Africa and her friends, and her mother was still alive.

From the day Fritz left, the sky darkened. We were ill-prepared for what was to come.

20

FRITZ LEFT AND A HUSH descended on Lido Court, Sea Point, all the jolly drained out of the air. My mother decided to visit my grandmother in Lutzville to clear her head. I stayed over at Griet-Blue-Beetle and her son Ivan's, as they lived close to my school.

When my mother returned, she lit some candles, and we sat outside on the stoep. She wanted to tell me something. During her visit to my gran, she'd met a man, Christie Kruger, who had gone to school with her. He was older, but so charming. He farmed with grapes and promised her the world. She was in love, and she was going to marry him. His farm, Dassieshoek in Lutzville, overlooked some vineyards and the Olifants River. It was also close to where my granny, Ouma Hansie, lived.

I didn't know how to process this. My world crumbled and I stumbled into the kitchen. My mom promised me that I could visit every school holiday, and she would also come to Cape Town regularly; she would need to see her friends.

The timing was right. She was tired of battling financially, in her early thirties and worn out from working non-stop. She also felt bitter about the Fritz saga. It was time for a new beginning. The angels had sent this man. He would save her. I would go and live with my father and his wife, Linda, in Gardens, within walking distance of my school in Kloof Street.

My father? Sam Korck? I wondered from where he'd suddenly appeared. How weird. Quite unexpectedly, he was going to feature in my life after years of absence. He'd never even paid maintenance.

I'd met him once. He'd fetched me in his car and driven very fast, wanting to show off. We drove through the backstreets of Vredehoek with screeching tyres and ran over a dog. The dog yelped and died. That scene never left me. My dad was also upset, but what was he thinking? It was someone's pet. A woman came out of a house, screaming.

A new pub, called the Vasco da Gama Taverna, had opened in Green Point. It was 1972. My dad said we should go there; he needed a drink. In the pub, the kids sat apart, sipping Cokes, while the men hung onto the counter drinking brandy and Coke. Eventually, my father got maudlin; he had dronk-verdriet over the dog. What a sorry sight.

I'm still a regular at that pub today. If I look carefully, I can see my dad's shadow lurking next to the counter, crying over the dog.

21

EVERYTHING HAPPENED SO FAST. MY father came to fetch me, and my mom married Christie. Off they went, to Lutzville, a God-forsaken backwater in those days, with gravel roads, searing heat and alcoholics. The farmers lived in luxury, the workers in abject poverty.

My life changed abruptly. The block of flats I moved into with my dad, whom I called 'darra', and Linda was named Avignon Court. It was an old Art Deco building in Union Street, Gardens.

My mom and dad were two very different people; the one was an extrovert, while Sammy, as he was known, was more of an introvert. Linda was, and still is, a darling woman, but in the beginning, she was quiet, reserved.

Although Sammy wasn't loud or talkative, he did have a way with people. He could be charming to such an extent that he may well have almost hypnotised people. One woman in our street confessed that she would love to marry him. She walked past our block of flats about ten times a day.

Sammy's quiet charm made him a top car salesman. When I visited his work and saw him in action, I, too, was mesmerised. He turned into another person. Sammy regularly won the Car Salesman of the Year award. When I moved in, he was working for a prestigious Peugeot dealership in the centre of town.

Sammy insisted that I read all the dailies: the *Cape Times*, the *Cape Argus* and *Die Burger*. Over weekends, *Rapport*, the *Weekend Argus* and the *Sunday Times*. His philosophy was that you should read them all and make up your own mind.

Linda worked for Nedbank. I felt lonely and like an outsider. It wasn't their fault, but I missed my mom. I was grieving for my life with her in Sea Point. My mother's move to Lutzville triggered a deep depression, taking me back to how afraid and lonely I'd felt in the orphanage, and during my stay with my uncle, Braam Lategan. This was the third time I was ripped away from my mom.

It broke me; I felt hollow, black on the inside, like the dark side of the moon. I lay awake at night, pining for her, listening to Springbok Radio because I could not sleep. I would listen to Robin Alexander, who called himself the 'Minister of Midnight Affairs', till the early hours of the morning. He was an invisible friend.

When I walked in the streets, I would get excited when I thought I saw my mother's face, only to realise that it wasn't her. I stared at women, hoping to one day spot her. At school I didn't take part in much; during breaks, I sat alone. My marks were good, but I had no social life. In hindsight, I realise this was when my addictions kicked in.

I would rush home after school to listen to Esmé Euvrard and Jan Cronjé on Springbok Radio; they had a food programme called *So Maak Mens*. After that, there was a serial, *Dans van die Flamink*. During these programmes I would sit at the kitchen table and eat Marie biscuits. Up to two packets at a time. I would dip the biscuits in black coffee, and I couldn't stop.

I ballooned, but food lifted my mood; it was a drug. It was my primary and first addiction. Feel lonely? Have a big black hole in you? Fill it with food. It was tough.

Opposite us lived two young boys, Grant and Peter, roughly my age. I started visiting them, and soon we became friends. They partly ended my loneliness. They built a tree house where we would lie for hours, reading comics. Some days we would spray people passing the house with a hose-pipe and then quickly run inside, locking the door. We would roll around laughing.

Other days we would phone strangers and, in a fake voice, tell them that we were phoning from Radio Good Hope, as it was called then, and that they were the lucky recipients of a huge amount of money. On boring Sunday afternoons, we would knock on people's doors, waking them from their afternoon nap, and ask them if 'Mr Smith' lived there. Most people just slammed the door in our faces. Childish, of course, but fun.

On some Sundays, Sammy would take us for braais on the slopes of Table Mountain and Signal Hill, when it was still legal to do so. When the sun set on Signal Hill, thousands of fireflies would appear from the bushes and light up the veld. They enthralled me.

The Kloof Street Public Library became my regular hangout; not so cool or sexy for a youngster, but nevertheless a building that opened many new emotional paths for me. My first visit was to read about fireflies.

I learnt that fireflies use their flashes as mating signals and that some of them flash in unison. Those were the ones on Signal Hill. The mountain would light up as if a huge UFO with bright spotlights was making a sudden landing to warn Earth of its impending doom.

Over the years I would return to this spot. The braai area doesn't exist any more. Once, it got dark, and I sat down on a bench and waited. But the fireflies didn't appear, ever again.

Near the library, just a few blocks away, I rediscovered the Labia, the theatre where my mom took me when I was younger. It was now a cinema, where I started watching arthouse movies, mostly from abroad. Years later, when I wrote an article on the Labia, the actor Richard E. Grant told me that during his student years at the University of Cape Town's drama school, which was opposite the cinema, the place was like his second university. The quality movies he watched there opened the world of cinema to him; also, the tickets were cheap, and sometimes he would watch the same movie over and over.

I decided one day that, as I was an only child, I would immerse myself in movies, books and, of course, Springbok Radio, which was on twenty-four hours a day. Fighting loneliness was my mantra. It was the early seventies. TV only came to South Africa in 1976. The atmosphere in the Cape was that of a small town.

One pale and windy Saturday afternoon, I was walking down Adderley Street, aimless and window-shopping, as people did in those days. At the top of the street, I saw a poster advertising the film *Enter the Dragon*, starring Bruce Lee. It was showing at the Pigalle tearoom cinema, where you could watch three films for fourteen cents. I went down some stairs and pulled open a dirty old curtain.

A glass case, with a green Formica counter, displayed pies, Coke, chips, cigarettes, popcorn, chewing gum, red toffee apples, candyfloss and other sweets for sale. Large cans of Ricoffy and Five Roses tea were set out on a trolley. You helped yourself and drank the beverage from white polystyrene cups.

I paid the woman behind the counter, who slapped the change down hard on the Formica surface. She had a cigarette in the corner of her mouth and looked like a displeased Dowager Countess of Grantham, as played by Maggie Smith in *Downton Abbey*.

I pulled open another curtain, and there I was: in a theatre with a big screen. The light on the screen was pale blue, because so many people were smoking. Everywhere, just fumes. I sat down and watched all three films they were showing that day. My relationship with bughouses started right then. The audiences were rough and often sat there the entire day, till late into the night.

One day I saw an article on the front page of the *Cape Argus* about a young man I used to see there. He fell asleep right at the back of the cinema, and when they closed one Saturday night, they didn't notice him. The poor guy had to sit there, in the dark, until Monday morning, when they opened again.

Remember, it was the seventies. The church was strict, so no movies on Sundays. Later, this was circumvented by midnight shows, which started at exactly one minute past twelve on a Monday. Oh, it was always nice to show a middle finger to a bunch of fuckfaces.

Soon after my visit to the Pigalle, I discovered the Piccadilly tearoom cinema in the old Picbel Parkade, which showed mostly Westerns. These were wild, violent movies where men on horseback shot at each other and beat each other with long whips. Of course, the best scene in every film of that genre was when the men were sitting in a hot, seedy bar drinking whisky. Outside, someone would tie up his horse, hat on his head, after which he would kick open the bar's swing doors and shoot into the ceiling with two guns blazing, and then, for good measure, at a few people sitting at the bar.

Outside, women in white puffy dresses would run screaming into their homes. There would always be one waiting for the wounded killer, and she would gently take care of him while they declared their love for each other. The killer would then slowly die in her arms. The camera would pan away from her where she lay on the bed crying, and hover over the barren plains while the acknowledgements and actors' names started to roll: John Wayne, Charles Bronson, Clint Eastwood ...

Another cinema was the Roxy, a stone's throw from City Hall. After paying, you had to descend a set of stairs deep into the dark heart of the theatre. On the left was a large kitchen where you could order hamburgers, hot dogs, pies and many other foods. Each seat came equipped with a small tray and an ashtray. It was a place that, under the radar, allowed in people of colour; the management looked the other way. The Roxy's speciality was Elvis Presley movies, and there were many.

Behind the theatre was a room known as the Crying Room, where women could take their babies if they started screaming. Over time, this became a room for making whoopie.

One event that stands out was the night when a large group of ducktails came to watch Elvis Presley's *Jailhouse Rock*. When the movie ended, pandemonium erupted. The ducktails jumped up from their seats and pulled out chains from under their leather jackets, took to the streets and started smashing car windows under cover of darkness.

The crowds quickly cleared away, the Roxy emptied and soon there were police, blue lights, sirens. Then followed a stunned silence. The ducktails were gone. Only the broken shards of shiny glass sparkled under the lampposts.

As Sundays were so boring, with everything closed, I would cycle through the empty streets of Cape Town with not a person in sight. On your own, on your bicycle, you are young … Throw in the raging southeaster, and depression kicks in. I would cycle to Sea Point, just for the sake of nostalgia, and because at least there was some life, action, drama, people, restaurants …

The game with my two friends, where we knocked on people's doors and asked for Mr Smith, eventually got us into trouble. We stopped.

Kloof Street back then was another world. If you look at all the restaurants and cars that line the street today, nobody will believe how dead it was then. Many of today's bars and restaurants were houses, with huge gardens, where elderly women lived. Often, a photograph of a man in uniform, allegedly a fiancé who had been killed in World War II, would be proudly displayed on top of the piano.

These kind women, who invited me in for Oros and Marie biscuits, would stare longingly at these photos and tell long, sad stories about the men. Later, when I was less naive, I realised that the women were lesbians. The photographs were both a sign and a cover-up. Lesbians had it hard. Polite people never used that word in company; they just pretended lesbians didn't exist. How painful it must have been for those women to live such invisible lives, hiding their relationships behind a facade of a fiancé killed in a war.

One day I cycled up Kloof Street and, overnight, demolitionists had knocked down Radyn, the boarding house, opposite Topolino Café, where I'd lived for a while. For years afterwards, it was just a parking lot.

It was another bleak Sunday afternoon when I discovered Tommy's Exchange and Second-Hand Bookshop. It was next to a supermarket called Punky's. Odd people shopped at Punky's, like the rotund woman of a certain age who arrived every Saturday morning and, before taking a trolley, would first march up and down the aisles whistling the theme song of *The Bridge on the River Kwai* so loudly that the whole supermarket would come to a standstill. Accompanying her was a tall, thin man with a trimmed moustache and a baton under his arm. He would march behind her.

After marching through all the aisles, they would stop and select a trolley, salute, and start shopping. The thing about Cape Town is that it's never had a shortage of crackpots. Never.

Tommy's bookshop was a picture show on its own. The two owners, who were spouses, should have been cast in films. Tommy had bags under his eyes and was as pale as a Weisswurst (a white German sausage). He looked like Harry Dean Stanton as the world-weary Travis Henderson in the Wim Wenders movie *Paris, Texas*. Tommy loved a tipple and hid his brandy behind the counter.

His wife was of a large build and wore tight dresses. She looked like Hattie Jacques, the matron in the *Carry On* movies, her face covered in white make-up. She smelt of baby powder and always had a cigarette in her mouth. When she laughed, she'd throw her head right back, howl like a dog and slap the counter so hard that it was on the verge of breaking. A cheery one indeed, in sharp contrast to her hubby, Mr Watery Eyes.

The pair took to me and I to them, and they allowed me to sit in their shop and watch the customers, who popped in and out. One day, Mrs Watery Eyes gave me a book by Ed McBain. The books were cheap, about two cents each. I became addicted to these fading paperbacks and started reading Louis L'Amour, Leslie Charteris, Ian Fleming, Raymond Chandler and Isaac Asimov. Although they weren't all literary heavyweights, I absorbed more of the English language through them than I did at primary school.

I remember primary school as being boring and a drag. One day I felt like making trouble, so I gave someone a chocolate-flavoured Brooklax. It tasted like delicious chocolate, but it was a tablet to make your stomach work. Well, this boy's stomach worked, and he pointed at me and told the teacher it was because of something I gave him. They found the Brooklax on me and I was ushered to the headmaster's office. There, the teacher, a vile man who had no future, told the principal that this was how drug dealing starts. Drug dealing! I received a hiding but never spoke to that teacher again, except once.

One day I was talking in his class, and he called me to the front. I had to show both my hands, palms facing upwards. He hit both hands twice. As I walked back to my desk, he asked the class if anybody else wanted to be spanked. I was furious, so I walked back to his desk and held out my hands.

He gave me two more spankings. I looked at him with dark, dangerous eyes, like a child in a horror movie, and said: 'You enjoyed that, didn't you? I wonder why?'

22

MY FATHER STARTED STAYING OUT later and later after work. Late, as in stumbling in at around midnight. I could hear the keys rattling in the door. The Oranje Hotel was right next to us.

Linda and I ate alone at night. She would put his food in the Defy 418's warmer. After midnight I would hear him in the kitchen, unscrewing the bottle of Cane, opening the can of Coke and pouring himself another drink. Sometimes I would get up to look at him, sitting alone at the table, drink in hand, staring straight ahead. He was not an exuberant drunk; instead, he grew quiet and morose.

With his endless drinking, he would lose his job like clockwork. Then he would drink the entire day, pass out and start again. The atmosphere in the flat was unbearable, suffocating. He would smoke and drop ash all over the place, stumble, or just sit. He would think nothing of dropping his cigarettes in the toilet and just leaving them there. It was disgusting, like living in a pub.

With her tiny income, Linda kept the show on the road. Sammy demanded money for alcohol, and if she didn't give it to him, he became violent. This, after my life with my mother, was unfamiliar territory to negotiate. I fell into a deep, deep depression, or I would dissociate, as if I were functioning outside my body.

I developed obsessive-compulsive disorder and would clean up behind Sammy every day. My room was impeccable, my cupboard perfect – I saw to it that everything was in the right order. I would walk to school and wonder if I'd put the toilet seat down. It gave me a sense of control over the chaos.

It made me despondent that I could never invite friends to our flat. I never knew in what state the place would be, and it looked poor. There was hardly any furniture, as Sammy would pawn it for alcohol. Not that I had that many friends to invite over, but sometimes I would have liked to. But we lived like paupers.

One day we went to Killarney to watch motor racing. We went in Linda's car, as Sammy didn't have one at that stage. On our way back, he was drunk. When Linda complained about his driving, Sammy lost his temper, stopped the car and told her to get out. It was dark and the flat was twenty kilometres away from where he pushed her out.

He raced home at a hundred-and-twenty kilometres an hour, swerving across lanes, hooting, flashing his lights. At home, he double locked the door. When I woke up the next morning, I could hear him begging her to forgive him. And did she have cash so that he could buy his Cane and Coke? Linda lost weight; she hardly ever laughed.

One could taste the darkness in No. 5 Avignon Court with its view of Table Mountain. I was deeply aware of how miserable my living arrangements were.

One day, our class went on a school picnic to The Glen. It was a lovely spot, with grass, a river, plants and tall trees. The rugby player Jannie Engelbrecht was there, with his beautiful wife, Ellen. They were the hosts, as their son Jean was in our class.

Although the Engelbrechts would divorce decades later, they shone with happiness that day. They were so decent, well-dressed, classy, warm. It entered my mind that I didn't know such happiness between a mother and a father. In my home, thunderous clouds of alcoholism were casting a long shadow over my childhood. I lived with a father who was a drunk, one who had achieved nothing in his life.

It hurt me so much.

23

I'M NOT CERTAIN, BUT BY now I must have been around twelve years old. My memory might be playing tricks on me, as I was going through so much trauma. I blocked out huge chapters over the years, and then a smell, a sound, a song, triggers a flood of recollections.

I do remember phoning my mother every Friday. The first school holiday I went to visit her, I took the Bitterfontein train. Sammy, inebriated, took me to the station in his safari suit. He wore aviator sunglasses.

It was exciting to get away, to see my mother and to travel on a train dragged by an old steam locomotive. The benches had green upholstery, and on the outside the trains were painted a deep red colour.

I rode with the window open, and we stopped at tiny stations, each with its own character. Sometimes I would share a compartment with an array of odd people: some drinking brandy from polystyrene cups, others slowly eating their padkos of boiled eggs, frikadelle or boerewors, washed down with tea from a flask.

The train left in the late afternoon and chugged along through the night. It was lovely to clickety-clack through the veld, watch the stars, smell the coal, lie under the warm bedding and listen to the whistling of the locomotive as we sped along.

On my first visit after my mother married, she and Christie both waited for me on the platform. It was early morning; the air was fresh. I saw little, red face-brick railway houses, my favourite architecture to this day.

Both seemed friendly, but his face had the hard look of Charles Bronson. My mother just looked uncomfortable. I was seeing her for the first time in six months. Her spontaneity, her vibrant personality, was gone.

We got into Christie's old, green Chevrolet bakkie and started driving to the farm, Dassieshoek. We all sat in front. My mother was fidgeting with her wedding ring; he stared straight in front of him. We crossed a bridge over the Olifants River, then turned onto a gravel road. When Christie stopped the bakkie, I saw an unassuming farmhouse with hardly any architectural grace, as well as a steep hill where the workers' houses were situated.

The homestead overlooked some vineyards and a river filled with reeds, just as my mother had told me. It was hot and the sand was red. The sound of cicadas filled the dry air. So, this was it. There was also a little gazebo beside the house. My mom and I would later sit inside it and chat for hours.

But first they took me to my room, a sombre space with an olive-green carpet and an old dressing table with a mirror. The curtains were thick, and the window looked out over a dry piece of veld and a koppie. It was quiet.

My mom and I went and sat outside. She told me that I would spend a week with her and Christie and another week with my gran in the village. I thought it a bit strange, as I'd come to visit my mother. I liked my granny, but why?

I soon realised that Christie did not like children. My mother protected me, especially at night. When the sun set, Christie would pour his first drink: brandy and water. After a few drinks, he would start screaming and moaning. I noticed that my mother had also started drinking more. Christie would scold her and call her a whore, and I was a hoerkind, the son of a whore.

The sins of the fathers, and how the wheel turns. Decades later, Christie's nephew, a man called Martin Visser, was the new owner of Dassieshoek. In 2018, a court convicted him for the murder of a farmworker, Adam 'Mannetjies Dukvreet' Pieterse. Visser beat him with a spade and then dragged him behind his quad bike before forcing Pieterse's two friends to bury him alive among the remains of dead animals. Before killing him, Visser had called him a hoerkind.

Why this family had such an affinity for this word, hoerkind, and violence towards and hatred for farmworkers, leaves me bewildered. While Visser was in the cells in Vredendal, he tried to take his own life. When Judge Nathan Erasmus sentenced him to life imprisonment, he said in his judgment: 'A human being's family has been robbed of the opportunity to just know he is alive; to know what happened to their brother. They don't have that, only the findings of the court.

'Martin Visser still hasn't told us anything. I don't want to send a message that farmworkers' lives are cheap. It's not. He disposed of the body, not only in a place where sick and dead animals are buried. He buried him like an animal.'

The pathologist, Dr Esme Erasmus, said Pieterse's remains had been at an advanced stage of decomposition. 'He had a cut on his left upper arm, resembling a defensive wound, and his genitals and perineum – the area between the anus and the scrotum – had been mutilated after his death.'

Meanwhile, Christie shouted, screamed and became more violent. My mother often crept in behind my back when I slept, out of fear of what he could do to her. She told me he was a fraud. Before the wedding, he'd pretended to be kind and sensitive. After six months, the facade could not hold, nor could the centre. He had become abusive, both physically and emotionally.

As soon as the sun set on the farm, I would start tensing up. The nights were endless. One night I woke up and Christie was trying to penetrate me from behind, his fat cock hard and drill-like. He was intending to rape me. My mother hit him over the head, I can't remember with what. He got up and fetched an axe from the garage.

We locked my bedroom door, but he started breaking it down. Terrified, we jumped out the window into the darkness, stumbling over rocks and bushes. On the hill, we found solace with the farmworkers. We were safe there; it was the last place he thought we would hide.

The workers often looked after us. Anna and John Takkies were a lovely couple. In Namaqualand, the two names would often join, so they were known as AnnaJohn. They gave us blankets to sleep on until it was safe to go back, often only the next morning. The hospitality of the farmworkers, poor but willing to share, will always remain with me.

These people had a huge influence on my psyche. Christie called these quality people by a derogatory term, volk, an Afrikaans slur for farmworkers. They were thin, tiny people, their skin wrinkled from working in the sun. Maria and I would regularly spend our nights with them, huddled around the fire, listening to tales of yore. Stories about the stars, the moon, the wind, animals, old people, children, that went back centuries, when their forebearers roamed Namaqualand.

They had more quality in their souls than someone like Christie and his ilk could ever have. While we listened to their stories, we could hear Christie carrying on like an animal roaring at the moon. We dared not go back; he was sure to murder us.

One night, when he started, my mother was boiling the kettle behind him. She calmly poured the piping-hot water over his head. He ran to the bedroom and grabbed his gun. He fired one shot, and a tiny piece of shrapnel hit my mother's nose. We ran out of the kitchen towards the vineyards with him shouting behind us, shooting aimlessly.

It was dark, I stumbled, and I could hear his footsteps coming closer. I lifted myself up and sprinted as fast as I could, pulling my mom by her hand, into the vineyards. There, we crouched while he kept shooting, and then, suddenly, he stopped. We could hear him mumbling as he walked away.

That was not the only time he showed how evil he was.

My mother had a cat that she loved dearly, called Gesiggie, the Afrikaans word for little face. She was lonely on the farm, and he kept her company. When she called his name, he would come running out of the bushes and jump into her arms. 'Oh, my child of the wind,' she would say, holding him against her face, kissing him.

One day Christie picked the cat up by its tail, swung it around and threw it into the bushes and rocks and red sand. Two days later, Maria found him dead. She buried Gesiggie and put a white wooden cross on the tiny grave.

Not long after that, someone removed the cross. That person broke it into little pieces and scattered it over the ground.

24

MY SO-CALLED HOLIDAYS ON DASSIESHOEK got worse with every visit. Christie insisted that it wasn't a holiday farm and that I needed to work in the vineyards. I went into the hot sun, a mere teenager, and worked like a slave. He paid me no money. I had to work in the heat just to see my mother, that's what it boiled down to.

Christie was a scrooge and complained that my mother and I used too much toilet paper. He allowed us two squares each and even rationed our food portions; we had to eat less. I was also admonished for walking on the carpets too much and ruining them.

Christie and Maria never went on holiday; he never took my mom to a well-known romantic steakhouse in Vredendal, a mere twenty-minute drive away. Once, only once, for their honeymoon, did they go away, to Mauritius. From what I could gather, it was a holiday from hell, much like the second season of *The White Lotus*.

My mother's world shrank. She started suffering from trichotillomania, a disorder where you pull out your own hair, strand by strand. There was a small bald patch on her crown. She developed chronic obsessive-compulsive disorder and would shift vases and ashtrays around for hours, until they were arranged perfectly.

Her days passed without any social interaction, and she drank heavily. Wine and grape farms produce a drink called vaaljapie, a wine of inferior quality. It tastes like dogfood, and the next day your hangover lasts for hours. My mom would start in the morning and mix the vaaljapie with Oros to make it look like cooldrink and enhance the flavour. By late afternoon, she would be smashed. It enraged me.

I had to live with a raging alcoholic in Cape Town, and now, over the school holidays, I had to endure another two drunkards. Begging my mom to leave Christie didn't help. He had broken her down; she had no confidence and believed she would be incapable of living without him. At least she had a roof over her head, she claimed. Shit is warm, so you stay close to it.

With every visit I noticed the decay, the way they were both deteriorating;

even the farmworkers were not immune. Christie would pay them with dop. After their work in the vineyards, he would compensate them with an old tin jug or two of vaaljapie. The workers became dependent on these drinks and turned into raging alcoholics. They would call him baas. When they called me kleinbaas, I asked them to stop. Christie was furious; I could see he wanted to slap me.

Most of the farmers in those days practised the dop system, which created a huge problem – mass alcoholism, with many babies being born with foetal alcohol syndrome. What terrible lives: working in the harsh sun, living in tiny shacks, yearning after vaaljapie, never going anywhere except to Lutzville on a Saturday morning to buy the bare essentials.

The workers had to use a separate entrance at all the shops, the post office and the butcher – apartheid was in full swing. Two signs: Blanke and Nie-blanke. Christie was aggressive towards the farmworkers, who had no power. He wielded it; he was baas van die plaas. He swore at them and some-times beat them with a sjambok. Once I intervened, but I was still smaller than he was, and he slapped me hard in the face. I fell to the ground, and he kicked me in my ribs.

The inhabitants of Lutzville and his family knew what was happening on Dassieshoek but chose to look the other way. There was an omertà, a mafioso type of silence. Deadly silence.

Under the blue sky, the white sun, the endless screeching of the cicadas, there were ominous secrets. My poor grandmother was too weak to help my mother; she trembled when she saw Christie. When my gran was younger, she broke one of her legs. At the time, she lived on a desolate farm, no doc-tors. The leg healed, but it never straightened properly. One day Christie told her that when she died, they would have to break her leg again. That was the type of man he was, with his churlish, scary sense of humour. It hurt her.

The plight of the farmworkers broke my heart. Their stories about Namaqualand and their idiomatic way of speaking nourished me. Those farmworkers didn't know it then, nor did I, but my love for languages was a seed they planted.

If a story told around a fire in the dark could captivate you to such an extent that it broadened your emotional range and gave you fresh insight into people and the world, then that was a gift to a young boy. Can't all literature, theatre, movies, art be traced back to that primal warmth around a fire, where the voice of the storyteller holds you spellbound? They must all be dead by now, but if I could personally go and thank each one of them, I would.

On one visit I remember my mother befriending a praying mantis. Yes, that's how lonely she was – an insect became her friend. It was astounding to see how this little stick insect ate pieces of mince out of her hand. She called him Albert. Somehow this camaraderie reached the ears of a community newspaper editor. They sent someone over to interview the two of them.

In the mornings, we would all walk right past one another. My mom would widen her eyes at me, which meant 'be quiet'. Anything could happen. Lunches were like those at my rich Lategan family, eaten with only the clatter of knives and forks.

As the sun started setting, I would become terrified. 'One day he will succeed in murdering us,' I thought. When the sun set, the alcohol appeared. Although my mother drank her 'Oros' during the day, brandy would make an entrance in the evenings, and a dramatic one, too. The admonishments and name-calling would start.

Every night Christie called me a hoerkind moffie gemors; my mother would be the hoer. One night he told my mother that she had whored for the furniture. These were the items she'd brought from Sea Point, which seemed like a distant chimera. She jumped up and pushed all the furniture outside and fetched a big can of petrol from the garage with which she soaked the furniture before setting it alight. The furniture exploded in a cloud of large, licking flames, and every item burnt out to ashes and black sticks. Gone.

I dreamt that one day I would succeed in getting her away from there to give her a new life or take her overseas.

Then, just as I thought it couldn't get any worse, it did.

My mother developed breast cancer and had to undergo a mastectomy. It came as a shock to me, but not to Christie. Before she even had the operation, he ranted at her about how much it would cost him and that she might as well become a man. He's not sleeping with someone who has one breast; sorry, no thank you.

On her return, he banished her to the spare room. She accepted it, that their marriage was dead. Not a night passed without him telling her how expensive the operation had been and how ghastly she looked with one breast. In those days, the early eighties, people attached a stigma to mastectomies. My mother had no psychological aid, nobody to talk to – she was on her own.

One night, when Christie was blind drunk, he hit her with his fist on her mastectomy wound. I grabbed him from behind, but he snatched a bread knife and held it against my throat. If I hadn't managed to kick him between his legs, he would have slit my throat. My mom and I ran in the dark to our saviours – the poor farmworkers – where we hid behind closed doors, trembling.

25

DESPITE ALL THIS, THE VISITS to my granny in Lutzville were wonderful. People called her Hansie, though I never knew what her full name was. To me, she was just Ouma. She was the widow of a farmer, my grandfather, who died before I was born and who'd retired to the village.

She lived in a small, neat house, surrounded by a huge garden that harboured a guava tree. When the guavas ripened, she preserved them; I remember the accompanying aromas well. I used to play and read books under that guava tree. Decades later, when I visited the house again, the tree was still there. 'Where was that little boy?' I thought.

My gran's home was a safe place. In the evening, she lit candles, as there was no electricity. The roads in the village were all gravel. The place was so small that everybody knew each other. My granny couldn't just walk to the butcher, because at least four people would stop her for long conversations on the way. Nobody just walked past one another. Sometimes the butcher's delivery man came on a bicycle to deliver the meat, which was beautifully wrapped in brown paper.

My granny's friends spoke openly and often about death; not like today, when people consider it impolite or morbid. Talking through their trauma was a form of healing; they didn't pretend that death didn't happen or stigmatise it as if it were a battle lost. They would casually talk about a deceased as if the person was still alive; the dead remained part of their lives.

Funerals were a huge event; the entire village would flock en masse to the Dutch Reformed Church. The ceremony was a sombre affair; everybody dressed in black. There was a huge tree outside the church, under which the hearse parked. I recall it being always hot, hot, hot. Too much.

The organist would pound the keys as if the end of the world was approaching, while the dominee ascended, as he always did, the stairs to the pulpit dressed in a long, flowing robe. He would lift his arms as if he were conducting an orchestra, close his eyes and pray with a sanctimonious expression on his face. A slight ennui was affected for extra drama.

Then everybody would sit down while the dominee spoke in a deep, sombre voice about the life of, let's say, Tant Gesie. He'd mention her unselfish service to the community, and that she had been a loving mother and a commendable wife to Oom Klaas.

The community would also remember Tant Gesie for the melktert she baked for the church bazaar every year; a tert that made acolytes of her baking flock to her table. The money made from those terte contributed to the upkeep of the old-age home. Everybody would nod in agreement: Tant Gesie was the best.

Her life had been a fruitful one, but now she was sitting at the feet of Jesus. The men would stare into the distance and the women would lift their veils and sob quietly. I remember those funerals so vividly. It seemed that each time I visited on a school holiday, someone would pass away.

After the church service, a cavalcade of cars and bakkies would slowly follow the black hearse. The shimmering sun, the red sand, the dry bushes next to the road and the berg wind all combined to create an atmosphere reminiscent of a cowboy movie.

Once we reached Koekenaap, where the graveyard was situated, people would walk to the grave, but super slowly. The sky blue, with a few fluffy clouds.

The farmworkers would form a choir, away from the coffin, and begin singing as the dominee read the final passages from the Bible and sprinkled red sand on the grave. I get goosebumps just thinking about those songs; they were so raw, so sad, and sung from the heart. The workers had to use separate entrances in daily life and white people treated them like scum, but at funerals, even if they stood to one side, they shone. And the whites knew it; their songs were so genuine and full of emotion that they resembled an art form.

Afterwards, everybody would go to someone's house, where copious amounts of snacks and tea would be served. The workers had to stand outside, but they, too, would get plates filled with food. They had their own enamel plates and cups, usually in green or yellow. To this day, when I see those metal cups and plates, I think of how black and so-called people of colour were humiliated in those days, but this awareness grew more vivid as I became more conscious of the world around me.

The funeral snacks would always include frikadelle, sandwiches, little homemade pies and melktert. For a few months following the funeral, the villagers would return to check on the bereaved person, always bringing food.

My granny had strict rules: she woke up at 05:00 every morning; there was no time to sleep in. I had to sweep the stoep and dust inside, while she baked fresh bread and started lunch: always meat, potatoes, rice and a green vegetable.

Breakfast was at 06:00. Lunch was at 11:00. Dinner was at 16:00. At 19:00, we had to be in bed. It drove me crazy, just lying there in the dark. Before going to bed, I had to wash in a skottel with warm water that she boiled on the Dover stove. My granny chopped her own wood. There was no bath.

One day, my cousin Eric arrived on his motorcycle. He was older than me and also the son of an alcoholic. We knew what it was all about. He told me to hop onto the back of his motorcycle for a ride to Vredendal, just to break the monotony of being in a dorpie. There, we would sit in on court cases; that is how you get into the dark vibe of a village.

Today, I find it unbelievable that we chose to sit in a magistrate's court in forty-eight-degree heat, listening to stories about stolen bicycles and bar fights, but yes, it did happen.

After a few hours of local drama, it was nice to ride through to the Olifants River and go for a swim. My memories of those days in the river, as well as those with my grandmother, are the only fond ones I have of that place.

26

MEANWHILE, BACK IN CAPE TOWN, life with Sammy took a strange turn. It appeared that he could stay clean for six months, but for the other six months, he drank. It was a merry-go-round of troubles.

The sober Sammy was a kind man who worked hard. He was a good salesman. When a business was doing badly, they would rope him in to turn it around. We drove in a wide variety of cars, as Sammy had to test-drive them, and some were frightfully grand. It was fun to sit in the back of the latest Mercedes-Benz or Jaguar, or even a second-hand one, and pretend that we were rich.

When Sammy had money, he was quite the dandy. Well-dressed, not a hair out of place, and he was a gourmand savant. We ate at only the best restaurants. His sweet tooth kicked in when he stopped drinking, which often happens, as the addiction shifts. He would gain weight.

Driving there in our luxury car, we'd patronise the restaurant at the Ritz Plaza Hotel, or the fancy Van Donck in the old Trust Bank building. Money wasn't an issue. Sammy also liked delis. There was one in Buitenkant Street called Millie's, which imported tinned frogs' legs and chocolate ants, all of which I loved.

Sammy also bought me an expensive rugby kit, a sport that I, at that stage, despised. I used it once. Then he bought two expensive miniature sausage dogs, which we called Boesman and Lena, after the Athol Fugard play. They were lovely dogs; he adored them.

We often went to the Goodwood Drive-In, also to the Hell's Angels held at the Goodwood Showgrounds. And we saw Demis Roussos live at the 3Arts in Plumstead. Let's say, when Sammy was doing well, he was on a roll.

Sammy liked to listen to cassette tapes in the car, a musical mix of The Shadows, Neil Diamond, Electric Light Orchestra, Creedence Clearwater Revival, Pussycat and Elvis Presley. He always drove with the window open and his right arm resting on the frame. Sammy had a permanent boere tan, as it was known. With his aviator sunglasses and an unfiltered Gunston cigarette hanging from his mouth, he looked quite the man of the moment. From the backseat, I sometimes spotted him looking at himself in the mirror.

He was one of those men who winked at every woman he passed. Today, the authorities would lock him up. Sammy was an impulsive man. During one of his drinking sprees, we went for a drive in a large Jaguar. The car had two petrol tanks; I'd never heard of anything like it in my life. We were going to Blouberg for an ice cream. It was just the two of us. Impulsively, he put his foot down and we sped in another direction.

I asked where we were going. To Port Elizabeth, as it was called then. I was astounded, but it felt exciting, so I sat back and went along for the ride. Sammy said that he would tell the school that I was sick. This was on a Sunday. We arrived in PE that same day and booked into the Holiday Inn.

While Sammy went drinking, I spent time in the pool. Then we drove around PE. One night an Afrikaans pop duo, Herbie en Spence, who were big in the seventies, performed at the hotel.

And that was it. After a few days, we drove back to Cape Town and life carried on, back to its usual rhythm. I often wondered what had gone through Sammy's head that day, this sudden trip to PE. Was he going to look up some woman? Or was he fleeing his own darkness, which always fell upon him eventually?

27

SAMMY'S DOWNWARD SPIRALS WERE ALWAYS evident when he started making a habit of getting home later and later. Each time, drunker than before. Then the familiar sound of the bottle top being unscrewed slowly, so that Linda and I couldn't hear. Cane and Coke. Three in the morning. I would be listening to Springbok Radio, the Minister of Midnight Affairs, but I could still hear him. Then he would lose his work.

During the day he would sit on the edge of the bed staring into the unknown. He tried Alcoholics Anonymous; he tried self-help books. A favourite was by a doubtfully named Dr Tuesday Lobsang Rampa, an author who specialised in paranormal and occult fiction. He turned out to be a fraud, but somehow Sammy was spellbound by his writing.

Alcoholics like to have drinking buddies; my dad had a friend called Peter. Peter would pop in as I left for school, and he'd still be there when I got back. They would be so hammered that they spoke no sense. Peter was a useless man; he never worked, and his wife supported him. A thin, pale guy who existed just for drinks; that's it. The two of them once went into business installing burglar alarms, but it lasted hardly a month. Both were too feeble because of the drink.

To supplement my pocket money during lean times, I started delivering *Die Burger*. My beat at one stage was in the old HF Verwoerd building opposite Parliament, where cabinet ministers from the National Party had their offices.

We would collect our papers from a bakkie at about 04:15 near a garage. There were a few of us; some delivered in Oranjezicht, Tamboerskloof and Vredehoek. The HF Verwoerd building was an austere, unfriendly place, its corridors hard, permeated with the stench of power. I had to drop off a paper, sometimes up to seven, in front of each office.

On a few occasions I put the newspaper on John Vorster's desk while he was working, as he would sometimes be there as early as 04:30. His door would be ajar. His nose was often red, and he would greet me politely. Later, I could imitate his voice, to the great amusement of my friends.

I delivered the papers diligently, with a friend, in summer and winter. Winter was hard because it rained and it was dark and cold. We also had to drop papers at a large house next to Tuynhuys. We were convinced the ghost of Jan van Riebeeck hung around there. A huge tree shook when the wind was blowing. When it rained, it was even more sinister.

My friend and I had to choose which of us was going to drop off the paper. We took turns. One wet morning I sped past and threw the paper against the front door. The door opened and a woman screamed at me that I should stop throwing it against the door. She was wearing a white gown … she certainly looked like a ghost.

I got such a fright that I fell off my bicycle and scraped my knee. But, in a flash, I climbed back in the saddle and sped off. I can't remember if I ever returned to that house.

I needed the money for movies, for escape, to get away from the raging alcoholism. Sammy had started disappearing for weeks on end. Later, we would receive a phone call from some pub somewhere in the platteland; he would slur. Sometimes he stayed away for up to two weeks. During this time, Linda looked after me, fed me, bought me clothes, kept an eye on me. Sammy didn't give a fuck.

He blew his money on wine and women, which is obviously why he stayed away for such extended periods. I was deeply hurt when he wasn't at home when I started Standard 6. All the other children's parents were dropping them off, waving tearfully, because they realised that their kids were growing up. It was like Sub A. Nobody was there to wave me goodbye, to hold my hand.

Two important rituals in a young child's life. I was on my own.

28

ON THOSE SCHOOL HOLIDAYS WHEN I didn't visit my mother, I went to another place. Linda's mother, Tannie Elga, and stepfather, Oom Hannes, lived in a dorpie called Van Wyksdorp in the Klein Karoo, between Riversdale and Ladismith. Those were the days before sleepy hamlets became fashionable tourist attractions and featured in glossy magazines.

Van Wyksdorp was the real deal: authentic, isolated, deeply rural. I have wonderful memories of it, as opposed to Dassieshoek outside Lutzville, which I associate with violence and hatred.

Oom Hannes and Tannie Elga's farm was called Karree Kamma; they were humble but productive and farmed with apricots and sheep. The farmhouse was big, with a door that opened onto the Groot River. There was also a plaas-dam and fields filled with sheep. The dam had a windmill and Elga grew aloes, which she sold for medicinal purposes.

I had a good relationship with the farmworkers and they, in turn, liked me. Gert Makriga showed me how to milk Blommie the cow before sunrise. He was a kind man, and I spent some time with him looking after the sheep and herding them back into the kraal.

Gert had a donkey cart on which I rode all the way to the village, about five kilometres from the farm. For a child from the city, this was a wonder-world. In the late seventies, Van Wyksdorp and surrounds had fewer than eight hundred inhabitants. I would have guessed even less.

On hot days, and there were many, I swam in the farm dam in the bliss-fully cool water. Oom Hannes and Tannie Elga had a laatlammetjie, a girl called Trui, and we became friends. Along the Groot River were patches of trees, which lent some shade. I sat there and caught geelvis, which Elga pickled and with which she made curried fish, which I can taste to this day. Oom Hannes showed me how to catch this particular fish. You took a tiny ball of curried mieliepap and attached it to the hook. The smell of the curry attracted the fish.

The farm had no electricity. At some stage, Oom Hannes acquired a generator. But, until then, the milk from Blommie was kept cool in a makeshift fridge in a little building built with rocks from the veld and covered with wire netting. A water tank and some coal perched on the roof and the water would slowly run down the walls. This makeshift fridge was situated under a tree, in the shade, where it would be cooled by a light breeze. It was primitive, but it worked. They also kept meat and cheese in that plaas fridge.

The toilet was an outside long drop. When I had to go, I feared that a snake would bite me on my bum. It was particularly scary at night, when you had to go outside with a candle and darkness surrounded you.

When you wanted to bath, there was a large, round, tin bathtub outside. The water had to be carried from a huge tank close by. If I remember correctly, a small fire warmed the water from underneath the tub. Thorn trees provided some privacy on the one side. The sky was always blue, the air fresh, so an outdoor bath like that was such fun. Where were those days? I was happy.

Tannie Elga pickled peaches picked from the orchard. She also made karringmelk with the milk Blommie produced, and with that she baked buttermilk rusks. We washed those down with moerkoffie brewed on a wood stove in an old green kettle.

To iron clothes, Tannie Elga used a heavy black iron that she also warmed up on the stove. Remarkable that so much could be done with so little. For eggs, there were chickens, which were also slaughtered for their meat: a large, plump one sacrificed for Sunday's roast. That was quite a story on its own (this is a trigger warning for vegans).

Once the chicken's head was chopped off, it could still run around for a few seconds. Alternatively, a sheep's neck would be slit. The blood that squirted out was used for sausages. They used every bit of the sheep: the trotters, offal, wool, head … nothing was wasted. The woman who worked in the kitchen, Loetie Opperman, often prepared one of my favourite dishes: kaiings (sheep's fat crackling) pan-fried with salt, which she served on freshly baked bread slathered with farm butter. Better than the best French food, let me tell you.

Loetie was also an expert at making a braai, for which she made roosterkoek with bread dough, shaped like a small cake and cooked on a grill over coals. I think of all these people with great fondness. I was lucky, in retrospect, to experience a farm with such embracing warmth. The way Oom

Hannes treated his farmworkers was so different from Christie Kruger in Lutzville. They weren't thin and emaciated, quivering with fear and subjected to the dop system. They lived in a little valley in neat little Karoo cottages right next to the orchard.

There was a big, old, black bicycle on the farm, with thick tyres and a dynamo to light up the front light at night. If I didn't walk or go with Gert on his donkey cart, I rode into the village on that bike.

Tannie Elga was a dynamic but fragile woman; she exuded a type of lingering sadness. But she told wonderful stories. She'd studied drama at Stellenbosch University, which, I suspect, was why I felt such a strong bond with her. Actors, artists, performers ... they don't have as many filters as other people. They are more open.

Tannie Elga loved sleeping outside in summer. We would throw down a large blanket and lie on our backs staring at the stars. The days before electricity and TV, you found joy in the stars, the river, the smell of apricots.

29

ACK IN CAPE TOWN, SAMMY announced that we were moving from Union Street in Gardens to Sea Point. Things were looking up; he was off the bottle and was making money again.

We moved into a flat in Illovo Court, right next to the Metro cinema and those previously pink Twin Towers, between Beach and Main roads. The Ritz Plaza was visible from my bedroom window, as was the sea. I often swam in Three Anchor Bay, still in the habit of trying to spot my mother. Sometimes I passed the places we had frequented, and the block of flats where we'd lived, and a longing so intense would take hold of me that I felt it might be better to die.

The situation in Dassieshoek was so desperate by now, there was no way I could visit. My mother's personality had changed; I suspected she had brain damage. I wasn't safe; I would have been killed.

My dear granny had had a stroke and was paralysed, confined to a bed in a retirement home in Vredendal. She couldn't speak ... the cruelty of it all. My visits to Lutzville were over. I chose to spend my school holidays in Van Wyksdorp or at home.

From Sea Point, I rode to school on a bicycle, all the way through Green Point, then Long Street, up Kloof Street, and parked the bicycle on the school grounds. Saturdays, I spent time with friends at the school's swimming pool. I was an excellent swimmer. Schoolwork was boring but, somehow, I did well. I did, however, enjoy English, Afrikaans and art, even woodwork.

Writing essays became a motivating force; I liked to spend hours on them, finding just the right words. During this time, I started playing truant. I would cycle the entire day or just read. Sometimes, I cycled all the way to Bloubergstrand or Camps Bay. The cracks were starting to show. Unresolved trauma frequently causes self-sabotage. I forged my sick notes. Sammy was indifferent to us. Linda spent her weekends filling in crosswords.

We still had the two dogs, Boesman and Lena, as well as two black cats, Squeaky and Jetty. I took the dogs for walks on the promenade. There was a putt-putt course in Mouille Point, and the cinema, where I spent a lot of time, was nearby.

Next door to the cinema was a restaurant called the Watney Girls, owned by two wild women who drove a red Ford Mustang. At night I would walk past and watch the grown-ups partying, going wild. There was something decadent about the place that appealed to me. Chris and Barbara Barnard used to hang out there. I thought, that's the type of place I'll go to when I grow up.

At home there was a strange sense of normality, but Linda and I knew that nothing was ever certain. Yes, life is unpredictable, but living with an alcoholic is another story.

Then it started. He stayed away over weekends. This time, he was open about it – he was having an affair. Her name was Merle Theron and she worked for a bank. She had permanently pouting lips that would have driven any man crazy. Linda was devastated; I was shocked. How to deal with this?

We continued in a liminal space, between then and somewhere in the distance. Every weekend, Sammy was away. Eventually, he lost his job. We plunged back into poverty. One day, when I wanted to take my bicycle to go to school, it was gone. He also sold my fishing rod, which had given me endless joy.

Sammy was desperate for alcohol. We had a bottle of KWV perfume, and he was so frantic, he drank it. That he didn't die from organ failure was a miracle. One day he was so drunk, I had to help him to the loo so that he could urinate; I had to hold his penis.

It made me think of a time when we went fishing in Gordon's Bay and I caught a huge stingray. It was strong and Sammy had to come and stand behind me and hold the rod, and together we roped in the fish. I was much younger then.

This time, I was standing behind my drunk father helping him to pee.

Linda and Sam got divorced.

I remember the day because they gave me a lift to school. Then they were going to the courts. The atmosphere in the car was terrible. Linda was sad. I didn't know what was going to happen to me. What was going to happen to her?

Sammy moved in with his mistress and just dumped me on Linda. Abandoned, just like that. One night, however, I did stay with him and Merle in their rented house in Sea Point. I knew my dad had sleeping tablets, and I had battled for long enough. I went to his cupboard and took them all. When

I woke up, I was in Groote Schuur Hospital, vomiting. This was my first attempt at taking my life. I was sorry to have survived this one. Years of Dassieshoek and then living with an unstable man who was sober one moment and drunk the next had taken their toll. I was an only child; I had no siblings with whom to share the pain.

The worst was when my father took me to the aptly named Greek restaurant Sloppy Sam. Here he told me, without a hint of irony or any insight into his own life, that he might not be the dad I wanted, but was I the son *he* wanted? I remained calm. It reminded me of Maria, who'd told me one day that she had been hoping for a girl, but then a boy popped out. In retrospect I find it such cruel behaviour, bordering on child abuse.

Not only did I feel rejected by my parents, the Dutch Reformed Church, Christie Kruger, not only did I feel like an outsider in society, that I was unwelcome, an unwanted guest, but it was clear that I was a whore child, with all the stigma attached to it.

In the meantime, Linda could not look after me. She told me that I had to go to boarding school, as she was leaving to start a new life in Windhoek. She wanted to get as far away from her old life as possible.

In Windhoek, she met a man who loved her, the radio broadcaster Peter Merrill, who was working there after the demise of Springbok Radio. They spent three happy decades together until he died in his nineties.

And so, in Standard 8, I moved into the school's boys' residence, high up against the mountain in Tamboerskloof. A new life was unfolding. I had no idea what lay ahead of me.

One of the saddest days of my life was when I heard, just before I left, that Merle, Sam's paramour, or he, had had all four of our pets put down. Boesman, Lena, Squeaky and Jetty. Gone.

I was on my own; I was so scared.

30

IN THE BEGINNING, AT BOARDING school, I was bewildered, confused, hurt. It felt like I was being chucked away, going back to the orphanage. A whole new world, however, unfolded for me. New friends surrounded me.

I realised how isolated my life had been as an only child, and even though I had friends, they were only a handful. But now I started flourishing socially and shared a large room with three other guys. The sombre atmosphere at home, the fear of living with an alcoholic, was gone.

At night we lay in our beds, telling stories to each other. I felt light; my depression lifted. Friends invited me to their homes for weekends and even school holidays. I still think of them to this day, and their parents, who always made me feel welcome: the McGregors, Oliviers, Müllers, Davels, and others.

There was a lot happening at school: there were the debate and drama societies, the school choir and the school newspaper, *Onze Jan*, of which I was a founding member, and which exists to this day. I participated in every debate possible, attended choir practice and competed in swimming competitions. There were eisteddfods. My social life was wild and busy. I was thriving.

But in the meantime, there was a secret sideshow in my life, one I hardly shared with people. It involved the father of one of my close friends, a man with whom I had an ominous, complicated relationship.

31

COENIE SLABBER WAS THE ARTS editor for *Rapport*, the second-largest Sunday newspaper in the country. It was so popular that at one point it had a circulation of 500 000. I was about twelve or thirteen when I met Coenie.

We were still living in Union Street, Gardens, and one of my best friends lived in the same street. He and I shared a love for chess, movies and swimming. At one stage, we also delivered newspapers together. He was an introvert, clever, with a good heart. We would play chess in our humble, poverty-stricken flat, but when Sammy was on a binge, I kept the boy away.

I started visiting his home occasionally. His mom, a music teacher, was a kind woman who showed a genuine interest in me. One weekend, my friend invited me along to his father's flat in Bloubergstrand. It was one of the first high-rise buildings in that area, with views of the ocean. I was looking forward to the visit, just to get away from the suffocating atmosphere at home.

Coenie and I got along immediately. I started visiting often. Because Coenie was an arts journalist, he knew many writers and actors, and frequently spoke about them. I was young and easily impressed, as I was interested in that world. His taste in music was cosmopolitan: he listened to Melina Mercouri, Édith Piaf and Marlene Dietrich. He had a large library and the flat's walls displayed his good taste in art.

I felt at home. On beautiful days, my friend and I would go fishing. We plucked mussels from the sea, which Coenie prepared at night with cream and garlic. He was hospitable and took us out for pizzas. In the evenings, we listened to music, and I listened attentively to his stories about the theatre and well-known actors.

I developed a great admiration for him. Later, I went to the theatre with him, without his son. He had a press card and could go to the movies for free. I noticed that Coenie had a passion for edgy movies, like *Quadrophenia* and *Urban Cowboy*, featuring rebellious, damaged young men. As the months went by, I learnt a lot from him.

There was a thirty-year age gap between us, so he felt like a mentor and

substitute father to me. I had just turned thirteen. One morning, I was standing in the bathroom, brushing my teeth. He came and stood behind me. He
slowly pushed his hand down the front of my sweatpants. It was a strange
moment; I didn't really know how to react, so I just laughed.

That day, we didn't speak about it; we just pretended that nothing had
happened. In the evening we all sat down, and Coenie made pizzas for us.
Afterwards, my friend and I went to the spare room, where there were two
beds, and went to sleep. At 03:00, I woke up. Coenie was standing next to
my bed. What the fuck was going on?

This towering presence in the dark … He pushed his hand under my
pyjama pants and started playing with me. It made me so uncomfortable,
yet I got an erection. My biggest concern was his son, my friend, sleeping in
the other bed. What would happen if he woke up? Should I have screamed?

His son was one of my best friends. I enjoyed my weekends in Blouberg.

I froze and had an out-of-body experience, like astral travelling. It felt as
if I was floating above my own body. He lifted the sheet, pushed his head
under it, put my penis in his mouth and raped me. To call it fellatio is too
much of a euphemism.

I reached orgasm, unwillingly. He left the room quietly. This happened
while his own son was lying in another bed, in the same room.

32

THIS WAS THE BEGINNING OF a strange tango with the unknown, a web of deceit and emotional manipulation; it was, again, uncharted territory. The next morning, everybody went about their business as if nothing had happened.

I told nobody, but later I did tell other close friends. None of them knew what to say. How does one make sense of something like that at that age? This continued for some years. I was a hostage, really. I didn't know how to get out of it. He groomed me and he groomed me well.

At one stage, Coenie moved to Johannesburg. He bought me train tickets and said I should visit him. Why didn't I say no? Because he was sly; he knew he had me by the balls. In Johannesburg, we would go to the movies or attend the theatre every night. When he visited Cape Town, he would meet up with me and take me out for dinner. I remember one night we went to the old Carousel; he plied me with Chateau Libertas. We ate pizza.

My own father was a miserable shell of a man, hollowed out by alcoholism. My mother was on a farm far away, a rag doll. Coenie was a father, mentor, friend, but also my molester. Later, when I moved into the school res at sixteen, he continued to stay in touch, more often than ever before. He even took me on a holiday to the Wilderness with his two sons.

He continued to rape me at each place we stayed; nobody spoke about it. Did they know? I doubt it; he was a sly snake, an expert Svengali. It happened in the Wilderness, Johannesburg, Bloubergstrand. I remember a time when his son and I accompanied him in his car from Cape Town to Johannesburg. He somehow wangled it that I sat in the front passenger seat, next to him. We drove through the night and my friend slept on the backseat. Or so it seemed.

Coenie put his right hand on the steering wheel, and with his left hand unzipped my trousers and masturbated me. Again, I froze; my friend was lying on the backseat. Did Coenie have no control over his lust? Evidently not. I felt dirty and started blaming myself. Was this my fault? Did I provoke him?

There came a stage when I could not look his children in the eyes, let alone his ex-wife. It was sick, and I had no parental guidance on what to do. Coenie knew this; he knew I was wounded. He could feast off my wounds.

On one visit to Johannesburg, I felt like a sex slave. He was living in a house in Bez Valley, which he shared with a female journalist. I won't mention her name, but that she just looked the other way is still a cause of annoyance and hurt. She was an adult, come on.

During the day, Coenie was at work. At that stage, I felt like a possession. I had to sit at home like a good boy while he went to work. He gave me no pocket money; I was a schoolchild. The money I made from delivering newspapers did not stretch that far.

There I sat during the day, like someone under house arrest, and at night I was expected to perform. He told me that I was fat. A few nights in a row, he fed me a slice of brown bread with some cucumber from his garden.

Yet, he was a clever little trout. He took me to Sun City to watch Liberace. It was a huge occasion, high camp, the twinkly lights; all the press was there. Coenie arranged for us to stay over – what else? The show was a bit of a spectacle, with Liberace arriving on stage in a limousine. His handsome chauffeur opened the door for him, and he climbed out wearing pink fur and a gold, glittering coat, his hair in its usual bouffant style.

The driver was topless, tanned, well-built and wore tight black leather trousers and a cowboy hat. He flashed a sexy smile at the crowd. It was typical eighties' excess, a Las Vegas feel, ostentatious. A candelabra in the shape of a miniature Eiffel Tower stood on top of a grand piano. Liberace swooped to the front of the stage and showed the audience his jewellery; each finger on each hand boasted a huge diamond ring.

'Do you like them?' he asked. 'Yes,' the audience replied. 'Well, good, darlings,' he said. 'Because you paid for them!' His music was kitsch, but he knew how to put on a show.

Liberace died of AIDS-related illnesses a few years later. His boyfriend, whom he hid from the world, told publications afterwards that Liberace was so boring at home. He never played the piano but loved to cook and played endlessly with his highly pedigreed dogs.

After the show, he received a ten-minute standing ovation, then got into the limo and was driven off the stage, waving. I sat there, thinking, 'What a different world from my alcoholic father and Dassieshoek, where a gun would be aimed at me.'

That night, I saw Coenie's vindictive side. He was friendly to Barry Ronge, who was at the height of his television career, but openly rude to the female journalists from various publications who were there. I remember how hurt by his attitude one woman was. In retrospect, I realised that Coenie wasn't only a paedophile, he was also a misogynist who suffered from internalised homophobia. He despised himself as a gay man and policed me so that I would behave like a straight man.

Once, I was looking at my fingernails, thinking it was time to cut them. He scolded me and said I looked at my nails like a woman does, by stretching out my fingers; according to him, a man folded his fingers into his palm to look at his nails. This from a man who was sucking a teenage boy's cock. For fuck's sake.

The next day, we met up with Coenie's friends, the Van der Lugt family. The father was a dominee and the mother an odd woman who suffered from various ailments. I had a good relationship with the one son; there were three. Jozua and I shared a passion for the theatre. He became an actor and later switched to teaching and sub-editing at a newspaper. We are still friends to this day.

We also had something else in common. He, too, was molested by Coenie, but for him, it started at the age of nine. Later, when we were much older, we spoke about the effect that period of our lives had on us as grownups. I felt that sex was dirty; I felt guilty about it, and that there should ideally be something secretive about it, like a quicky in a dark alley. Jozua and I also discussed our low self-esteem and how our self-confidence had received such a knock, it would forever have a negative impact on our careers and relationships with other people.

Coenie had robbed us of reaching our full potential. For years we spoke about it, to try to make sense of it all. It remains traumatic and unresolved.

Years later, with the help of *News24* editor Adriaan Basson, we could get closure. Coenie had raped another teenager: Theunis Engelbrecht, a writer and journalist. Ironically, our tormentor had brought us together and, decades after the abuse, with the help of *News24*, we went to the police, where we laid criminal charges against Coenie. You need three accusers to lay charges before you can expose the perpetrator's name.

Two other youngsters had also fallen under Coenie's spell, but as adults, they didn't want to be part of the effort to expose him. I can't mention their names, but one, a famous Afrikaans singer, killed himself in his forties. The remaining one wanted nothing to do with it, which I found both sad and infuriating.

Before *News24* published the article, the journalist contacted people who knew Coenie from the old days. Coenie had often spoken about Breyten Breytenbach, the famous poet. I was deeply under the impression back then that Coenie knew Breytenbach, because at one stage he'd won a major literature prize sponsored by *Rapport*. How could he *not* have known Coenie?

Breytenbach was angered by the journalist's phone call and claimed that he didn't know who Coenie was. This was not how I knew Breytenbach, who is a true gentleman and usually soft-spoken. I assume he thought that he was being implicated in some scandal, which was certainly not the case. The journalist was simply looking for a quote. Along with Barry Ronge, Coenie had been one of the leading arts journalists in South Africa.

The story ran and caused quite a ripple, with people asking us the usual questions about why we'd waited so long to report him. A tired trope that illustrates the ignorance and hypocrisy of a society where these issues are best ignored. I know that people gossiped behind my back; I don't give a fuck. One day, the journalist who was working on the story, Riaan Grobler, went with a camera operator to Coenie's flat in Blouberg.

Coenie was astounding; the vitriol he spouted about me was shocking to see online. He said I was vendetta-driven, that I liked to gossip and that I'd always had a rich imagination. At first, he claimed that he couldn't remember much about me, but when the camera arrived, he managed to dish up some details about my apparent demonic personality. The man suffered from a sense of hubris that knew no bounds. He told Grobler that I was angry because I'd felt rejected by him when he stopped seeing me. Really?

What I should mention is that ten years before we went to the police, I made an appointment to see Coenie at his flat. I wanted to confront him. Once there, it was a creepy experience. The flat was a time capsule; hardly anything had changed. He sat at the window in a chair with the sun reflecting off his lips. I looked at them and thought, 'With those lips you stole my youth, you raped me. Not only me, others as well.'

I couldn't get myself to talk about the past. Instead, I became like a little boy seeking his approval. I left feeling rattled, and as I was leaving, there was a knock on his door. In came a striking black teenager, no older than fourteen. My heart sank. Coenie told me he was helping him with Afrikaans lessons. I knew he was lying; he was still up to his old tricks.

In my car on the way home, my cellphone rang. It was Coenie, who said that there were certain things in his past that he felt ashamed about. It was an odd call, as if he wanted me to say that all was well. Yet he had no shame luring a teenager, one I had just seen with my own eyes, into his flat.

As the case was mounting against him, Coenie died at the age of eighty-two. Odd, as his one neighbour claimed that he'd still taken the stairs up the seven storeys to his flat every day. He died of natural causes, a vague term if ever there was one. Perhaps the stress of a looming court case had become unbearable. But I often wonder whether paedophiles ever feel any guilt. At least that phone call of his proved that there was some measure of shame.

What a tragic end to one of the country's top arts journalists, a man who was respected for his work, who could have been a mentor but became a predator. When he died, I decided to forgive him, move forward and get on with my life.

33

AFTER COENIE'S SOJOURN IN JOHANNESBURG, he moved back to Blouberg. He continued taking me to opening nights at the theatre. One day, he invited Jozua van der Lugt and Theunis Engelbrecht to his flat. I was there too. We soon realised what his plans were – he wanted an orgy. It didn't happen, as we decided to talk right through the night until Coenie went to bed.

But Coenie, as low as a snake's gut, always had a surprise up his sleeve, to lure you back into the fold. One day he announced that he would be taking me and his son to Spain. I was thunderstruck. My parents were poor and would never have been able to send me overseas, so this was a chance of a lifetime. I knew, however, that there would be a price attached.

34

WE FLEW TO MADRID, WHERE I was beguiled by the architecture, art galleries, aromas, backstreets and beautifully dressed people. At night we went for dinner at 23:30, the little back alleys packed with people, the energy high-octane.

While I was there, I started wondering, 'Is this what rent boys do? Has the whoreson, hoerkind, become a whore?' What did my friend think when I shared a room with his father at night? I didn't have the emotional abilities to process it all. After Madrid, we went to Seville, Ronda, Granada, each place a cultural learning experience.

It was in Spain that I realised how travelling can expand your emotional world. The last place we visited was a kitsch tourist spot, Torremolinos, with a beautiful beach. I was young, trim, tanned and hunky. I caught Coenie taking photographs of me on the sly as I came out of the water wearing a gold Speedo. Back in Cape Town, I couldn't stop talking about my adventure, but those old feelings of confusion, smuttiness and guilt came back to nibble at me.

35

MY SCHOOLWORK STARTED TO SUFFER. I couldn't concentrate. I was sound academically, but I lost all motivation. Looking back, it's no wonder my schoolwork was suffering – I had nobody to talk to. I was ashamed. For days I would write meaningless lists, like places I wanted to visit in future, the titles of books I would like to write … endless, endless lists, while I should have been studying.

In other areas, I thrived. I was elected as head of the drama and debating societies, I sang in the choir and started a school newspaper, I entered national essay and poetry competitions; in fact, I did everything except study. Then I started taking photography and music lessons. I made friends easily; my social life was busy, busy, busy.

To keep his tight hold on me, Coenie offered to pay for drama studies at the Academy for Dramatic Art under my old teacher, Babs Laker. I would study improvisation, accents, movement; the world was my proverbial oyster. Despite everything, I never received any acknowledgement from my parents. Whether I did well, or badly, or won a prize, they simply didn't care.

One day, some random teacher chose me, along with four other pupils, to drive in a Kombi to an unknown destination. We were excited to get away from school, so we all jumped in. Never mind where to, we were getting a break. Off we went, towards the city centre, where we parked right next to the HF Verwoerd building, where I used to deliver *Die Burger*. We were ushered into the building, in our school uniforms, and into a lift.

The next moment, we were in an office and asked to wait. In walked Prime Minister PW Botha, smiling from ear to ear. We were dumbfounded. He introduced himself to each of us and asked questions, as if he was genuinely interested. Then a cameraman popped up and asked us to stand in a circle, with the Groot Krokodil in the middle, holding an open book. We had to pretend that we were looking at this book. The camera flashed, PW shook our hands, and off we went, back to the Kombi, back to school. Not one of us understood what had just happened; it was Dadaistic.

The next morning, there we were, on the front page of *Die Burger*. The caption read: 'Young Nationalists enjoy some time with the Prime Minister, PW Botha, discussing the future'.

What a liberty. That was sly public relations at its best. At the time, I identified as a communist, just because it sounded like it was anti-establishment. To identify as such was like showing a big middle finger to the world … not that I knew much about communism, I must add.

One Friday afternoon I went into town to drum up some advertising for the school newspaper, as the school itself wasn't going to contribute anything. I endured, got funding and a printer, and off we went.

The first editor, John Ross McGregor, was a brilliant photographer; the rest of the small editorial team wrote articles. The first issue was a mixture of profiles, sport, music, poetry, photography and gossip.

The then administrator of the Cape, Gene Louw, wrote us a letter complimenting us on a job well done. The only problem was that the school principal was furious that a story on Rastas had appeared and asked us why we had black people in the newspaper.

Another teacher told us condescendingly: 'Brave effort.' Once I left school, I sometimes bumped into her, and she always had an aura of delusions of grandeur about her, as if she were some grandee. In hindsight, she was a parvenu suffering from the Dunning–Kruger effect.

To spite the principal, in the next issue we ran a story on the white gangs in our school, who all rode motorbikes and caused havoc at Topolino Café on Friday nights.

He was furious.

36

A T THE SCHOOL RES, I became friends with a suave, sophisticated guy named Grant Doidge. He was sardonic, had no time for authority, dressed fashionably and was a social butterfly. He was also a good artist. We both knew that we were gay, but I still had some girlfriends, informally. I was a teenager and discovering my sex life, away from Coenie, who symbolised evil.

One night in Fresnaye, at a huge house party, I had sex with a girl on the bathroom floor. We were both sixteen. There were no condoms, but we used a Jiffy bag. We still laugh about it. We were young, bulletproof. Life was for living. Once a red-headed friend of mine told me that people with red hair have a whiff of curry underneath their armpits and in their nether regions. He lifted his arms and I smelt it: pure curry. I'm sure he was sending me up, as he'd had curry the previous evening.

Through Grant, I became friends with an avant-garde clique at school, all attractive, defiant. We smoked cigarettes, dressed up when we went out and started clubbing. We listened to Grace Jones, Nina Hagen, Klaus Nomi and Maria Callas. With Grant, I started frequenting art galleries in town, where you were given free cheese and wine.

We would get drunk and flirtatious and start oozing and schmoozing with artists, photographers, fashionistas, actors, punks and journalists from underground publications. We befriended Rastas on Greenmarket Square, went home with them to Salt River and smoked dagga.

On Saturday nights, Grant and I went to a nightclub, Club 604, on top of the old Trust Bank building, where you could dance with the city lights in the background. The dancefloor was made of see-through Perspex, underneath which colourful lights flashed. Disco balls sparkled and swung around above us.

Next to this club was a restaurant called Van Donck, where a woman in a long evening dress used to sit and play a huge harpsichord. Grant and I would sneak out of res at around 23:30 and get back at about five in the morning.

Because we were young, we hardly ever had to buy our own drinks. In Sea Point, we frequented the old President Hotel, where they had a disco called Raffles. It was always packed with people who dressed in the latest fashions for the occasion. It was only a bit later that we developed a taste for more grungy nightclubs like Rita's and Scratch, and gay pubs like the Wine Barrel.

Grant met a man called Bernard Sach, a wealthy restaurateur, who lived in the stately Mimosa Court, right opposite La Perla restaurant and the old Carousel. Bernard was a bit of an *arriviste*; he took us out to the best eateries, where he would take out a twenty-rand note, tear it in two, and give one half to the waiter. If the service was good, the waiter would get the other half.

Grant had expensive taste, and Bernard bought him many things, but one day poor Grant would pay a heavy price for this friendship.

Later in life, a friend reminded me what Grant always said: 'When someone asks how you are, always say, "I am very well." Little did we know about the darkness behind his words.

37

THE END OF THE YEAR was lurking, which meant exams. I was in Standard 9. Coenie was still hovering like halitosis horribilis in the background, but it turned out that he wasn't the only horribilis. It was also an annus horribilis. I failed my school year.

I was seeing Coenie too often, and my mood swings were out of control, my boundaries non-existent. I said and did anything that came into my head. I also drank too much over the weekends. Instead of the school offering me psychotherapy, or help of some kind, I was left to my own devices. I find it incredible how nobody noticed I was a trainwreck about to happen. I didn't notice it either.

I didn't allow self-pity to inhibit my life at school, so I tackled my second year in Standard 9 with even more fervour. Debates, essays, parties, a whirl-wind of bonhomie.

At the end of that year, I was elected as deputy head boy of both the school and the res. How weird was that?

I passed that year, but a great disillusionment was awaiting me. I had to say goodbye to my dear friends, as they had now matriculated and would go forth to start their new lives.

So, they left, moved on, and I was stuck at school. A great, great sadness enveloped me.

38

M Y MATRIC YEAR WAS A fiasco, as in a *huge* one. I suffered from a paralysing sadness, pining after my old friends. Some went to university, others to the army, two became exchange students.

I made new friends, but my heart was with the others. My way out was to take the train to Stellenbosch University every weekend to visit my friend Jozua van der Lugt, who was a first-year drama student.

I would stay over, and because most of his friends were also drama students, or artists, or studied philosophy, they were more rumbustious, spontaneous and adventurous than, say, a student of theology. Here I met people like the journalist Murray La Vita and the singer Koos Kombuis. We were all incredibly young.

At school, I became progressively impossible. My drinking over weekends was starting to take its toll. One day, my Afrikaans teacher read one of my essays to the class and had the temerity to ask me if I'd really written it. I lost my temper, jumped up, grabbed the book from his hands and tore it in two. He was a large man and had once been a train driver; his face turned red. 'Papa' Driese was an old barfly just like my dad and often stumbled out of the Oranje Hotel in Union Street.

Driese was a maverick who had studied teaching part-time; he could speak Latin and Greek fluently. His problem was his permanent babelaas and the rage that accompanied it. When I tore up the book, his face exploded. He was so angry, he came running after me with his fists and wanted to donner me. I ran to the school principal, a man nicknamed Bees (Ox).

Bees despised me and insisted that I hand my deputy head boy badges back to him. I wasn't setting a good example for the other children. I felt nothing; I was on my own rampage. I was a renegade, and nothing was going to stop me.

At the next debating evening, I pretended I was going to discuss something innocuous, like should boys and girls mix on the playground. Little did they know I was going to out myself as gay and a communist.

I spoke with fervour; I had rehearsed the speech for hours. The audience was speechless, floored, wide-eyed. When I left the hall and walked down the passage, Bees was waiting for me outside his office. He dragged me inside and screamed so loudly at me, the whole school could hear him. He expelled me with immediate effect. I could come back to write the last exam, but other than that, I wasn't allowed to set foot on campus. It also meant that I had to vacate the res.

It was June, it was winter, I had nowhere to go. Destitute.

39

I HAD TO PLAN AND MOVE fast. My mother's friend Griet (with the blue Beetle) and her son, my childhood friend Ivan, lived in a big, old, double-storey house in Hofmeyr Street, just behind the school. I knocked on Griet's door and asked her if I could please stay with her; I had nowhere to go. The house had many rooms and so I moved in. It suited me well, even though I felt guilty that Griet had to look after me.

I became joyless, sombre. Friends came to visit, and slowly I started feeling a new freedom, a new happiness. There was no spiteful bully of a school principal to ruin my newfound serenity.

One day Coenie Slabber traced me to Griet's house. The phone rang and it was him on the other end. He demanded that I move in with his ex-wife. My old schoolfriend, his son, was studying at Wits and I could stay in his room. His ex-wife was a schoolteacher, and she would keep an eye on me while I studied.

Oh, he was cunning ... up to his old tricks. I'm surprised that I said yes. I still don't know why.

The next day I thanked Griet, said goodbye to her and moved in with Coenie's ex-wife. I was back in Union Street, where I'd once lived with my alcoholic father and his then wife, Linda. I had a large room, with views of Table Mountain.

I woke up during the night and wondered what I'd done. Coenie's daughter and other son lived in the same flat. How had I decided to move in here when this woman's ex-husband had molested me for all those years? Was I a traitor, a little minx? I felt remorse, like a villain sullying the lives of innocent people.

In between these maelstroms of burdens, I had to study. It was boring, as the subjects left me unchallenged. I stared for hours at Table Mountain. It was October and the southeaster was howling; it was also hot. My body felt tired, numbed.

To whom could I turn? I would walk for hours around the reservoir right opposite the flats, the same little park where I'd walked Boesman and Lena. I missed them. They had been put down. Murdered.

At my desk, I would stare at the trees bending in the wind. What a disaster. During the day, when my flatmates were all gone, I would read newspapers and books, fooling myself that I had been studying.

The exams crept ever closer. The situation was insufferable. I had studied nothing, not a word; the pages were dead to me. I felt like that little boy in the orphanage who had lost the ability to speak and had become mute.

With the first exam, I walked to school feeling terrified. I had gained weight again, having turned to food, my old friend, to alleviate the horror I felt. My legs were chafing against each other as I walked into the hall. People stared at me. I thought, 'I am a sex slave masquerading as a matriculant.'

I left the pages blank for a while. I saw nothing and could hardly answer anything. Today, after years of therapy, I realise I was suffering from a deeply complicated post-traumatic stress disorder. That I even got out of bed every morning was a miracle.

In between exams, I befriended an older Afrikaans actor called Limpie Basson. I would visit Limpie and we'd drink tea and talk about interesting stuff like movies and theatre. He took me to see Pieter-Dirk Uys at the Baxter Theatre, when he appeared as the camp and witty Evita Bezuidenhout for the first time in Cape Town.

The show was called *Adapt or Dye* and took place in the big theatre, and it was packed. It was circa 1981. We spotted the security police in the audience; we just knew: the clothes, the moustaches, the hairstyles. They were there to report back on this man who criticised the National Party so vehemently, but I don't think they were ready for what was to come. A waving Tannie Evita arrived on stage with a bunch of proteas and a huge presence.

To the security police, this woman looked like their moms, aunts and grannies. How could she speak like that about their leaders? Critically, as if they were jesters?

But she did, and she got away with it. And they were left speechless.

Desmond Tutu was in the audience and Evita also sent him up; Tutu laughed and laughed. Piet Koornhof, a cabinet minister known as Piet Promises, was also in the crowd. When Uys lampooned him, Koornhof was big enough to laugh at himself. Koornhof was a man who had caused immeasurable pain to black South Africans. Laughing at himself, while knowing what he had done, was macabre.

When the show ended, Evita walked up the stairs carrying her flowers and waving at everybody. The then South African flag was wrapped around her. As she arrived at the top of the stairs, where the members of the security branch were seated, she stopped and blew them kisses. Then she walked to a vintage coupe limousine, got into the car and sped off. The crowd loved it. At last, we could laugh at the Nats.

That night, something also shifted in my head – it was possible to send up the establishment. With Evita's satire, I started becoming conscious of what was really happening in South Africa.

After the show, Limpie took me backstage to meet Pieter-Dirk. It was quite something to see Evita take off her wig and remove her make-up to transform back into her real self, Pieter-Dirk, in front of your eyes.

It was then that I realised that theatre and acting were powerful tools, capable of changing people. A way to shine a torch into the abyss. I liked Pieter-Dirk at once, and over the decades, we stayed in touch. He was a prime influence on my young mind.

Later, in the same theatre, I saw Athol Fugard's play 'Master Harold'... and the Boys. The production was initially prohibited in South Africa, which illustrates just how dire the situation was. In this play, a young white man spits in the face of an older black man, in this version played by John Kani. I froze. I realised, as if a wave had engulfed me, that there was something terribly wrong with this country.

Another evening, during the same period, and also at the Baxter, I saw John Kani in Miss Julie. Sandra Prinsloo played the title role. In the play, their characters had to kiss. A white South African woman kissing a black man, in public, on stage, during the reign of PW Botha! The opening night was like waiting for a time bomb to explode.

Would they kiss, or skip the scene? Then, John Kani came closer to Sandra, and they kissed. The audience gasped; some people got up and left. The security police stood around, waiting to pounce, but the play went ahead unhindered.

This was the first time a black man had kissed a white woman on stage during the apartheid regime. The next day, the story was on every front page; some people were furious, others rejoiced.

Both Kani and Prinsloo were escorted into the parking lot by security after each performance, as there was a high chance that they could be attacked by right-wingers. Prinsloo received obscene hate mail and death threats. What a palaver over nothing. South Africa was isolated and parochial, and sometimes that mindset still pops up today. Way too often, in fact.

In between these happenings, I was still writing exams. Eventually, the exams ended. Coenie, as I'd expected, wanted his pound of flesh. I had to take the train to Johannesburg to visit him. My plan was to study drama at the University of Cape Town, or UCT, for which I had to do an audition, but I could do that in Joburg.

Coenie was his usual cloying, soppy self. I was done with him, but I was trapped. Meanwhile, I went for the audition and was successful. Out of the many who had applied, only a few were accepted. For a change, I felt good about myself. Nobody ever applauded anything I achieved; I had to do it myself.

Then Coenie said that we were driving back to Cape Town. A female friend of his would accompany us, thank heavens, because I shuddered to think what I would have had to do in that car.

Little did I know what was awaiting me.

40

WE DROVE BACK MOSTLY IN silence. The friend in the back spoke now and again. We dropped her in Rosebank in Cape Town, and Coenie and I drove on. Then it hit me: I had nowhere to go. Coenie didn't want to talk to me about it. The next moment, we pulled up at 110 Buitenkant Street. Coenie opened the boot and dropped my luggage off at the front door.

Somehow, the journalist in him had discovered where my dad lived. We were at his cottage. Coenie got back in his car and drove off. We wouldn't speak for decades. After years of abuse, he'd discarded me like a used condom.

It was the best thing that could have happened to me. I realised that, at eighteen, I was too old for a paedophile; I'd overstayed my welcome. But Coenie's departure didn't mean that I was free. The damage he'd caused would endure for the rest of my life.

I knocked on the front door, with trepidation. My father opened, drunk. He looked a mess. I walked inside and the whole place stank of alcohol and cigarettes. It was grubby. At school, I had received a small amount of money every month from a charity that the school was connected to. Now I had nothing.

UCT had not started its year yet, the matric results had not been made public. All I knew was that I had passed the audition. I had to plan, to keep standing; I couldn't disintegrate.

I had a roof over my head, but no money. One of my old schoolfriends, Johann Müller, had just returned from the Netherlands, where he'd been an exchange student. He, too, needed money. We decided to apply for jobs as waiters at the Inn on the Square on Greenmarket Square. Although the manager decided to employ us, it was as bouncers stationed outside the busy pub. Johann and I were young and strong; the manager needed that look.

This was the third job I'd ever had; the first was working as Christie's slave, harvesting grapes in the heat, the second was delivering newspapers. Johann and I had to wear suits, and, by some miracle, I actually owned one. The Inn was a swanky bar with a wild side. Our job was to keep the sex workers at bay. It was a tricky situation, as you couldn't just assume that a woman was a prostitute. What does a prostitute look like? I remembered them from my childhood in Kloof Street, but they had all looked quite glamorous to me.

Soon, I became friends with the prostitutes and allowed them all entry into the bar. When the manager found out, he transferred me to the restaurant. From grape harvester, to bouncer, to waiter. My résumé was starting to look impressive. I earned good money there – certainly more than I was used to.

One night, I arrived home after a long shift and Sammy was smashed. He attacked me and grabbed all the money out of my pocket. He pushed me against the wall, but I was bigger by now and kicked him in the stomach.

Some arbitrary woman in the background, who looked like one of the junkies from *Trainspotting*, came running up to me, screaming: 'Give us the money!' I was furious. I grabbed them both by their necks and pulled them to the front gate. They were too pissed to fight back.

I threw them out of the house and latched the door. They would have to climb over the wall to get back in. Despite the state he was in, Sammy managed to do just that. But before he could get inside, I ran to the kitchen to get a bread knife. I slit his one finger; it did not deter him. He was on a mission: money and drink.

He was wild. I locked another door, but I didn't realise just how desperate he was. He kicked in the glass door, bleeding and in a rage. I phoned the police, who came quickly. The cops put them both in the back of the van and drove off.

I had the glass in the door replaced with extra-strong glass and changed the locks. They didn't come back.

A schoolfriend, Petro Davel, moved in with me to share the rent. She had wild red hair, also with a whiff of curry, and could make heads turn when dancing in a club. On nights out, we went to a club called Scratch. Dancing consisted of jumping up and down in one spot, and the bands who played there performed hard punk and electro-pop … anything that was so loud you couldn't hear a thing for two days afterwards.

Goths were big at the time, and if you performed, you had to have attitude, and I mean a *moerse* attitude. Also, reggae. The men played topless; one night, I saw a woman throw her bra into the crowd. And did she shake those tieties!

At the local all-night café, Cadiz, formerly known as Zippy's, we lined our stomachs with soggy pies, curry and rice, Russians, hamburgers, or half a loaf of white bread with slaptjips covered in salt and vinegar. By 03:00 in the morning, the place would be pumping. It was open twenty-four hours a day, seven days a week. The prices of items changed depending on the hour of the night or day.

Cadiz had Pac-Man machines and ciggies. Most people had to hang onto the counter. They were finished. Klaar. Op! Dagga and alcohol.

A man of Dutch origin, called Pops, had run Zippy's. Pops wore a knitted beret and sported a long white beard. He only had one tooth, but at one point, he'd had two. He was rude and grumpy, but sometimes also quite endearing. If there was a fight, he had a cup of vinegar ready and would throw it into the renegades' faces. That made them stop quickly.

He also wielded a sjambok, which he would hit sharply on the floor. The pellet gun he discharged a few times was a bit scary, but nobody was ever gravely injured. Pops wore braces over brightly coloured tie-dye T-shirts. He had tons of badges stuck to his beret and shirts, but what they stood for, nobody knew.

Someone mentioned that his flatmate wanted to impress a hot new girl and got Pops's permission to put a nice little table, complete with a white tablecloth and a candlestick, in the middle of the shop. Pops served the girl samoosas on good china.

There was also a place called Roma by Night near Rita's, and the Moulin Rouge opposite Roma, where Russian strippers performed pole-dancing during the day. Roma was known for its wide variety of colourful night flowers (hookers).

The survivors of that era, I'm afraid, are now rusted wrecks like me, residing somewhere in a scrapyard. At least we have the memories.

Over weekends, the friends I had made in Stellenbosch came to stay over and enjoy the city's nightlife. They would take the train back to Stellenbosch the next day. Once, one of them fell asleep on the train and woke up in Paarl.

During this period, I also reconnected with an old schoolfriend, Belinda Voges, who had the campest mother. Trix, as she was known, drove a huge Jaguar and dyed her beehive hair poodle blue. She wore stilettos, white catsuits and big gold belts. Her lips were always painted a ripe watermelon red, and her toenails pink.

Trix often accompanied us to Rita's, where she would be the main attraction on the dancefloor, looking quite out of place, but with a hint of Amanda Lear. She loved the song 'Vicious Games' by Yello and would twirl to it, then stand still and blow a kiss into the air.

Through Belinda I met a young man, André Carl van der Merwe, who would later write the book *Moffie* about his time in the army. Who would have thought, way back then, that the book would become a heart-wrenching movie with the same name. When I saw the film decades later, it upset me so much, I had to leave and go back to watch it another time.

André would accompany us to Rita's and agreed that Trix was like someone from the Weimar Republic demi-monde. At that stage, André had a stall on Greenmarket Square, which was the hottest place to hang out on a Saturday morning. Young fashion designers sold their own designs, and they were good. The smell of dagga hung in the air. A gramophone was always going, on which were played songs by Jennifer Ferguson, Via Afrika, éVoid and Bright Blue, popular bands of the time.

Everybody had a fuck-you attitude and a babelaas. We knew the country was at a tipping point, that change was in the air. But not quite yet.

41

IN THE MEANTIME, MY MATRIC results were released, and they were a tragedy. I was furious that I'd been lured into studying at Coenie's ex-wife's flat, as the atmosphere there was unbearable. I felt guilty staying there, not to mention soiled.

I know the ex-wife meant well, as she obviously wasn't aware of Coenie's dark, paedophilic side. Besides, the school should not have expelled me at the most important period of my school career, and Coenie should never have told me to move into his ex-wife's flat, as if I were his concubine.

To think, these were adults playing around with a teenager's life, his future. How much could one person endure? Where did boundaries start; where did they end? I didn't know. I had no examples to follow.

This lack of boundaries followed me for quite a while; it still does. I would spontaneously grab a woman friend's breast, for example. Just because I'm gay doesn't give me the right to do that. One night at a dinner party, I grabbed a man between his legs. I had no hidden agenda, it was Bacchus talking. His wife, rightly so, threw a glass of wine in my face. That was the end of the dinner party. You just don't do that.

I often find myself saying outrageous things on social media. There are times when saying nothing would be better, but no, I steam ahead. Afterwards, I self-flagellate; I get so angry with myself. From my early years, I acted the court jester in company. Let them laugh, chuckle along … just don't let them see the sheer mortal terror behind the mask.

Later, on my own, after the party was over, I would often ask myself: 'Is this it? Is this what life is about?' I would contemplate self-annihilation.

Then there were days when I would wander aimlessly around the streets of Cape Town, assessing all the high-rise buildings. I would look up and wonder from which window I could jump.

One day, I was on the twenty-first floor of the Ritz Plaza Hotel in Sea Point. In the men's toilets, right next to the urinal, was an open window. I noticed that it was quite large and that I could easily fit through it. I popped my head through the window and looked down, down, down, onto the street far below. For a moment I wanted to jump, but then I pulled my head back and left the men's room.

I ran back to my table at the revolving restaurant, made jokes and laughed, pretended that all was festive. The place was alive with flambés and harried waiters running around, while outside the city lights sparkled and white waves broke in the ocean below.

Despite my bad matric results, I enrolled at UCT; I did, after all, pass the audition. Nothing to be sniffed at, I thought. This was around 1984. My old schoolfriend, Johann Müller, who'd worked with me as a bouncer, had an old, wonky, light-blue Toyota. A tiny car, but dependable. The car's name was Blikkies. This tiny car, built like a dinky toy, became a strange leitmotif in my life. In a movie, it would be known as the getaway car.

Johann drove us to UCT's Upper Campus, where we had to register in the blazing sun: he for law, I for a diploma in theatre and performance. Unfortunately, my time at UCT was short-lived, as the head of the department, Professor Robert Mohr, called me in. Despite passing the audition, I'd have to rewrite two subjects to stay on.

The prof was a kind man who listened to my tale of woe; he made quite an impression on me. He told me that although my other subjects were excellent, those two needed more work; he said he knew I could do it. He got up and gave me a hug.

Of course I could do it, but my head wasn't ready. One of the people whom I met at UCT, and whom I still admire, was Melinda Ferguson, who would become a well-known writer and publisher. Her sister, Jennifer, was already a well-known singer. Melinda was at the start of her adult life.

Another job that I could add to the list of jobs I'd dabbled in was that of being a lighting controller at one of Jennifer's shows. The show took place at a cabaret venue, Garbo's, near the Castle; it was one of those places where you simply had to be seen.

The walls were black, the interior dark; candlelight was the only illumination. A touch of the Weimar Republic, decadent, before the fall. Garbo's held late-night live shows, and Jennifer needed someone to control the lighting for her one show. I had no clue how to do this, but it was such an honour to be asked, as I was a big fan of hers.

So, I did it. There I stood, behind the control switches, while Jennifer sang all the songs I knew so well. When she sang louder, I turned the red light up, up, and when softer, a touch of yellow, sometimes a bit of darkness; unexpectedly, a white light. It was a great night; I'll never forget it.

Jennifer's sister, Melinda, and I got along as we both had a quirky way of looking at the world, and she was an empath. Melinda's life crumbled later when she became a full-on drug addict, living a hard life on the streets of Hillbrow. But she eventually got clean and wrote a riveting book, *Smacked*, about her recovery. And what a recovery it was. Today, she is one of the big names in the local publishing industry and has made a success of her life. She has also helped many aspiring authors to become published writers.

After my chat with Professor Mohr, I felt both relieved and disappointed. Relieved, because I realised that I wasn't focused enough and would probably waste the year. I had too much trauma to work through. But also disappointed, because I now found myself in a liminal space, a train between stations, dangling between destinations.

I occasionally bumped into the prof in the Company's Garden. He would talk endlessly about theatre, and each interaction was like attending a masterclass. He died, unexpectedly, in 1984, which came as a shock.

One day I was walking rather aimlessly in the Company's Garden, thinking about the future. A homeless man came up to me and asked me for money. He told me that he was staying at the Salvation Army, that tall, faded-red face-brick building on the Foreshore.

I glanced at this unshaven, barefoot man with his dirty hair and grubby clothes, but, when I looked closer, I saw that he was my father, Sammy Korck. I had no money on me, so I walked away, and the wind came up and blew through my young hair. This was too much, too much; hold, heart, hold.

I stumbled back to 110 Buitenkant Street and closed the door. One day, an ex-girlfriend of his told me that Sammy was sent to prison for two years, for fraud. It was in the stars; it had to happen. His alcoholism had turned him into a devil with only one thing on his mind – alcohol.

That day, when I walked away from him, was the last time I would see him. Years later, when I was around twenty-seven, there was a message on my answering machine. It was from Linda, Sammy's ex-wife. She told me that Sammy had died. He had choked to death in a steakhouse in Port Elizabeth, of all places. I always wondered what his connection was with PE, as I remembered the day we drove there in a Jaguar.

I had guests at my place that night. In the background, I could hear the laughter of my friends. I listened to the message again. After a few seconds, I phoned Linda, and she told me that Sammy would have a pauper's funeral.

Poor Sammy, a life that ended by choking in a steakhouse, after a jail term, then buried in a nameless grave. The irony didn't escape me: he'd died doing what he liked best – drink in hand, eating a steak in a steakhouse.

I returned to my guests and, in passing, mentioned that my dad had died. My friend Suzy Brokensha, who years later would become editor of *Fairlady* magazine, went pale. She asked me how she could help. I said that the party must go on, that my dad and I weren't close; he'd died, that's it. I poured more wine and the evening continued.

The next day I sat in the bath, held my knees, bent my head and wept. I cried for a man whose life had been such a waste. An intelligent, charming man. I bawled over my lost childhood.

It was the end of a miserable chapter. Or perhaps not.

42

THE RESTAURANT THAT I WORKED for, closed. It was around the mid-eighties: the country was going bankrupt under the Nats, as sanctions were being imposed on South Africa, and everyone functioned under a state of emergency. I couldn't get work and had no money.

Petro, with whom I shared the house, became a gallerist and moved to another place. For a few days, I, too, worked in a glamorous gallery, where everything was white, including the floors, the ceilings, the walls ... even the owner was blonde. I lasted only a few days, as she could not pay me. Then I applied for a job at the post office in Cape Town, in the old Stuttafords building in Adderley Street.

My job was to search for errors in the telephone directory. It was very odd. I sat in a huge office, going through each name and phone number and phoning people to ask them if their address was correct and their surname spelt correctly.

My colleagues were all Afrikaans, as it was the time of white Afrikaans affirmative action. They mostly looked at me as if I were an alien. I don't know why; I wore a tie and looked decent. An air of desperation hung over the place, and I would say a lack of ambition was evident. People spoke for hours in little groups and showed no interest in their work.

It was a dreadful job. At the end of the first day, I felt like one of the Angry Young Men of the British literary movement. Was this how life would pan out for me? I don't job shame, but that was just so ho-hum. The second day, I could hardly get myself out of bed, but I arrived at my little desk in the huge room, sat down and started the endless phone calls.

Some of my colleagues were lonely, and they would strike up long conversations. I could entertain them for a while, but I had to move on; the boss, Mr Louw, kept a strict eye on my progress. He was probably in his early sixties, of huge build, with a face that was a mix of John Vorster and Danie Craven. Mr Louw barked in staccato when he spoke. When he went out, he would put on his hat, take a yellowwood walking stick and light his pipe.

Everybody in the office lit one cigarette after the other; the place was billowing with reefs of smoke. By the end of the second day, I felt so defeated, I wanted to cry. I thought of the novelist William Faulkner, who was fired as a small-town postmaster because of his bad work habits. If Faulkner could work in a post office, maybe that was a sign, I thought. Start writing. I didn't have a typewriter, but when I got home, I sat down and wrote some trashy thoughts in a big black book.

On the third day, I crawled out of bed, walked to the office, entered … and turned around. I was already mentally unstable, but here I would finally be certified. For my own mental health, I had to run, and fast.

The reality was, I was now destitute, penniless, in the gutter, just as Tina Lategan had predicted. I had to eat. The thought of becoming a rent boy crossed my mind. I walked all the way down Buitenkant Street, past the Kimberley Hotel, to Greenmarket Square. At night, it was a hotspot for rent boys.

It was a warm night and I leant against a lamppost. A slender, attractive man with black hair came up to me. In a German accent, he asked me if I would like to go out for dinner. There was a popular restaurant where actors used to hang out, called Backstage, just up the road.

I was very nervous, but I led the way. A French couple owned the place, and they hosted cabarets and offered new singers a chance to test out an audience. Mara Louw performed there one night, which was risqué as it was a crime for blacks and whites to mix. Backstage had a diverse clientele.

When this man, my potential client, and I sat down, I was famished. The food was wonderful, but I think at that stage I could have eaten a live puffadder. I started to panic about what was lying ahead. Had the whore's son become a whore? The words 'in the gutter' echoed through my head again.

I have nothing against sex workers, but right there and then I realised just how vulnerable and exploited they must feel. No, no … I jumped up and ran out.

But I had to think fast, as I couldn't pay the rent and there was no food in my fridge. Once, through Coenie's ex-wife, I'd met a man called Pieter Serfontein, a retired opera singer who used to sing under the name Christiaan Stern. He was running Ankerhof, one of the last remaining boarding houses in Kloof Street. A number of drama students boarded there, as it was only one block from UCT's drama school.

I knocked on Pieter's door and told him my story. He offered me a room, with no strings attached, and he stuck to his word. He saved me, at least temporarily, from a life on the streets.

43

PIETER WAS A WORLDLY PERSON and, I suspect, a loner who was looking for some company. The usual Athol Fugard-esque cast of underdogs, brittle birds and oddballs filled the boarding house.

One such person was a woman called Lilla Koen, a beauty in her day, but with a palpable melancholy in her heart. Her face was always downcast, even when she had on her signature bright-red lipstick. In the evenings, she would make a dramatic entrance, descending the stairs while reciting sad poems by Sylvia Plath and Elisabeth Eybers. She often cried.

Pieter would listen to opera the entire day while typing away at his novel, set in Russia. He was friendly with opera singers like Wendy Fine, Marita Napier and Marita Knobel. One day, he and I went to the old Nico Malan Theatre to meet up with Mimi Coertse, who was rehearsing for an opera. She was completely different from what I'd expected. I thought she would be an old, sour, haughty tannie, but not a damn – she swore and told dirty jokes, laughing so hard that the cutlery on the table rattled.

Opposite the boarding house was a video shop, where you could hire arthouse movies on those old VHS tapes. Pieter and I spent hours watching those and reading books from Ankerhof's library.

I was aware that my life was going nowhere, but I needed a break, just to catch my breath. It was a transitional period or threshold, I told myself yet again, a period of uncertainty and ambiguity, where my identity, values and beliefs were in a state of flux.

Nevertheless, life was going swimmingly until, one day, a letter arrived. It was from the South African Defence Force (SADF); they were my call-up papers. I had to serve two years of enforced military service to maintain the apartheid status quo and to give the original state capturers the power to keep going. If you refused to go, you could get a six-year prison sentence.

It was winter, it was cold, the mood was sombre. You could feel it on every street corner. I tore the paper up and flushed it down the toilet. I had to plan an escape, disappear. They had my address; they could send the Military Police and lock me up. The country was teetering on the edge: there were daily riots, states of emergency, gun shots, teargas. PW Botha was always wagging his finger on TV. No way was I going to be a part of all that.

Pieter sponsored me for a few weeks in a guesthouse in Faure Street, in the backstreets of Gardens. Next door was the Monte Rosa old-age home, and opposite a hall owned by the Dutch Reformed Church. Perfect camouflage.

I spent my days in hiding, conjuring up plans to escape. Pie-in-the-sky stuff, because how could I? Where would I go? It was a miserable experience. Dismal.

Coenie Slabber's ex-wife got to hear about my predicament – I still don't know how and why. But she was very convincing, regaling me with scary stories about jail and years of my life that would be wasted behind bars.

She took me to see a chaplain in Panorama, a suburb which, on a cloudy day, could inspire suicide. The chaplain was your stereotypical Afrikaans dominee; he prayed and read a verse out of the Bible before we began.

He told me about the necessity to defend my country against communists, black people, Cubans and Russians. I sat there feeling so sad, until I had another out-of-body experience. My soul left my body; I was adrift against the ceiling. I was not there, sitting in front of him. I longed for a lobotomy.

The next scene of this sorry saga was the train. I was sitting in one, on my way to Grahamstown, for basic training. A young man and I shared a coupe compartment. His hair was thick, long and black. He had lost his father in a plane crash, which was why he was a month late for his basic training. But he was looking forward to it.

My excuse was that I'd hid in a guesthouse behind the Labia, with no clue what to do, or how to flee, or where to go. And no, I wasn't looking forward to what lay ahead. I looked at his hair, and mine in the mirror, and thought, 'It will be gone tomorrow. They will shave it off.'

The soundtrack for that trip was the Thompson Twins singing 'Doctor! Doctor!' This guy played that song over and over on his little cassette player. I started to enjoy the trip. As the landscape went by and the sun started to set, we created a private mood, a cocoon. We were both young, in that little cabin on wheels, with no clue what was going to happen the following day.

The next morning, we awoke to a sight that was so spectacular, it was like the opening scene of a movie. We both sat in shocked awe. Hundreds of bright-pink flamingos were standing to attention in a big vlei, like a platoon of soldiers welcoming us.

The train slowly entered the station. A new life awaited. I could feel the fear, as if a spider was running down my back.

44

GRAHAMSTOWN IN WINTER WAS BITTERLY cold. The air was heavy, grey, hostile. They used coal to keep the ovens in the kitchens going, and I don't know what else; all I knew was that coal was burning twenty-four hours a day. So, there was lots of dirty-smelling smoke; it was everywhere. Sometimes there was even something oddly comforting about the odour.

A huge barbed-wire fence cut us off from the outside world. Some days I would stare through the fence at the Monument Theatre, yearning for freedom. At night, sharp white spotlights shone on strategic areas. Soldiers stood guard, rifles in hand. You might as well have been in a concentration camp.

My hair was shaved down to the skull. The huge barracks I stayed in had a long green floor that was polished to a shine; for the rest, everything was in military brown: the blankets, the trommels, our balsakke, clothes, underpants, boots, socks. Brown, the colour of chocolate. Or shit.

I knew nobody and was a month late, so the rest of the troops had already bonded. Sometimes one of them would fart loudly at night, while others burped; the one in the bed next to me was a masturbator who whimpered quietly when he came.

There was a guy, the main farter, who asked for a match when he could feel one coming. He would bend over, and someone had to light a match as soon as he let go of his wind. The flame of the match would double in size; once, it burnt his bum.

A siren woke us at 04:00 in the morning. Our beds had to be made perfectly, our boots had to shine, the floor had to sparkle. A corporal would walk down the barracks, inspecting everything. If your bed was not up to scratch, he pulled off all the bedding and screamed at you as if you were a child.

Afterwards, we had to form a platoon at parade: attention, march, salute, and get another scolding. Vastly different from opera, poetry and arthouse movies. The food consisted of overcooked veggies, tasteless meat, and eggs that turned blue from being kept warm for too long. It was all served in things called varkpanne.

Breakfast was mieliepap. Oh God, it was a nightmare – cold, thick and far too sweet. At night, a little cafeteria would open, where some of the troops could play snooker or buy a hamburger and a Coke. I would hang out there, but I felt like a misfit.

Letters from friends arrived, which brought some relief. Pieter-Dirk Uys as Evita sent me a postcard wishing me the best of luck. 'Liefde vir 'n linkse meisie!'

Pieter Serfontein wrote, as did old schoolfriends; nothing from any family.

During the day, we had to practise with our guns in a forsaken veld, crawl under and through barbed wire, and pretend we were shooting at an enemy. A terrorist.

One night I felt so down and out, I knocked on a medic's door. He was blond and friendly, that's what I remember – a kind face. He tried to talk sense into me, but he was my age; what did he know? I listened in silence while sitting on the edge of his bed. We moved closer to each other, and I could sense that we would end up hugging. He gave me a sleeping bag in which I could sleep on the floor in his tiny room. The next morning, I was afraid. What would they do if they knew I hadn't slept in my own bed?

The head of the camp called me in and wanted to know where I'd been. I told him that the medic had kept an eye on me, as in a suicide watch. He wanted to know if we'd slept together, and I said no, because it was the truth. The man looked at me with venomous eyes; clearly, he didn't believe me.

The days grew colder and darker. Cleaning a rifle was one of the worst things I ever had to do. Weekends, an ill wind blew in from the veld. There was nothing to do but hurry up and wait.

Sometimes a little sunshine fell on the camp, and you could turn your face towards the sun, though it was weak and had no strength, as if it were dying up there in the sky. There would be a group of us, sitting in silence, faces turned upwards. Young men who should never have been there.

I had worked out a detailed plan on how to go AWOL. One night I sat with a fellow troep and we discussed my plan for hours. We would run away the following night. But he turned out to be a traitor and informed the head of the camp. I was furious.

We got one weekend off, and an SAA plane loaded with troepies flew from PE to Cape Town. It was a strange experience, the army paying for the flight.

When we saw Table Mountain, we all started clapping. The plane flew over

False Bay and slowly came in to land. It was like a chimera. As we landed, everyone applauded again. Pieter Serfontein fetched me from the airport. I stayed for two days, too exhausted to talk. I knew I would have to go back.

45

ONE NIGHT, THEY WOKE US up at 23:00. We had to change into our uniforms, take our rifles and put on our helmets. Outside, large army trucks were roaring. It was raining; I could sense terror, danger. We got onto the back of the trucks, which started driving off in a convoy. Nobody knew where to.

The rain pelted down. We arrived in a township. Sharp searchlights were attached to the roofs of the trucks and aimed at the houses; outside, children, the elderly and adults were standing, shivering. We were there to intimidate the inhabitants; it was a show of force and a reminder that whites were in charge and had the weaponry to enforce their dominance.

We were ordered off the trucks; me too. Carrying our rifles, we had to run to the front door of one of the houses and kick it in. The door broke open. We ran inside with our torches, and the one troep screamed at two people lying curled up in bed. They turned their faces to us; it was a mother and her child. The look on their faces still haunts me to this day.

In another room, a young man lay shivering, clad only in his underpants. I could see the whites of his large eyes and his thin, frail body.

Something in me gave way and snapped forever, to this day. I ran outside and sobbed. Nobody noticed; it looked like rain pouring down my face.

The next day I got hold of a bottle of Panado and swallowed the whole lot down with water. I needed to die; I'd had enough. But I started to vomit, and someone heard me. I was carried on a stretcher to the clinic on the base. Lying there, I thought: 'I'm state property. Trying to take your own life is inflicting damage to state property. You could go to the detention barracks for that.'

An irritated nurse shoved black fluid down my throat, which made me vomit even more. They kept me there for three days.

In the room next to me, a young man was suffering from malaria. He was yellow. I had never seen anybody that yellow before. At night, I could hear his screams and rapid breathing. When they discharged me, the clinic sent me to see a psychologist.

I never heard what happened to the yellow boy. I hope he survived, that he had a long and fruitful life. One wonders.

46

THE PSYCHOLOGIST I SAW WAS young, too young. He hardly had any experience and was of no help at all. He just nodded his head at everything I said. They then sent me to see one in Port Elizabeth, my father's old stomping ground. I took one look at the place and saw the horror of it: a faded, drab, old city, a backwater, and much too windy. I felt even more down in the mouth. I was projecting my joyless life onto the city – perhaps 'suicide village' would have been a more apt description.

The new psychologist was another catastrophe. I had to repeat my whole life story all over again, to no avail. I realised I had to get out of Grahamstown. My basic training was ending, and then it would be off to the border. I had to be inventive.

One dull Sunday I sat down with an old notepad and wrote down my experiences in the army. Where I got the guts from, I don't know, but I marched into the office of the base commander and asked him to please send the letter to the Minister of Defence, Magnus Malan. I explained that I would be of more use to the army as a journalist than a soldier, which is what I was pleading for in my letter. Oddly enough, he listened to me, though I don't know what he did with the letter.

I gained some insight into my personality that day. I was either on the floor, with no self-esteem, or I was on top of the world, full of bravado. This fluctuation was exhausting, but when I was confident, I could achieve near miracles. When I was low, I self-sabotaged.

I left the base commander's office and life went on, with the clock ticking closer to the date of departure for the bush. One day, the commander called me to his office. I had to pack my balsak; I was off to Cape Town and had to report to the Castle, where I would work for their media (read propaganda) department and write articles for their publications.

Pieter Serfontein gave me back my room in Ankerhof, and this time I could pay him for it, as I was receiving a stipend from the army.

I walked down Kloof and Long streets, then turned into Darling Street, and the next moment I was at the Castle. We had to line up for a parade at

07:00, after which we'd march to our offices. I considered the parade a total waste of time. I even had to stand guard twice a month, right through the night. What for?

The articles I wrote appeared in publications on the Cape Flats, or in a magazine called *Paratus*. They were all positive stories about the army. A team of us interviewed everyone from high-ranking officers to ordinary troops who had interesting stories to tell. The set-up was very professional, with an arts and layout department, writers and a photographer.

I collaborated with Guy Tillim, who went on to great heights as an internationally renowned photographer. He taught me something that has stayed with me my whole life. We had to interview the flower sellers on Adderley Street about their Christmas plans. Our uniforms looked a bit scary, although Guy, with his kind face, could never look threatening. He always had a serene presence.

Guy noticed that my interviewing style was quite aggressive and told me that I should learn to 'read the room'. These were harmless women, no threat at all. With a softer approach, I would get more information out of them.

Afterwards, I thought about this and wondered whether the aggression I'd had to endure during basic training had provoked a fight response in me. Years later, when I met up with people my age who had also gone through basic training or had been deployed on the border, I realised that they, too, had a seething anger underneath a thin veneer of calm.

I know one man who, after serving on the border, was never able to hold down a job. His family looks after him. No career, no ambition; he just sits, doing nothing, the entire day. Apartheid left a terrible psychological scar on black people, but I wonder what those broken white men do with their demons. Are there forums in which group therapy takes place? Do they have someone they can talk to about their experiences?

For a while, I was also the editor of a little newspaper at the Castle with a print-run of about five hundred. I don't know who it was aimed at; I can't even remember its name. I made all the decisions and confidently approached possible contributors. I even walked into the offices of the *Cape Times* and asked the then military correspondent, Willem Steenkamp, if he would write something for me. And he did.

Then I went to Nasionale Pers and asked the cartoonist at *Die Burger*, Fred Mouton, if he could supply me with a cartoon relating to a troepie. It took chutzpah.

47

THE NEXT PERSON I APPROACHED was the author Uys Krige, who was elderly by then. He was staying with his daughter in Tamboerskloof. Krige was the first person of note I interviewed, and it was also his last interview. We went to Zerban's Cake & Coffee Shop, a well-known deli-restaurant in the Gardens Shopping Centre in those days. If you wanted to be seen, that was the place; it was always packed.

Krige knew about war, so I asked him about his time abroad. During World War II, he had worked as a war reporter for the South African Army during the Abyssinian and North African campaigns. The Italians apprehended him during the siege of Tobruk in 1941 and sent him to a prisoner-of-war (POW) camp in Fascist Italy, from which he fled two years later, following the downfall of Benito Mussolini.

I was nervous and studiously wrote everything down in a big, black schoolbook. Krige gave a riveting interview about his time as a POW. Luckily, I was familiar with his work, so that was an icebreaker. Afterwards, I thought how humble and kind it was of him, then in his mid-seventies, to accommodate a nineteen-year-old troepie.

His health was a tad frail after a car accident some years earlier. Krige said that after the accident, he learnt that kindness was the most important attribute in a human. He never fought with anybody again after that.

When my little newspaper appeared with all these different stories and the cartoon, the bigshots at the Castle were mighty impressed. Not, however, for too long. Typical of my young life, it was an ever-changing set design, as if I was living in a play.

48

M Y POLITICAL AWAKENING HAD ALREADY started in a small way with my mother and her strong-minded female friends. Her open-minded attitude to gay people and the way she interacted with people of colour influenced me tremendously. Regarding apartheid, I was too young then to really understand the economic and psychological implications of this illogical policy.

But that night in Grahamstown, I reached a tipping point when I saw the fear in my fellow South Africans' faces, the sharp lights, the torches, the rumbling Casspirs and big, brown military trucks, the loud noises, the smell of petrol and terror, the Vektor R4 rifle in my hands …

I started trying to make sense of it all. One day – again, pure synchronicity – I noticed a poster on a lamppost in Adderley Street promoting a meeting of an organisation called the End Conscription Campaign (ECC). I'd also read about the United Democratic Front (UDF) and felt myself attracted to their values and ideas.

Dr Ivan Toms, a gay Christian physician, was the speaker at the ECC meeting. He had a practice in Crossroads township, outside Cape Town. White people hardly ever ventured there, as the political atmosphere was too volatile. The inhabitants treated Toms like a hero. He'd turned against the army and police when he saw how they broke down people's homes during surprise raids. There, he had reached an Aha-Erlebnis, just like I had in Grahamstown.

I suspect Toms's humanitarianism and progressive thinking started at university, but Crossroads was a gigantic shift. In February 1985, he went on a three-week hunger strike in St George's Cathedral to protest the government's decision to bulldoze the township. Archbishop Desmond Tutu supported Toms, and they became close friends.

Crossroads' destruction resulted in violence and the deaths of residents who tried to resist the demolition. During his hunger strike, Toms said: 'As a Christian, I am obligated to say no, to say that I will never again put on that SADF uniform.'

In 1986, the SADF officially annexed Toms's busy and essential health clinic. In July of the following year, Toms defied the SADF when they called him up for one month of mandatory service. In 1988, the court sentenced him to twenty-one months in jail for defying the order, and he eventually served nine months in Pollsmoor Prison.

Those were the times we lived in. That a productive doctor could be locked up by the apartheid state was shocking. Of course, Toms wasn't the only one. Later, when we became friends, he never spoke with bitterness about his ordeal.

I would later start attending UDF meetings, where speakers like Cheryl Carolus, Trevor Manuel and Dr Allan Boesak made a huge impression on me. The ominous presence of the police lurked in the background at every peaceful meeting.

Another man who made a considerable impression on me during this time was Professor Farid Esack, who addressed a crowd in my *heimat*, Sea Point. It took place in the Civic Centre, next to the Sea Point Public Library.

Esack spoke about how white people could never be free while they were holding one foot firmly on the necks of their fellow South Africans. They were depriving themselves of broadening their horizons and of a wider and enriching multicultural experience.

A crowd of frightened and brainwashed whites heckled him. Although the political situation is dismal today and not the type of utopia we expected then, at the time we thought speaking up was the right thing to do. I know of old lefties, also original supporters of the UDF, who are intensely disappointed in how power and greed have turned South Africa into a carcass. Useful idiots, that's what we were.

That the just struggle for freedom resulted in South Africa becoming another post-colonial wreck is just depressing.

49

I WAS READY TO GET MORE involved with, specifically, the ECC. Somehow, I couldn't get hold of Ivan Toms; I think he was away. I needed a foot in the door and would do anything to help. It was urgent. One day I picked up ECC and UDF pamphlets, and on each one the printer was identified as one Trevor Manuel. He was already known in struggle circles, but I didn't know much about him.

There was a phone number. I dialled and asked to speak to him. Trevor Manuel came to the phone, and I told him my story. I asked him if we could meet in public, at the Inn on the Square. When he heard my surname, he wanted to know if I was Colonel Lategan. I said no. Understandably, he was hesitant to meet me and said goodbye.

Activists were justified in feeling paranoid during that time, as many spies had infiltrated organisations like the UDF and the ECC. From then on, I realised that it was going to be difficult for a young white male to get involved in the real 'struggle'. How I despise that word now. What a joke.

One day, however, I attended a huge gathering of young white men from the ECC, where we signed a document expressing our disapproval of the SADF's murderous role in the townships. The next day, it was splashed all over the newspapers.

Ankerhof was still my abode, and one morning I got up to take a shower. I had just got back to my room with my towel still wrapped around me when my door was violently kicked open. It was a captain from the Castle, along with some troops. I had to change into my uniform and accompany them.

They shoved me into a vehicle and sped off. At the Castle, I was subjected to a disciplinary hearing and found guilty of going AWOL. Then, the horror: they produced photos taken of me at ECC and UDF meetings. As a journalist in the army, I was part of intelligence. I was not supposed to be connecting with the enemy.

What was I doing at those meetings? I was sentenced to two weeks in solitary confinement at the detention barracks in Wynberg.

It all happened so fast. One moment I was in Ankerhof, the next I was in the back of an army van peering through the bars, on my way to their prison.

The punishment did not fit the 'crime'. But worse events were about to unfold.

50

W HEN I ARRIVED IN WYNBERG, they locked me up in a single cell, where I had to stay for fourteen days. I looked at the walls folding in on me. There was a makeshift toilet, a few pieces of toilet paper. I was on my own, buster, nobody to help.

The only time the warders allowed me out was when I had to shower. I saw an old friend from my childhood, Paul, whom I greeted. We used to hang out back in the day when I lived in Union Street with my dad. It was great to see someone I knew, an old tjommie to reach out to under scary circumstances. Just as we started talking, I was taken away, back to my cell. I would never see him again.

I was desperate, miserable, lost. There was no way out, nowhere to turn. My life-to-date came back to haunt me: the orphanage, the near-death incidents at Dassieshoek, being expelled from school and molested for years, my short-lived drama studies at UCT.

But the one person who came back to haunt me most was Tina Lategan. I was in the gutter, as she'd foretold. After a week, I felt as if I was entering a state of psychosis.

One morning, I was called for kitchen duty. I could not believe my luck. Just to get out. My job was to peel potatoes. While peeling, I thought of the knife. I looked at it. Then I took it and started cutting my left wrist, but the knife was quite blunt. I had to slice really hard.

At last, blood shot out like a fountain. Just then someone walked into the kitchen, grabbed a cloth and wrapped it around my wrist. They took me to 2 Military Hospital, on the same base in Wynberg.

In the operating theatre, I saw another guy from my childhood; he had been at school with me. I felt ashamed, as here I was, lying flat on my back, and he was one of the medics attending to me. His face was sullen; he showed no mercy. Nor did the doctor, who just looked irritated. He worked roughly with me and I'm certain he botched the job out of spite. To this day, part of my hand has no feeling and I have an unsightly scar where the tendon forms a lump. This time, the army did charge me with damage to state property.

State property… let that sink in.

51

FTER THE OPERATION, I WAS whisked off to the psychiatric ward, where once again I was subjected to a psychologist who was green and inexperienced. I had to repeat my whole life story for the umpteenth time; it was so dispiriting.

A bunch of overmedicated young men sat in the TV room, staring in silence at the screen. The corridors were white, the floors shiny, the rooms lit up by neon lights.

What was I doing there? The head of the ward, a man with a Vlakplaas face and the eyes of Wouter Basson, called me in. He was a colonel. He sat behind his desk, staring at me. Then he took out a thick file with my name on it and showed it to me. Again, the silence, the staring. What did he want from me? I was irrelevant, a buzzing mosquito on the peripheral. Not a head honcho in uMkhonto we Sizwe, the military wing of the African National Congress (ANC).

The place reminded me of South Africa at that stage: suffocating, parochial, paranoid, bureaucratic, driven by fear. It reeked of a mortuary with clean floors. I thought of how I wished I could fly away, beyond the borders, away from this country. If I could stand on the tarmac, before boarding the aircraft, I would turn around and spit on the ground.

I looked into the eyes of young men, just teenagers, who were bosbefok, as they had seen too much. They were bossies. Landmines exploding, machine guns rattling, the feeling of a hand grenade in your young hands before you hurl it at someone and see their body explode in front of you. These were the youths who were incarcerated with me.

This was before the experts realised the immense psychological effect of post-traumatic stress disorder. Decades later, when these men were middle-aged, they disintegrated. They turned on their wives, drank too much, got overly aggressive. Often, they would commit suicide. There was no forum for damaged white South African men to talk about the horrors of the Border War or their experiences in the SADF. They were forced into something that they had not planned for and didn't want to be a part of.

I remember, I had a schoolfriend who lived just one street up from our school. We would walk the streets together, talk, play in a stream behind his house, catch tadpoles and throw them back into the water. There were trees, with birds, and in winter you could smell the fresh soil. But as soon as you entered this boy's house, you were accosted by a murky, melancholic atmosphere. The curtains were always drawn, the windows only slightly open.

The boy's mother would serve us sandwiches, but she hardly ever spoke. I never asked him where his father was; they didn't mention him. There was a room with a door that they kept shut. I often walked past it, and one day I asked my friend what was in the room. His mom was away that day, and he put his finger to his lips. 'Shhhhht,' he said. Don't tell her. He opened the door. Inside was the room of a teenager. It was untidy; the bed was unmade. T-shirts were lying around. On top of a cupboard was a balsak and an army helmet. Posters of pop stars adorned the walls.

My friend told me that it was his older brother's room. He'd died on the border.

His mother had kept the room just as he'd left it a year ago. The only possessions of his that were added were the balsak and the helmet, which the army had returned the day they came to inform her of his death. The room was a shrine, as were so many rooms throughout the country. Empty.

I was remembering this tragedy as I lay on my back in the army's psychiatric ward in Wynberg. Next to me was a young man to whom I'd introduced myself; his name was Craig Oakley-Brown, and he was a trolley dolly for SAA, he told me. Out of this meeting of two people adrift in a sanatorium, something good came about. Craig had a stack of magazines next to him, those glossy things that people read before the internet. Craig often flew to New York and London and had brought them back with him.

Bored, I started reading them. A shift happened; it was a door opening to a new world. I read *The Face*, a top British music publication. The writing was brilliant. Craig also gave me Andy Warhol's *Interview* magazine, *Esquire*, *GQ*, *The New Yorker*, *New York* magazine ... I couldn't stop reading. There was nothing like that in South Africa.

The layout, the quality of the articles, they were so smart and witty. It dawned on me that, as a product of Christian National Education, I had no idea of the big world out there. I lived a small-town life.

One day I received the news that Craig had jumped from a building. It saddened me; he had been my friend in that ward. Was he one of the army's statistics? Did his unresolved issues come back to haunt him?

While in hospital, Coenie's ex-wife came to visit me. She had the cheek to tell me that my friend from school, Grant Doidge, was an alcoholic and that I should stop seeing him. I was stunned. Her ex-husband had raped me over many years, she'd taken me into her house to study for my matric, which contributed to my bad results, she'd made me see a dominee who talked me into going into the army, and now she had the nerve to visit me in a psychiatric ward to tell me one of my best friends was an alcoholic. Really?

After two weeks, the colonel informed me that I could go. 'Where to?' I asked. 'Home, the army is discharging you. You're a security risk,' he said. In my dismissal letter, a psychiatrist wrote that I was untrustworthy because I was obviously gay and therefore could not keep a secret. This was too risky for a member of their intelligence unit.

And as an obvious supporter of 'communist' movements like the ECC and the UDF, I was even more dangerous. 'At last, I'm a communist,' I thought to myself. I should just convert to Catholicism, then I would belong to all three gevare: the Rooi Gevaar (communism), the Roomse Gevaar (the Catholic Church) and the Swart Gevaar (black people).

The report also proclaimed that, from a psychological perspective, I was incapable of being rational or solving problems. Well, well.

And all this in perfect Afrikaans. Bless.

52

PIETER SERFONTEIN CAME TO FETCH me, and I moved into my old room in Ankerhof, Kloof Street. What now? Where to now with my life? Again. I was so tired of being in limbo.

There was a tickey-box in the foyer. One day, it rang. I ran down and answered it. It was my friend Theunis Engelbrecht, whom I had met through Coenie Slabber. We'd kept up our correspondence, and Theunis was a musician and journalist by then. Could he bring a guest? he asked. They wanted to stay over for a few nights.

Pieter was fine with it. Business was a bit quiet at that stage. Theunis's friend was a child psychiatrist from New York, Casper Schmidt, an expat, who'd returned for a brief holiday. Casper was an avant-garde Afrikaans poet and artist but preferred New York's cultural and psychiatric scene to what was going on in South Africa. He fascinated me, as he truly had an unusual way of looking at the world.

While he was here, we would drive to various locations, and he analysed people as we drove past them. It was like a voiceover in a movie or a documentary, but with running commentary from a psychiatrist. A black man stood by the side of the road and pushed the button of the traffic lights to stop the traffic so that he could cross the road. Casper said this was a man who felt powerless over many issues in his life; he was emotionally paralysed, and by pressing the button, he felt a sense of power.

Casper stayed for a while; a few days became a week. We attended off-beat literary parties, which was quite different from my days in the army. Casper would play a big part in my life, sooner than I thought.

53

A T ONE OF THESE PARTIES, I bumped into my surrogate mother, whom I have not mentioned until now. Sheila Cussons was an influential Afrikaans poet whom I'd met at the age of fifteen after I'd read one of her poems. I was a mere schoolchild, but I decided to write her a fan letter.

To my surprise, she contacted me at school and asked me to join her for coffee at Zerban's in the Gardens Centre. I was nervous and wondered what we'd talk about.

Sheila had been injured in a gas explosion some years before we met, which left her disfigured and fragile. I had no problem recognising her, as I had seen photos of her scarred face. I introduced myself, feeling so terribly nervous in my school uniform. But it was a match that was meant to be. My own mother was decrepit from alcohol abuse, and here I had met a woman who would shower me with maternal warmth.

This must have happened in the late seventies. With Sheila was the woman who would look after her for over two decades, until her death, Amanda Botha. Amanda has been a part of my life for decades; we are friends to this day.

After that first meeting, the three of us continued to meet, sometimes in the old Company's Garden Tea Room or Café Mozart in town. Sometimes I would pop over to Sheila's flat in St Martini Gardens in Queen Victoria Street just to chat.

Later, I helped her with chores like shopping; things she needed and could not carry herself. I could talk to her about issues a young person would discuss with his or her parent.

During that period, I befriended quite a few Afrikaans literary figures, as I was enthralled with their knowledge of the world. I realised that I liked older people; they had so much to teach me. And not everybody wanted to exploit me like Coenie Slabber.

May I interrupt myself here and mention that although my Afrikaans memoir, *Hoerkind*, received glowing reviews, for which I am eternally grateful, some readers complained that I was a name-dropper. I'm not: in an autobiography, you surely mention the people who crossed your path and who shaped or abused you, otherwise what's the point? An endless internal dialogue that goes nowhere ...

Let me move on to another interesting person whom I met when I was about eighteen. There was a gay bar in Cape Town called the Wine Barrel, which I've mentioned before. It was a tatty little English-style pub where you could play snooker, eat pork pies, or just drink and talk kak.

Here, I met an older man called Ismail, who also went by the name John. Sometimes he dressed casually in trousers and a shirt and wore sandals on his feet, while on other days he would arrive in a long white robe. John talked with insight about politics and poetry; he also told me that he had grown up in District Six and had spent time in prison during some war. I was too young to really take notice.

Sometimes he became maudlin, and he would cry. A few times I saw him getting into screaming matches with the bartender; once there was even fisticuffs. Ismail was wearing his long, flowing white robe that day, and it tore. I stayed out of it, as he was in a rage. Later, he disappeared. I thought I would never see him again, and I missed him.

Years later, I spotted him in Long Street, coming out of a mosque. I ran over to him, and he told me that he had been in jail and was living in the Bo-Kaap. He'd been in prison because of his involvement with uMkhonto we Sizwe. My mouth dropped to the floor ... I couldn't believe it.

During his time in the military wing of the ANC, they'd called him Grandfather Africa. He took my hand and said, 'I'm now called Tatamkhulu Afrika.' It turned out that he was a respected South African poet and writer; I never knew. In 2002, he was knocked down by a car and died at the age of eighty-two.

54

IT HAPPENED BEFORE I TURNED twenty-one, around October 1985. One day, the tickey-box rang. I picked up the receiver and it was Casper Schmidt, whom I had met a few weeks earlier. He was single, older, and said he would like to be my mentor.

Casper told me that he had heard about my background and what had happened to me in the army. He would like to buy me a return ticket that would be valid for one year so that I could experience New York City. I would be his general factotum and help him with some chores and at his publishing company, Ombondi Editions. Casper needed an Afrikaans proofreader, and I would be able to obtain a working visa on those grounds.

A ticket from Cape Town to New York cost R999 back then. I could sense that there was no sexual pay-off or vibe of any sort from Casper's side; he genuinely felt that he had the money, so why not give a youngster a chance at a bite of the Big Apple.

I moved fast. The next thing I was on a plane; the world was my oyster, with New York the pearl. Up in the air, I thought of the life I was leaving behind. I had made the right decision. I had the chance to start over. The soundtrack of that flight was a-ha singing 'Take On Me', which was played continuously. How apt.

On landing in New York, Casper was waiting for me. We climbed into a yellow taxi. I stared at the cityscape as we slowly drove off. Would New York be a pleasant revelation, or would it be torture?

The windscreen wipers went swoosh, swoosh, swoosh, swoosh, as light snow started falling. It was late afternoon.

Casper said the strangest thing to me and the taxi driver. As he studied his reflection in the rear-view mirror, he said: 'It's terrible to be ugly, terrible.'

55

MY FIRST IMPRESSION OF NEW York was that I was on a movie set, yet this was the real deal. I recognised many of the high-rise buildings from movies and photographs, and also the black limousines ferrying glamorous women around, the yellow cabs hooting and the drivers shouting, the accents, the pavements (or sidewalks, as they say), packed with people walking with a mission.

I saw the hotdog sellers with steam bubbling from their steel carts. We passed Zabar's on Broadway, where people were standing outside eating bagels and sipping coffee. An image that stuck with me was of a man sobbing bitterly outside a hamburger joint. He was crying into his hands, his body shaking. Later in my life I would see other people crying in public. It always upset me.

We arrived at Casper's magnificent apartment block on the corner of West 82nd Street and 98 Riverside Drive, overlooking the Hudson River. It was a grand old New York block straight out of a Woody Allen movie. The orange-and-brown brick building made a gentle curve along Riverside Drive. I had never seen anything like it before, except in the movies.

We walked into the foyer, where a uniformed doorman welcomed us. The carpeting in the foyer was thick and luxurious. The door to the lift opened and an elevator operator took my luggage (one small suitcase!).

That Casper was thriving in New York was obvious, and I would soon discover that he was one of the city's most respected child psychiatrists. As an urbane, cultured man with many interests, New York certainly was a better choice than a country isolated through sanctions from the international cultural thrust that was happening in 'The City So Nice, They Named It Twice'.

Casper put me up in his study, as his apartment was large but only had one bedroom. He suggested that I first settle in and then start looking around for roommates or digs. I looked down from his lounge window onto the Hudson River. On the street below, I saw a row of kindergarten children walking, all dressed up warmly in bright jackets.

That night Casper and I went to a sushi restaurant, unheard of in South

Africa in the mid-eighties. We were so isolated that we thought a fortune cookie was the height of cuisine. I noticed mixed couples, people from all parts of the world, different accents, a potjiekos of nations. At last, I felt a new freedom, away from Afrikaner Nationalism, the South African Defence Force, the security police, Casspirs, the Dutch Reformed Church, men with moustaches talking into walkie talkies, tannies wagging their fingers at you because you cussed.

There was, however, a dark side to New York, a dichotomy. The mayor of the city was a closeted gay man, Ed Koch. Gay people were angered that Koch had the opportunity to be a role model but instead chose to play politics. Ronald Reagan was in power, a nasty man who charmed people with his acting skills. Koch played to the gallery.

New York was experiencing an epidemic, an outbreak of AIDS-related illnesses that was clear everywhere you walked. Men, their faces covered in lesions, would pass you on the pavement.

Reagan had decided to release those who were diagnosed with schizophrenia from state mental-health facilities. Their families often rejected them, and they would become homeless, living on the streets, talking loudly to themselves.

There were the bright lights of Broadway and Times Square, but New York was also a place of immense turmoil and sorrow. The AIDS pandemic had hit the creative industries hard, but none of this was yet visible in South Africa.

Mayor Koch was a brash and blustery coward who once said in public: 'I am not a homosexual.' He completely distanced himself from the crisis that was unfolding. Simply by pretending that AIDS was a gay disease that didn't really exist, Koch stymied the AIDS charities that were trying to help the sick and dying.

A character based on Koch is featured in the 2006 John Cameron Mitchell cult movie *Shortbus*. This character talks to a young man to explain why he did so little at the time. 'People said I didn't do enough to prevent the AIDS crisis, because I was in the closet. That's not true,' the character says. 'I did the best I could. I was scared.'

One of Koch's biggest critics at the time was the high-profile activist and dramatist Larry Kramer. He was the founder of the gay human rights group ACT UP, and wrote an agitprop play called *The Normal Heart*, in which a group of young gay men try to convince Koch about the looming tragedy, without success.

In the end, more than a hundred thousand New Yorkers would die of AIDS-related illnesses, often shunned by their family and friends. The creative world was nearly wiped out.

I quickly became involved in ACT UP by attending the group's public meetings and reading as much of their literature as possible. One day, in a gay club, I kissed a man my age. The patrons screamed at us and told us to behave – we could be infecting each other and them. There was rage on their faces.

Sex had become a death sentence; even a kiss was dangerous. Night had fallen over Gotham City.

56

OR A WHILE I LIVED in Casper's study, and during the day I ran errands for him. I had to make deliveries in Brooklyn, Manhattan, Queens and on Staten Island, so I slowly got to know the whole of New York.

I also had to assess the viability of manuscripts for Casper's publishing company, Ombondi. In the meantime, I started looking for a place to stay. Eventually, I found a room in the West Side YMCA on 5 West 63rd Street, in the heart of Manhattan and close to the Lincoln Center. Wow, I still couldn't believe I was in New York.

But then Casper started behaving strangely. I often went to his apartment in the evenings to hear what my chores were for the next day and sometimes to watch TV. I had a key to his front door, but he would latch it from the inside so I couldn't get in. When I couldn't open the door, he would pull it open and ask me why I was battling to unlock the door. Casper was gaslighting me.

He also started analysing me and claimed that I had an unconscious fear of his apartment and his computer, specifically the latter. But in fact, it was his cat who needed treatment. Nobody was allowed to touch ET. One day, when I tried, ET bit me so hard, there was blood all over the place. This infuriated Casper, as he suffered from bouts of obsessive-compulsive disorder. Everything had to be neat and tidy and packed away. Some blood on the carpet and he flew into a rage. You even had to take your shoes off when you entered the apartment, as Casper was terrified of germs.

Poor ET was about ten and had never left the flat. He would stare out of the window for hours at a time, gazing at the birds in the trees down below, next to the Hudson River. When a boat bopped by, ET would look at it as if it were a way out.

Casper's OCD manifested in other ways as well. He could listen to the same record for weeks on end. *Götterdämmerung*: never in my life had I experienced a person so obsessed with one record. Another quirk was Casper's addiction to sitcoms. Here was this genius of a man, who watched *Who's the*

Boss? religiously. Every time it was on, he would roll around laughing at the slapstick jokes.

The gaslighting continued. Casper started sending me to places to collect parcels, but when I got there, they wouldn't know what I was talking about. Then I'd have to go all the way back to find out what was going on. Casper would be adamant that I'd gone to the wrong place and that he'd given me the correct address.

He started 'forgetting' to pay me. When I asked for my money, he would look shocked and pretend that he had paid me. He even asked me if I hadn't brought my own money from South Africa.

I had to think fast, so I decided to get a job as a waiter at a coffee shop in Greenwich Village, the gay and creative hub of New York.

Casper the friendly ghost (he looked like a mix between the cartoon character and Andy Warhol) had two sides to his character. On the one side was the friendly, warm intellectual, poet, artist and psychiatrist, and on the other, the cruel man who liked to play games with your mind. He once told me that he'd wanted to hire a helicopter when he'd fetched me at the airport.

57

EOPLE DID WARN ME ABOUT Casper and his shenanigans before
I went to New York, but I never believe anybody until I experience
something for myself. I should have seen the red lights on the dashboard, but no, I was a naive knucklehead.

In South Africa, I'd heard how he'd written poetic obituaries for his best friends, which he'd posted to them. Of course, they were shocked to the core, as he didn't save them from a tongue-lashing, highlighting their imperfections.

Then there was the time that he rubbed tons of garlic on the walls of the flat of a fellow medical student, who suffered from severe mental-health issues. Casper knew that his friend was fragile, but he went ahead anyway. He had the spare key to this guy's flat, which is how he got in. When the friend arrived home, the smell overwhelmed him. He panicked, as he thought he was having a schizophrenic episode, hearing voices and smelling strange odours.

I mentally prepared myself for what lay ahead; I had to be strong. I was in a big, strange city, with my support base back in South Africa. But I calmly went ahead and sucked the sweet juice out of each day. A friend from my army days at the Castle lived in New York. Irwin Weiner was studying interior design at the Fashion Institute of Technology and shared a flat with a friend. In a place like NYC, housing, flats, even rooms, were scarce. Many people slept on couches that doubled as beds.

Irwin had also just arrived in the city and wasn't flush; he worked fourteen hours a day. We managed to connect regularly and comfort each other.

One day, Casper again didn't pay me on time, and my tips from the restaurant were low, so I decided that I was going to do what I'd done in Cape Town. I'd attend art exhibitions, where I could enjoy free snacks, often top cuisine, and drink nice wine. Just enough to become pleasantly tipsy.

I bought a copy of the underground, counterculture newspaper the *Village Voice*, as they always had listings of the best art events, accompanied by great interviews with the artists. One of the founding editors of this newspaper was the writer Norman Mailer, who had a South African connection. His father, Isaac Barnett Mailer, also known as Barney, was an accountant from Johannesburg.

I started attending art exhibitions nearly every evening, as there were so many to choose from. Oh, it was bliss, because not only did I learn a lot about art, but I could also people-spot, drink wine and eat fantastic snacks.

One installation, in the Meatpacking District, stood out. It took place in a large butcher shop, which served as a pop-up gallery. Instead of animal carcasses, there were actual people hanging on the big hooks in the fridge. They were dressed in their underwear and their bodies were covered in blood. As you walked past them, they would snort like piglets and bellow like cows.

At another installation, also in a factory, snakes hissed at you from a birdcage while ancient traditional Japanese music softly tinkled in the background.

I attended exhibitions in Harlem, Greenwich Village, Little Italy, Chinatown and Hell's Kitchen. I often bumped into people I only ever saw in print or on TV. Yes, I was young and starstruck. I saw people like Andy Warhol, Keith Haring and Jean-Michel Basquiat. Warhol was an artist and the founder of *Interview* magazine.

The three of them moved around as a trio, and I stalked them. Once, I followed them to Warhol's studio, called The Factory, at Union Square West and 33rd Street. This was where he created his zany movies, pop-art paintings and psychosexual dramas.

Warhol was a pale man, always fidgeting with his glasses, and occasionally touching his signature wig. He hardly ever smiled. But he was observing everybody the whole time; he would scan a room. One night I followed them after an exhibition at The Factory and, in the dark, I saw Warhol kiss Basquiat goodbye. It was more than just a peck.

All three of them would die shortly after 1986. Andy Warhol died in 1987 from ventricular fibrillation. In 1968, the aspiring writer Valerie Solanas had shot Warhol in a jealous rage, and his health had never been the same after that.

Jean-Michel Basquiat died of a drug overdose in 1988, and Keith Haring in 1990 due to AIDS-related illnesses. They had been the rock stars of the art world.

Visiting art galleries was fascinating, and one day I started talking to a woman who told me that she was originally from Johannesburg. Her name was Ingrid Sischy. Who could have predicted that she would become the editor of *Interview* magazine in 1989?

Am I name-dropping? Unashamedly, yes. It's New York, where you bump into a movie star or famous person on every corner.

For a short while, I shared a room with a drag queen in Harlem, one who had a liking for hashish. During the day, he worked as a clerk for an accounting firm, but over weekends he turned into Aurora Borealis, a queen of note in Harlem's nightclubs.

I never smoked the hashish, as it made me paranoid. One day, however, I had to go to Casper's apartment. I tried to see as little of him as possible, so I decided to take a puff or two. I went into the subway wearing a brightly coloured jersey I had bought on Greenmarket Square. The noise the trains made on the tracks and the smell of fuel were noticeable. I thought people were staring at me.

So I exited the subway and walked down Broadway, and there, coming towards me, was Molly Ringwald, the actress from *The Breakfast Club*. I kept walking, right past her and her friends, but then I looked back. And they were looking at me, too. To this day, I still wonder if it was really Molly Ringwald or just a chimera conjured up by the hashish.

Later, I moved from Harlem back to Broadway, as Aurora Borealis had overdosed on drugs, lapsed into a coma and died. At the time, I enjoyed rough sex with volatile and druggy young men in back alleys, knives in their back pockets, tattoos on their bodies, the smell of jail and testosterone permeating them. I flirted with the possibility of being stabbed or kicked in the stomach.

Secret and seedy sex in dark alleys also added a frisson of being caught out. Afterwards I would feel guilty and dirty, yet only this excited me. I would later trace this form of sex back to its primal origin: the encounters with my molester, Coenie Slabber, had also been seedy and secretive, always with the potential of being caught out.

I moved to Broadway and West 86th Street, a few blocks from where Casper lived, where I shared a flat with a down-and-out actor who had no hope of ever making it. His pained face showed that he realised this. He watched MTV day in and day out. I can still hear Prince singing 'Kiss', the Pet Shop Boys performing 'West End Girls' and Robert Palmer crooning 'Addicted to Love'.

I slept on this guy's couch for a nominal rent, but the TV was always on. Once, as I was drifting off, I heard South Africa's Minister of Foreign Affairs, Pik Botha, saying at a Cape Town press conference that it was certainly possible that a black president would one day rule the country. The next morning, all the papers ran this as their front-page story.

Downstairs from our apartment was a supermarket called the Red Apple. One day, as I was taking some milk from the fridge, I noticed a man standing next to me. It was Kevin Bacon, who'd starred in movies like *Quicksilver* and *Footloose*. As he lived in the area, I saw him fairly regularly. It was a strange feeling to see someone as famous and sexy as him buying something as mundane as toilet paper. Movie stars, like the late Queen of England, didn't use the loo!

I continued my outings to art exhibitions, where I bumped into one of the scariest people I'd ever seen: Anna Wintour, then editor of *British Vogue*. She made a dramatic entrance at the venue and had a hard face that never moved, just like Andy Warhol's.

I attended talks by people like Susan Sontag, who pulled a huge crowd of New York intellectuals with 'Illness as Metaphor', which was published in 1978. Charles Bukowski gave a poetry reading while he was pissed, but he still manged to read well.

I certainly wasn't idle. I attended Norman Mailer's masterclass in New Journalism at New York University, as well as two masterclasses on the art of writing movie reviews by Pauline Kael, the film critic at *The New Yorker*.

Then there was the time I spotted William Burroughs sitting on his own in a dark pub. I was too shy to talk to him, but just seeing one of my favourite authors was a thrill.

That was New York for me – a place to ogle celebrities, but also to learn as much as I could. I absorbed each day like a flower turning its head to the sun.

58

MY STAY IN NEW YORK took another twist. Through Casper, I got involved with an organisation called the International Psycho-historical Association, whose goal was to study the backgrounds of politicians and try to figure out why they made certain decisions, specifically why they started wars with other countries. Also, why, in many cases, they self-sabotaged, or reacted in a certain way to catastrophes like the AIDS pandemic. The founder, Lloyd deMause, was the author of *Reagan's America*, *The Emotional Life of Nations* and *The Origin of War in Child Abuse*.

These psychohistorians produced papers in which they'd psychoanalyse political figures like Ronald Reagan, as well as racism and reactionary politics. According to them, early collective trauma in children had profound consequences on geopolitical events. It all sounded very interesting, but my interactions with them made me feel as if they were a cult. They examined every aspect of people's lives and would climb into one another's personalities, too; nobody was spared. They even had their own TV programme, which was recorded in a studio a few blocks from where Casper lived on Riverside Drive.

Casper asked me to be a general factotum and help with the set and behind the cameras. One of my tasks was to make sure that everything looked stylish and professional. I also had to type out Casper's handwritten notes on a variety of subjects and double as a make-up artist and hair stylist. Casper owned a pair of glasses that he would wear on camera, as they did not reflect light. He was so pleased with these that he couldn't stop talking about them.

Every second Friday, Casper hosted a chic cocktail party at his apartment, where he provided his guests with catered food and expensive drinks, all served by beautifully dressed waiters. Soft music played in the background, perhaps Burt Bacharach. The guests were a mix of artists, actors, academics and psychoanalysts. One woman, who always arrived in a limousine, took a shine to me, and at every one of Casper's parties, we'd have long conversations about South Africa, my background and her life as a Jewish person living in New York.

At one stage, when I was living in Harlem, I told her in detail about my life there. She had big, big hair, which she sprayed into what resembled a large, hairy balloon. I saw her as a character straight out of a Woody Allen movie; she reminded me of Eve, played by Geraldine Page, in *Interiors*.

In fact, her name was Flora Rheta Schreiber, a journalist and the author of *Sybil*, a book based on the true story of a woman who had sixteen personalities. *Sybil* was an international bestseller (hence the limo) and was turned into a two-part, made-for-television film starring Sally Field and Brad Davis. Davis was known for his roles in *Midnight Express*, *Chariots of Fire* and *Querelle*. He died from assisted suicide in 1991 after suffering from severe AIDS-related illnesses, which he'd contracted due to intravenous drug use.

Senior psychohistorians invited Casper to give a lecture in Washington based on an academic paper he'd written on the group-fantasy origins of AIDS – it blatantly supported AIDS denialism. The world of academia received his analyses with astonishment, polarising its members. One group of scientists considered it the best paper ever written on the virus, while another was so shocked by the content and the rambling esoterica, they didn't know what to say.

As someone who has read it often, I think it is a brilliant piece of work, even if it is complete blabber. Casper's premise was that gay men were the victims of mass hysteria, and that the pandemic existed only in their own minds. There was no virus that was killing them. Because society frowned on homosexuality, they were confronted with intense feelings of rejection and self-loathing, which contributed to a psychosomatic plague – gay people were 'thinking' themselves to death.

In one section, Casper writes: 'I posit that AIDS is a bio-psycho-social disorder. I argue that a sequence of group psychological events in the U.S. has shamed – and mercilessly so – the homosexuals and the drug addicts, giving rise to an epidemic of shame-induced depression.'

He continues: 'It is my contention that this mechanism of killing the shamed is one of the most powerful, though deeply repressed, dynamics of the AIDS epidemic: that which is enacted in real murder in the tribal culture, becomes a more sublimated but nevertheless equally venomous outpouring of death wishes towards drug addicts and homosexuals.'

'It is as if the shame of the offenders' misconduct were acutely felt by the rest of the group, so that only their elimination can remove the painful effects of the shame. These identifications are based on an unconscious resonance between the shamed ones and the rest of the group.'

Where Casper had found the time to research and write this fifteen-thousand-word paper is a mystery. There are one-hundred-and-twenty-three references, one of which is 'Mass Hysteria Associated with Insect Bites'.

Nevertheless, off we went to Washington on a high-speed train. As usual, Casper analysed everybody in our carriage while I read *LIFE* magazine and looked at some great photographs by the South African photographer Peter Magubane, which appeared in double-page spreads.

On a seat opposite me, however, sat an interesting young guy. He was in full-on punk regalia, with spikey green hair, and loads of earrings, tattoos and piercings. I loved the look, but Casper projected a whole lot of psycho-babble onto the stranger. Apparently, he had some unresolved childhood issues and suffered from an old trauma that was now manifesting itself in the way he dressed. I thought it strange that after living in New York for so long, Casper still had a touch of parochial South Africa in him.

We arrived in Washington, where it was cold and covered in snow. I did go and see the White House, but the architecture and spirit, or genius loci, of the place didn't appeal to me. I found it too generic, as all the buildings looked the same. Its inhabitants never made eye contact; it was boring. Too many politicians in one place and this is what you get.

Casper and the psychiatrist at whose place we were staying spoke end-lessly about the 'myth' of the virus. The hall where Casper was going to deliver his talk was packed with the crème de la crème of mind doctors. At the end of his delivery, Casper received a standing ovation. I couldn't believe it. In New York, you saw sick people on every street, yet the genius was in denial.

Later that night we went to Georgetown, a student hub, to celebrate Casper's successful talk. It wasn't during the student holidays – the students were all there – but dear heavens, there was no vibe. If New York was the sun, Washington had to be the moon. I would visit Boston later on, and that was a much more exciting city.

After Washington, Casper became obsessed, manic; he could not stop talking, working, going on about the virus. He was a good artist and took up painting again, working towards an exhibition, plus he was still seeing all his patients, and he was working on a collection of poems and short stories.

Where he found the time for all this, along with his TV programme and his work with the psychohistorians, remains a mystery to this day.

But change was coming.

59

I KEPT ABREAST OF WHAT WAS happening in South Africa by going to the embassy and reading all the newspapers there. They were only a day or two old, so the news was quite fresh.

I read about PW Botha with his wagging finger, I saw Casspirs in the streets, burning townships, teargas, a country teetering on the edge. So different from New York with its own social problems, but mostly bright lights.

One day, I picked up an old *Esquire* magazine featuring a South African, Rian Malan, on the cover. The cover copy read: 'My Father, My Country: A Powerful Story of Divided Loyalty by Rian Malan'. Inside, the article's headline was 'My Traitor's Heart', which later became a book.

Rian was in his early thirties and as good-looking as a movie star with his black hair and smooth skin. He wore a red shirt with a collar on the *Esquire* cover and the shirt featured a badge that proclaimed 'Free South Africa', with artwork by Keith Haring, the very artist I had been stalking.

I sat down in a coffee shop and started reading. The article took me back to my country and stirred in me feelings of loss, nostalgia, melancholy and confusion. Rian's writing style was vivid, poetic; it made me feel that I needed to start writing.

I shared Rian's sentiments, that the ANC should be unbanned. An office of the ANC, linked to the United Nations, was located in New York. I decided to look them up and found their phone number in one of those old telephone directories from back in the day. I spoke to someone there and they seemed keen to meet me; I arranged to pop in.

Once there, I couldn't believe that I was sitting in a banned political organisation's office. If I recall correctly, it was not large; small, two desks. Solly Simelane and Neo Numzana, the two head honchos of the ANC in New York, introduced themselves, and we sat down to chat. They were keen to hear about the ECC and the UDF and everything else that was happening in Cape Town.

We got on well. I asked them questions about the ANC, but I somehow had the feeling that they were a bit lacklustre. There they were, sitting far removed from where the real action was taking place, at the coalface in South Africa. For them, New York and all its trappings must have been quite alluring. I also got the impression that they didn't trust me, a young white Afrikaans boy from Cape Town trying to ingratiate himself with a prohibited liberation movement.

Nevertheless, I kept popping in regularly, even asking them if I could join the ANC. They looked baffled and gave me forms to fill in, which I did. I signed them and thought, 'Is that it? Am I now a member of the ANC?' Seemingly so, but I still felt like an outsider. In retrospect, I realised that I was naive, although what the ANC stood for, and their ideologies, which I supported, sounded right at the time. Decades later, I would, of course, realise that the movement was a front for criminals who felt nothing for South Africa, except to make money out of a business that was going bankrupt.

At this point, Casper started gaslighting me again and became increasingly manic. I realised that he was working through the night; he had the appearance of someone who'd worked non-stop in a coal mine for a week.

My work on his TV programme increased and I had to give up my job at the coffee shop, which I'd enjoyed. I was thus financially dependent on Casper again. Of course, he stopped paying me and pretended that I was insane to suggest that he hadn't. One morning I woke up in a fury and realised that it was time to go back to Cape Town. I knew New York would see me again one day, but the time had come for me to go home.

I booked a seat on SAA for that same day, but Casper still owed me money. So I packed my suitcase, went to his flat and took $400 out of the drawer where I knew he kept his cash. Casper was attending a conference, spouting forth his usual denialist drivel. The amount was far less than what he owed me, but I wanted out. I took a taxi to the airport, but I felt sad. Leaving New York was not an easy decision, but it was one I had to make.

I felt homesick and missed Afrikaans, the language that so many so-called coloured people speak. I had no idea what I was going to do or where I was going to live once I was home, but Casper was making me fall apart.

En route to Johannesburg, we landed on Ilha do Sal, an island in Cabo Verde, off the coast of West Africa. When I disembarked on this island, I had a panic attack, wondering what I had done. To leave New York, to go back to a land that was going up in flames? Huh? I thought of hiding in the restroom and starting a new life on Sal.

I went to a toilet and closed the door, my heart racing. Then I heard my name being called, as all the passengers had boarded. I ran to the counter, showed my passport and got onto the plane. Once we took off, another panic attack came over me. What if Casper had laid a charge of theft against me in New York? On my arrival in South Africa, I would certainly be arrested. I'd go to jail.

We landed in Johannesburg. At customs, I showed the official my passport, it was stamped, and I went through. I phoned my friend Theunis Engelbrecht, who had introduced me to Casper. He lived in nearby Bethlehem and insisted that I come and stay for a while.

Theunis fetched me, and he told me in the car that Casper had phoned a whole lot of Afrikaans writers and poets and told them that I had stolen money from him. I was persona non grata. Life is strange, as a few years later Casper would visit me in Cape Town to apologise and give me so many paintings and presents, I was quite embarrassed.

Bethlehem, of course, was not New York, but I had time to think about my future. One hot and quiet Sunday, Theunis took me to the petrol station on Bethlehem's main road. About ten cars were parked in a row, facing the highway. Inside each one was a family. With them, they had flasks of tea, sandwiches, frikadelle and eggs wrapped in tinfoil. Each item of food was neatly unwrapped from the tinfoil, which caught the rays of the sweltering sun, reflecting the harsh light. Slowly, the tea was poured while everyone sat staring at the road.

Theunis and I drove off, but two hours later, we returned. Most of the cars were still there. I asked Theunis what this was all about, and he explained that Sundays were so boring in Bethlehem, families came and parked their cars next to the highway to watch the traffic pass by.

It was time for me to leave. That morning at 03:00, I boarded a train. I opened my compartment's window and waved at Theunis ... goodbye. Twenty years would pass before I would see him again. The sound of the train's wheels on the tracks was like a butcher's blade cutting through meat. I felt very alone.

60

O N MY ARRIVAL AT CAPE Town Station, I wanted to sit on a bench and weep. Instead, I found a tickey-box and phoned my friend Johann Müller and asked him to fetch me in his tiny blue car. Poor Johann, always fetching me and taking me somewhere. This time, he took me to the YMCA in Queen Victoria Street. I exchanged my dollars for rands. I had no income and had to find a job, because how long would that money last?

I knocked on the doors of restaurants, but there was no work. Eventually, depression overwhelmed me, and I found solace at the Drag Store in Sea Point, where outsiders and misfits sat at tables on the pavement and got pissed. The place was owned by two glamorous women; unfortunately, their names escape me. One of them was once a finalist in the Miss Israel pageant. The Drag Store played Nina Hagen and partied hard. I spent all my money on alcohol, just to function.

A friend, Shaun Crause, who lived in Sea Point, offered his flat to me for three weeks, as he was going abroad on holiday. It was in a large block called the Bordeaux Residential Apartments, right opposite the Sea Point promenade and Graaff's Pool.

I discovered Shaun's Valium in his medicine cabinet. I lived in a haze, and I needed alcohol. My friend had left me money for household expenses, but that went quickly: not on food, but on alcohol. I'd sit at the Drag Store holding court; la dolce vita and all that.

I started thinking of ways to make money. Theft became a possibility. My plan was to rob ABSA bank in Sea Point, but for that, I would need a gun and a getaway car. An old schoolfriend, who was half in love with me, offered to organise me a gun, as she had 'contacts'. In the end that plan fell through, to my great chagrin.

Fuck that, I thought, I would sell my friend's microwave oven. Shaun, who had been so good to me. That was how low I sank, into the nether regions of Valium and the sauce. A man came and fetched the microwave after I advertised it in the *Cape Argus*. He paid me in cash. I was twenty-one and, after New York, truly in the gutter, as Tina Lategan had predicted. Again.

When Shaun returned, he saw that the microwave was gone. When he asked me what had happened, I couldn't think of an excuse. I just said that I didn't know. Shortly after that, the Sea Point police called me in, and I was questioned by a detective. I couldn't lie, so I just admitted it: I was a thief. I was charged with theft and had to appear in front of a magistrate, who gave me a suspended sentence. Now I was stuck with a criminal record.

Shaun forgave me, but he moved overseas shortly afterwards. We didn't see each other for decades, but one day we did, at the Hussar Grill in Mouille Point, and it was like the good old days before the microwave incident.

But my life certainly was far from hackneyed. Just as I thought it couldn't get any worse, it did. Much worse.

61

I FOUND MYSELF LIVING ON THE streets. I slept on a bench in the Company's Garden. Survival mode kicked in. I had to remind myself what I'd been through in the past and that I'd managed to overcome it. This went on for a month. During the day, I went to the soup kitchen at St George's Cathedral and used the ablution facilities in the Company's Garden. I wandered the streets and sat in the Cape Town City Library to pass the time.

The days were dark, but the nights were somehow better, because I could sleep and pretend to be dead. Sometimes I would snuggle up under a bush, as it was more comfortable than a bench. But I heard strange and scary noises in the night. Rats, squirrels, footsteps. Then, one day I got up and rose from my rags and my filth. I walked to the flat of an old schoolfriend's mother. Her name was Shirley van Jaarsveld. I knew my friend was studying overseas and her room would be empty.

I knocked on the front door of the Hof Street flat in Gardens, right next to the Mount Nelson. I felt ashamed, but I told Shirley my story, and this wonderful woman took me in. She gave me a bed, a roof over my head and food. Slowly, I started thawing and feeling human again. Over Christmas, Shirley invited me to join her and her ex-husband, Johan, at his holiday house in Gordon's Bay. This kind gesture did not escape me.

I walked to the Kaapse Tafel restaurant, which was about five minutes from Hof Street, in Queen Victoria Street, to ask for a job. The owner, Graham Hughes, specialised in Cape cuisine like bobotie, tomato and green bean bredies, and Malva pudding. I started the same day. Graham taught me about which wines went best with which dishes and how to deal with difficult customers. He was frightfully well-mannered, but not in a haughty way.

Next to the Kaapse Tafel was a filthy little hotel, ironically called the Carlton. Here lived one of Cape Town's most recognisable faces (during the eighties). She was of Dutch descent, a tall, thin woman who dressed up in a different outfit every day of the week. Everything would match: the gloves, hat, scarf, shoes, dress, from bright yellow, to pink, purple and white. She would walk like a queen and smile and wave at everybody.

Once she left the hotel, she would head for the Company's Garden. Then, as if on a catwalk, she would sashay into town and stop and talk to all the workers in Gardens, look at the flowers, comment on them, and then off she went to Adderley Street. All the cashiers at Stuttafords knew her, and she would pause to chat at each counter. Nobody really understood what she was saying, as she spoke in a thick Dutch accent. The flower sellers knew her too, and sometimes she would give them chocolates. Oh, she was gorgeously eccentric.

One day, she disappeared. I asked the owner of the Carlton where she was and he told me that he'd had to take her to a retirement home in Green Point, as she was showing signs of early dementia.

I tracked her down at this place, a beautiful old building with a large garden. I looked around the lounge and, in the corner, I saw a tiny woman with no make-up, sitting all on her own. It was her. Gone was the rouge and the colourful outfits; she was a grey, elderly shell with dementia, who didn't recognise me. I sat down next to her and held her tiny hand. She just stared in front of her. Later, they told me she died shortly after her arrival. Bless, she was one of the city's top characters.

Shirley, who had saved me from the streets, worked as a speech therapist, but also taught drama at the Academy for Dramatic Art. She secured me a place with my old lecturer, Babs Laker.

With the money I earned from the Kaapse Tafel, I also joined the Maas-Phillips College of Speech and Drama, named for its founders, Rita Maas and her husband, Maurice Phillips. Rita was a refined, elderly teacher, who had studied at the Royal Academy of Dramatic Art in London in the late 1930s. Rita spoke impeccable Queen's English. Her husband, Maurice, was a background figure at the school; he was more like a retired butler. It was another world from that of the earthy Babs Laker.

Rita instructed me to drop my Afrikaans accent and to speak English like a British person from the upper classes. For years I'd had a hang-up about my accent, trying to sound like the faux grandees from Kenilworth and Constantia. One day, I thought, fuck that, if I speak clearly, I will retain my South African Afrikaans accent. Instead, I joined the Community Arts Project (CAP), where I could study with black students and work on improvisation.

It was a politicised project, which suited me. I loved it, specifically because I could collaborate with black actors. One day, however, the head of CAP called me in.

His name was Derek Joubert, a man who looked like a half-day book-keeper who had lost all his money. He informed me that I was unwelcome there; I was too large and in charge, white and scary. I had a megaphonic voice.

In a moment of rage, I wanted to throw a pot of hot chicken giblets over his head; it was cooking in the kitchen next to his morgue-like office. Boom-ing voice? I thought acting was about speaking loudly, overemoting, so that the audience could hear you in the back, that you moved your hands and your body dramatically. I was wrong.

I left feeling like a total racist. An academic friend of mine always said that all white people are racists, so there's no way out. Stuck. After that I would see Derek cruising on the Sea Point promenade, and he could never look me in the eye.

I had an itch to scratch and thought that I should get involved with chari-ties. I went into town and knocked on the doors of Tape Aids for the Blind. They were in a building next to the Groote Kerk. They didn't pay, but I enjoyed reading those books, which also helped strengthen my vocal cords.

In the same building was Molo Songololo, an organisation that promoted and protected the rights of children and youth. They published a magazine, also called *Molo Songololo*, and I offered to translate it into Afrikaans. This boomeranged spectacularly on me one day when a Michaelis art student asked me why I was friendly with Pik Botha's daughter, Lien. She implied I might be spying on them.

I'd met Lien at the Academy for Dramatic Art. She was studying at the Michaelis School of Fine Art. We got along well and shared an interest in the arts. Lien had a little Volkswagen Beetle, and we would speed along to Camps Bay beach for a swim and a bottle of Tassenberg; we'd get tipsy and wallow in dronkverdriet.

I didn't even know who her parents were, so this was news to me. Even if I had known, how can you judge someone by their parents? It's absurd. So, I stripped my moer and stormed out. Oh, the irony. Here was a group of privileged, young, white students at UCT who looked down on Afrikaners; they were virtue signallers. When 1994 came, they were the ones who packed their bags and left (fled) for New York and London. The art student who tried to frame me as a spy also moved to New York. She's not living in the utopia she 'fought' for; strange that, isn't it?

Another, a well-known journalist, who also absconded to New York, has a Wikipedia page. It starts with: '[...] is a South African–born journalist and former anti-Apartheid activist.' Such great activists were they that they left the country. Always nice to throw in that you were an activist … one who left, that is.

My attempts at charity work at Tape Aids for the Blind also backfired. A new woman took over. The previous one had been a bit of a hippie from Noordhoek.

This one was an icy Wasp from Constantia who took against me.

A black, curly-haired boy of about nineteen walked barefoot from Hout Bay to Cape Town every day to work at Tape Aids for the Blind. Once the hippie from Noordhoek, the boy from Hout Bay and I took part in a protest on Greenmarket Square.

Suddenly, SADF Casspirs appeared; they were mine-resistant, ambush-protected vehicles. Other scary-looking army vehicles also arrived, and they started spraying us with purple dye.

We ran away, drenched in the dye. Soon, graffiti appeared on the city's walls, proclaiming: 'The Purple Shall Govern!' Graffiti sprayed on a wall opposite De Waal Park read: 'A Naartjie in Our Sosatie.' Clever.

On another day, we picketed outside Parliament. Fists in the air, screaming: 'Amandla!' The police came running towards us with sjamboks and Alsatian dogs. We ran. The dogs bit the barefoot, curly-haired one on his bum; I felt the whack of a sjambok on my back. But it was a kugel from Sea Point who really made it all seem a bit burlesque. As the police were chasing her, she ran as fast as she could on her stilettos. One broke and she fell to the ground, but effortlessly, as if in a ballet sequence. She burst into tears, dogs barking, big men surrounding her, and screamed: 'My shoes, oh my God, my shoes!'

My time at Tape Aids for the Blind ended; it didn't pay in any case, but I wanted to do some good. The new Wasp manager dropped all of us misfits.

I needed to earn more money apart from my tips at the restaurant, and as a result of my studies at the Academy for Dramatic Art, I auditioned for a TV dubbing job, from German to Afrikaans, with the actress Antoinette Kellerman, which took place at a studio in the city centre.

Antoinette was the director and kind enough to give me work that paid, but I was terrible. My nerves, my lack of confidence ... not a good mix. Antoinette just wanted to give me a break.

After that, I auditioned for Afrikaans radio dramas at the South African Broadcasting Corporation (SABC) in Sea Point. I passed the audition but found that certain older actors resented me. One old queen, Paul Malherbe, I'd thought was a friend, until we had to work together. Then, his displeasure at seeing me was obvious. I was paid, not much, but I continued to do some radio work for a few months.

Again, I realised this career path was leading nowhere, that I should move on. Although I loved theatre, I was not a performer.

62

IN THE BACKGROUND, THE BLACK dog was ever present; nonetheless, I realised that although the hubcaps may be off, the wheels kept on turning. I continued with my drama studies and enjoyed how it made me feel my way through words: the rhythm, meaning and musicality.

I didn't realise then that this training would help me in the future, to write movie and theatre reviews, poetry, short stories, essays and columns. Again, nothing that happens is wasted; somewhere down the line, it pops up as something useful.

A new underground magazine, called *Vula*, saw the light of day around the mid-eighties, and I visited their office, which was in a tiny house, off a tiny street, trying to get the feel of a magazine environment. It was all very exciting, and even though the editorial team had no money, the readers loved their countercultural approach to music, art and interviews.

Vula's covers were bright and colourful, and their fashion shoots differed from the norm. It reminded me of New York's underground magazines. The doyenne of the South African magazine industry at that stage was Jane Raphaely, and she wrote an adoring letter, describing *Vula* as a mad dog on Vitagen.

Nevertheless, *Vula* eventually folded, as advertisers were still too unadventurous to deal with anything but the mainstream. *City Late* emerged from the ashes of *Vula*, and I started freelancing for them. Then followed *ADA* magazine, which stood for art, design and architecture, which was also quite off the wall.

ADA delivered an alternative type of journalism; it was metropolitan, celebrating the resistance and transformation happening in the country at the time. Journalism thrived during the eighties; it was aflame with fresh rebellion. The *Weekly Mail* launched in 1985, and later became the *Mail & Guardian*. None of these newbies could really pay freelancers, but I knew I was onto something I loved. I was determined to build a portfolio of stories.

Things heated up with Max du Preez's first edition of *Vrye Weekblad*, published on my birthday, 4 November 1988. I still remember holding that first copy in my hands while standing in Adderley Street. I thought, 'No, this is impossible.' A newspaper in Afrikaans with content that resonated with me. I sent them some small stories, too demure to tackle bigger ones. But I kept at it.

I remember taking my handwritten articles to the *Sunday Times* in Cape Town and handing them to Glenda Nevill; I was too poor to afford a typewriter. We were living in wild times; you didn't know from one day to the next what to expect.

One day, I sat in a coffee shop on Church Square, with Parliament about two-hundred metres away. In my hand, I had an envelope with an interview I had handwritten for a magazine. It was a profile of Ivan Toms, with an added focus on the End Conscription Campaign. I was on my way to deliver it but decided to have a cup of coffee en route.

There was a TV set in one corner of the coffee shop. It was 2 February 1990; the state president of South Africa, FW de Klerk, was delivering a speech at the opening of Parliament. The coffee shop went quiet when we heard what he had to say: he was unbanning the African National Congress, the Pan Africanist Congress and the South African Communist Party. Within one moment, my article was dated and had no relevance.

I crumpled it up and gave it to the waiter to throw away. Life would never be the same again, not for South Africa and not for me.

63

I RESIGNED FROM THE RESTAURANT WHERE I worked for a more lucrative job as manager of an ice-cream parlour, Carvelle, in Sea Point. Another odd job that I could add to my list of experiences. It was fun, and busy. I played music loudly, as the Main Road of Sea Point was pumping; I was back in my favourite part of town. My time with Shirley van Jaarsveld, who had plucked me from the streets, was over. My gratitude was infinite.

Shirley died in 2022. At the time, I posted on Facebook:

'When I returned from New York in 1986, I arrived in Cape Town with a few rand. After the bright lights, big city, of the Big Apple, I had nowhere to go.

'My parents were alcoholics and were incapable of looking after me. I had no job. At first, I had some small change to live in the YMCA in Queen Victoria Street. But then the money ran out.

'I found myself sleeping in the Company's Garden. Poor, hungry, young, with no prospects. I had an aunt who once told me when I was small, that one day I would land up in the gutter.

'Well, how right she was. For food I went to a soup kitchen that was then in St George's Cathedral. One meal a day. The nights were cold and lonely, believe me.

'One night I simply couldn't stand it any more. I went to Hof Street and knocked on the door of Shirley van Jaarsveld. She was the mother of an old schoolfriend of mine.

'She opened the door, and I told her my story. For six months Shirley gave me a room, food, and the opportunity to find my feet. I suffered from terrible depression, and she would sit right through the night talking to me.

'I wanted out, I wanted to take my own life and I was only twenty-one. Slowly I became stronger and got direction. Shirley died last Sunday in her sleep.

'I phoned the actress Isadora Verwey who was also living in the same flat at that stage. She was studying drama at UCT, with Anna-Mart van der Merwe (who often brought freshly baked bread to eat) and Lionel Newton.

'I told her Shirley had died. In her sleep. We spoke about her huge influence on our lives and then we were silent. I was sitting in Melkbosstrand next to the blue ocean when her ex-husband, the filmmaker Johan van Jaarsveld, sent me a message about her death.

'He, too, was kind to me when I was down and out. With her death I was reminded about generous people, people who give you a break and help you along. Shirley van Jaarsveld was such a person. To my aunt who told me I would land up in the gutter – yes, I did. It was cruel of you to say such a thing to a boy of seven.

'But it was in the gutter where I learnt about surviving and compassion. It is a pity that you lacked that.'

I moved into a flat with my old schoolfriend Grant Doidge, and together we indulged in more late nights on the pavement at the Drag Store, a few metres away from our flat. Softie that I am, I started to give free ice creams to the local street children, as well as to famous people like Sipho 'Hotstix' Mabuse, whose music we often played in the parlour. I also gave my money away to the sex workers and homeless people I befriended.

I was on a roll again, but it was a downward spiral. Spending money, giving ice creams away, drinking too much, back on Valium.

One night my artist friend Lien Botha fetched me in her Volksie (it felt like everybody drove one in the seventies and eighties). I was out of control and begged her to take me away. We could go to Windhoek and start a new life. Away from South Africa, Windhoek would offer new opportunities.

Lien agreed that it was time for a change. We got into the Volla and off we went, into the dark night. I took a few more Valiums and drank a bottle of Tassies. I didn't even pack a suitcase. We just went. At the Green Point traffic circle, we saw them: the police. It was a roadblock.

Lien opened the window, and someone shone a torch on us. The police officer looked big and scary. Lien and I both summarily burst into tears and told him that we'd had enough of Cape Town, of life, and were on our way to Windhoek, our only saving grace. We were surprised when the officer said, that's fine, we could leave. Lien accelerated and we were on the flyover, descending into the city, when she had an idea.

'Before we leave, there's a party at Michaelis. We should just show our faces, have a few drinks, and then it's goodbye and good luck.'

We arrived at one massive party. The music was deafening, the place was shaking, it was a thunderous occasion. At one point, I was on a table dancing topless, screaming at the crowd to raise their fists and shout: 'Amandla!'

I lost track of Lien. When I woke up the next morning, I was in a Kombi with surfers in Fish Hoek. They'd parked at a beach and were preparing to go into the water.

One guy told me that they'd picked me up hitchhiking on what was then called De Waal Drive. It was all very odd.

I realised I had the day off, so I was going to hike back and go to Sandy Bay, a nudist beach right on the other side of the mountain. I didn't need a swimming costume, so the decision was made.

It was 30 December 1986; on the fourth of November, the month before, I had turned twenty-two. At Sandy Bay, I bumped into a friend, Joss Lewis, who had a stand on Greenmarket Square, and sat down with her. A young man came walking towards us. Joss knew him, and she introduced us. Once again, it was a turning point, but this one would change the whole trajectory of my life.

64

HIS NAME WAS GRAHAM SONNENBERG, he was twenty-six and an articled clerk at his deceased grandfather's legal firm, Sonnenberg Hoffmann & Galombik. I asked Graham if his dad was Dr John Sonnenberg, and he said yes. What a coincidence – that was the man who had delivered me.

Graham and I immediately felt a strong attraction, and I can honestly say that he is the love of my life. Without his constant support I would have been dead, or indeed in a gutter somewhere. We have been together for forty years, with a break in between. Although we are not romantically involved any more, we still live together and share a deep brotherly love.

The ancient Greeks would describe our love as having evolved from eros (sexual passion) to philia (deep friendship). It's remarkable to have someone love you for such a long time. Graham has seen me fail, grow and evolve over the years. He often sacrificed his own needs and desires to prioritise my well-being and happiness.

On that day in December, after making small talk in the sun, Graham and I headed over the rocks and up the hill to his blue 1982 Opel Kadett. We drove to the Carousel in Sea Point; it was summer, everything was fine.

The next day, I moved into Graham's flat in Melrose Mansions, in Green Point, an old Art Deco block built in 1929. I had no possessions, except for two T-shirts, one pair of trousers and one pair of takkies, without laces. No underwear.

We were poor, as Graham earned something like R650 a month as an articled clerk, and I worked in an ice-cream parlour. But we were young, everything was fresh and new, even the cheap pasta with frozen veg we had for dinner nearly every night.

Of course, it had to happen: the owner of the ice-cream parlour caught me handing out free ice creams to the poor street children, and that was the end of that. It was time to act. Again! At twenty-two, I felt exhausted, battling from one beginning and end to the next. There was no time to lick my self-inflicted wounds, as I was still studying drama and had to pay for my classes.

I managed to get a job as sommelier and waiter at one of Cape Town's top restaurants at the time, Rozenhof in Kloof Street. It was right opposite the drama school, which was perfect. Here I worked with Suzy Brokensha and the actress Bo Petersen. They were happy times; the staff was diverse, bright, all looking for an extra buck to get by.

My first mode of transport was a bicycle. I would cycle to drama classes and then pop over to Rozenhof for a shift. After each shift, we tasted the wines and got to choose an item off the menu. You had to know your story to recommend wine and food to customers.

I tried desperately to keep politically active in whatever way I could, even if it meant just wearing an 'Unban the ANC' T-shirt (blush) or 'Free Nelson Mandela' badge. One night I went to a movie in Sea Point wearing my Mandela badge. When I was leaving after the movie, an agitated, middle-aged white man ran up to me and screamed: 'You fucking terrorist!' I had forgotten about the badge, but soon a small crowd of angry people surrounded me. I turned and walked away from them as they screamed and shouted at me.

I continued writing my freelance articles. One day, I wrote a letter with a strong political message for *Vrye Weekblad*. The following night I was sitting in the kitchen at home, Graham was out, when there was a hard knock on the back door. Four police officers stood there, demanding to discuss the letter. I just laughed; it was a letter, not a letter bomb. They asked me a few questions and left. I closed the door and thought of that 1961 musical, *Stop the World – I Want to Get Off*. It was surreal.

I was on the verge of completing my drama studies while I continued freelancing and building up a portfolio. It was almost time to find a job on a paper or at a magazine.

Before that, though, the gay community would experience a crisis that still haunts me to this day.

65

AIDS WAS CASTING THE SHADOW of death over South Africa's gay community and, closer to home, our city of Cape Town. Recently, I wrote a piece for the *Daily Maverick* for World AIDS Day on 1 December 2022, as most people, including the gay community, have forgotten what it was like at the time.

In the *DM* piece, I wrote how news of friends of friends who had fallen ill started surfacing in pubs and at dinner parties. They lost weight and had lesions on their faces, then they started dying. Most of the heterosexual population looked away; it had nothing to do with them. Unprotected sex was still *de rigueur*. The attitude was that if you fell ill, you were looking for it; it was your decision.

The religious community said it was God's way of punishing the gay community. What did we know about condoms? We didn't even have dating apps; you went cruising in parks, on beaches and in pubs. Was it safe to touch people? Could you use the same toilet seat? What about kissing? Fellatio? Nobody knew.

My memory jumps around as to the timeline in which it all happened – it was so traumatising. When I was still working at the Kaapse Tafel in Queen Victoria Street, the owner asked me to take a plate of food to someone in St Martini Gardens, the block of flats next door to the restaurant.

So, I went to the flat, knocked, and after a while a thin man with spots on his face opened the door. His hands were flecked and looked like claws and he was unsteady on his feet. He took the plate of food and thanked me, but he looked away. I took food to him for about a month, and each time he looked worse.

One day, the restaurant owner asked me to stop taking food. He said nothing, but I knew. I never asked the man's name or found out what had happened to him.

Another time: Graham and I were on our way to Plettenberg Bay. Our neighbours had rented a house next to the sea. Two other people, called Peter and Christopher, would join us. When we saw them, we knew that they were sick. But nobody spoke about it.

On our last evening in Plett, Peter went on and on about how he was going to build moving pavements, like escalators, to transport the domestic workers to the homes of the rich whites for whom they worked. He would design them the moment he arrived home. He was, in hindsight, delirious.

It was to be Peter and Christopher's last holiday at the ocean. They both died shortly afterwards. We attended Peter's funeral, held in a church in Rosebank. It was packed. The then mayor of Cape Town, Patricia Sulcas Kreiner, arrived in a show of solidarity. It was the first time that we could palpably feel someone in power taking notice.

I remember how she slowly walked down the aisle, dressed in black. It was a big day for the gay community. We cried. By this time, the virus had spread through white, so-called coloured and black communities. We could spot the victims in the church. The bells rang, the service started.

Peter Moon was a ship's captain who lived around the corner from us in Green Point. He was a butch man and knew the sea, the tides, the waves. We called him Moon by day, La Luna by night.

When on land, he would invite us over for dinner. The food was awful, mostly boiled veggies. But his wine was wonderful, he swore like a sailor and he told delightful stories. His party trick, of which no one took any notice, was to take out his penis and swing it around. It looked like a large mushroom; it wasn't pretty. But no dinner party was concluded without this ritual.

One day, Peter told me that I could take his best wines. He started giving things away. He was a big man, but he, too, started wilting. We knew, but we never spoke about it; it remained unsaid. Again, the omertà. Peter sold his flat and moved to a house next to Marina da Gama, where there is a lagoon. There, he lay on a chaise lounge, staring at the water.

Peter had a boyfriend called Connel Fortuin, who took over. One day, all Peter's close friends were invited to a party at his house next to the water. We knew it was a farewell. Everyone was merry, we laughed, platters of food were passed around, we got drunk on Champagne. Peter loved the music of Michael Franks, who sang 'Popsicle Toes'.

A woman in a long flowing robe arrived at the soiree and proceeded to undress until she was completely naked. Then she walked into the lagoon and swam around in circles. For a moment, it felt like we were in a Fellini movie. People standing around, the indigo water, music, laughter, a blue, blue sky.

For the first time, I sat down next to Peter and wept. I held his hand. He cried softly and said: 'I don't want to die.'

That was the last time we saw him.

Next one: I'll call him X, as his family is still in denial to this day about how they treated him and have threatened legal action. X was a boerseun, but after finishing school, he fled the small platteland life for New York.

There, he studied fashion design and lived a large, cosmopolitan life, away from the narrow-mindedness of his rural past. He was vibrant, forward thinking, creative. X enjoyed the nightlife of New York, the clubs, the bars, the steam baths. After a decade or so, he returned to Cape Town and moved into a small bungalow in Clifton. I spent many weekends there, admiring the still, shiny water, the beautiful people. We partied; we were young, and life was good.

But then X also grew weaker; it wasn't noticeable at first. Eventually, he was reduced to a carcass and ended up on the seventh floor of the Somerset Hospital, which was called the AIDS floor back then. In those days, if you landed up there, the chances of leaving alive were slim. People would whisper: 'He's on the seventh floor.' That was the code; you didn't have to ask any questions. *He's on the seventh floor* became a mantra. Seven rhymes with heaven, but heaven it wasn't.

I arrived there one day only to see X lying in his bed drenched in vomit. Nurses tried their best but couldn't keep up. The wards were full. They, too, were scared, as information was scarce. Could you catch it by touching a patient?

Incidentally, the suicide rate among gay men spiked for a while. One drove off the cliffs of Chapman's Peak. When rescuers found the body, there was blood everywhere. He'd left a note. The next day, the papers were full of stories of how this man had exposed the emergency workers to the 'dreaded disease'. Another man gassed himself next to a road near Table View. Another note, another front-page report.

X left the seventh floor; he was lucky. He ended up in a hospice in Gardens, where Graham and I would visit him on Saturdays, with a bottle of wine. Not one of the people who had partied with him ever visited him. All those festivities – food, drink, hospitality – but when he fell ill, he became persona non grata.

His family came to fetch X, after which we had no communication with him for about a month. Then, one cold and wet night during a miserable winter, our doorbell rang. Two very straight-looking men stood outside and told us in Afrikaans to come down to their car; X was there. The rain poured down, drenching us.

The car was parked under a lamp and the light fell on it as if in a fifties' noir movie. X was on the backseat, paralysed, mumbling.

'Take him!' one of the men roared in Afrikaans. I remembered that our friend Stephanie, who lived near us in Sea Point, had a spare bed. I ran up to the flat – it was before cellphones – and made a quick call. Stephanie was frightened, but she said she was ready. They could bring him.

So, X was dumped at Stephanie's place like a piece of damaged furniture. The two men left without even saying goodbye. For the next few days, we popped in and out, and battled, as none of us had any training to deal with such a patient.

Somehow, X landed up in Karl Bremer Hospital. Before we could visit, Stephanie phoned to tell us that he had passed away. There was a little chapel inside the hospital, where we attended the service held for him. To this day, the horror: the only people there were Stephanie, my partner, the priest and me. X had died abandoned and alone, like so many others. Where had all the flowers gone?

Then 1999 arrived, the Mbeki era, and a prolonged period of more grief. The gloomy shade of more deaths and denial ensued. That, I'm afraid, is a story too sad to tell here; I leave that for others to write. Allow me to be sentimental and quote Shakespeare: 'Let me be boiled to death with melancholy.'

Around 1990, I joined a media company that marketed properties. It was excruciatingly boring. I was forced to wear a suit, be polite, and work from 08:00 to 17:00. There were two of us in the office. My colleague was Adele Shevel, who later went on to become a financial journalist with the *Sunday Times*.

The job forced me to write fast, with a word count, and to find new angles. Just how many words could one write about a showhouse? Estate agents had their own clichéd jargon, and the trick was to write around the hackneyed expressions to make the copy come alive.

I discovered that estate agents were, from an anthropological point of view, a rare breed. So much backstabbing, tears, drama, blatant hatred, jealousy, vendettas, blood on the boardroom floor ... Thank heavens I had Adele as a witness, otherwise nobody would have believed me. There must be a reality series lurking in the background called *The Dark Lives of Estate Agents from Hell*.

I kept my more interesting freelance work going on the side, otherwise I would have gone bonkers. Now I could add another job description to my list of work experience: public relations officer. But it wasn't for me. I was good at generating publicity, but my temperament wasn't suited to sucking up to journalists, smiling, waving, being nice.

One day, I heard that the *grande dame* of magazine journalism, Jane Raphaely, was launching a new magazine, *House and Leisure*. It was just before 1994, so people thought she was losing the plot. Many whites thought that a revolution was imminent, that the country would collapse, and here was Jane, launching a lifestyle magazine. I found out that the editor was Sumien Brink, so I sent her my portfolio of articles.

I didn't hear a thing for a while, but I was desperate to leave my PR job. Then, one day, my phone rang, and it was Sumien, who asked me to come in for an interview. At the same time, I arrived at work and saw a letter on my desk. I was being asked to leave the PR company. The boss, I later heard, had discovered that I was gay. I'd kept this from him, as I could sense his homophobia. Now I was out of a job.

This was not the first time I was sacked because I was gay. In my much younger days, I worked for Plaizier, a coffee shop in the city centre. Before I worked there, the place had pulled a gay crowd, but the new owner wanted nothing to do with that. When my gay friends started supporting the place again because I was working there, the owner pulled me aside and asked me to tell them not to come there; he didn't want homosexuals in his place.

Then he let me go. I went to a labour lawyer, Michael Bagraim, who managed to get me a nice settlement.

But now, I was desperate – I needed a job. *House and Leisure* would be a perfect fit. Look, it wasn't *Rolling Stone* or *The New Yorker*, but it was a new, glossy magazine with endless potential and a foot in the door of an industry that was difficult to enter. So, I went for the interview and was asked to write a few pieces.

In retrospect, the articles weren't that good. I think they were just being kind, as they wanted to give a young person a break in an industry that you would either love, or it would chew you up and spit you out. So, they were being kind. This would never have happened in New York, but our country was full of new possibilities; they took a gamble.

I learnt on the job, and I had to learn quickly. My features editor, Annelize Visser, and Sumien Brink became my mentors. They showed me how to avoid clichés, old, lazy expressions and tired words. Not that easy. I still fall back on them sometimes, but hey, no one is perfect. Sometimes I had to rewrite a piece, and every time it was a challenge I loved.

I had two columns, for which I had to do my own styling with a photographer, plus I had to write features. To work for Jane Raphaely, Sumien Brink and a team of professionals was like attending a masterclass at Columbia University. What better way to discover the inner workings of the media than being part of the machinery that kept the engine going? I was thriving.

Jane was a strict but fair taskmaster. She didn't hesitate to send an article back if it wasn't up to her standard. She was adamant that detail mattered and that, metaphorically, you should always come back from an interview with the name of the dog. Indeed, the devil is always in the detail – you must notice everything, even a small photograph hidden away on a sideboard.

66

M Y FIRST INTERVIEW FOR THE magazine was with the artist
Tyrone Appollis, who lived on the Cape Flats. His house was
humble, his art colourful. On the same day, I had to go to a fancy
block of flats in Sea Point to speak to some dreadful queen who took himself and his decor terribly seriously. Two total opposites in one day. Tyrone,
with his quirky, outspoken, unpretentious personality. Then, this man in his
opulent flat, who looked like a gay vampire.

Jane drilled it into us that, as journalists, we had to network, attend
launches, go for lunches, meet new people … that's how you found interesting subjects. And travel. It was a time where everything was blossoming, or
at least that's how it felt. New restaurants, like Bukhara, were opening. I was
the first person to interview the chefs and the owner. New art exhibitions
seemed to open every night and clubs were mushrooming all over the city.
Cape Town was growing into a cosmopolitan megalopolis.

I flew to Johannesburg quite frequently, either to attend art exhibitions or
openings of restaurants. It was a time of money, socialising, new experiences
– different from my life as a poor child, an orphan, a shipwrecked kid living
with an uncle and his wife who barely tolerated me.

We had a library in our offices with access to magazines from all over
the world. We could read a new edition of *The New Yorker*, *Esquire*, *TIME*
magazine, *Newsweek*, you name it, every week.

I was the first person to interview the artist Carrol Boyes. People who
have no interest in lifestyle journalism would, of course, roll their eyes, but
fuck them. It's easy to interview a politician, because you already know
that what they're going to say is mostly banal, generic, press-release drivel.
Give me an artist, a murderer, a psychopath, people on the outskirts, any
day. I have no interest in journalists who think that writing about politics
pushes you up the hierarchy of writing.

The day I arrived to interview Carrol Boyes, hardly anybody knew about
her; I didn't either. I'd read up about her, titbits, but there was hardly enough
information on this woman. I arrived at her house on the edge of Sandy Bay

with a blank notebook. She took me into her studio beneath her house, where she showed me the cutlery she'd made from pewter. I'd never seen anything like it in my life: salad spoons, knives, forks, all in different shapes and sizes. It was art.

My features editor, Annelize Visser – a clever sausage if ever there was one – wrote this headline: 'Sculptures You Can Touch'. And that was what they were, and still are, today: sculptures.

Shortly after the article appeared, there was a knock on our back door. Fortunately, this time it wasn't the police coming to interrogate me, but Carrol, who'd brought me a complete set of her cutlery; I was one of the first people to own and use them. I was sad to hear that Carrol passed away from cancer in 2019, at the age of sixty-five. She'd lost her life partner, the ceramicist Barbara Jackson, to breast cancer in 2010.

While working at *House and Leisure*, I made lifelong friends with people like the journalist Marianne Thamm, whose whimsical way of looking at the world had a big influence on me. She was working for *Femina* magazine, which belonged to the same company. Marianne believed in fresh experiences, new people and looking at the world with a third eye. Later, when we both went freelance, we phoned each other every day to stay in touch and motivate each other to persevere, to endure, to push on and keep going.

67

I WAS GIVEN THE OPPORTUNITY TO fly to Sydney to write a travel article, my first trip abroad since that appalling trip to Spain and, of course, my sojourn in New York, which is a whole book on its own.

A travel story is not an easy piece to write, as you could fall into the trap of 'easy writing' and come up with something that reads like a travel brochure. My favourite travel writers were people like Bruce Chatwin, Jan Morris, AA Gill and the Dutch writer Adriaan van Dis. They were hard acts to follow. What made it even more of a challenge was that it centred around Sydney's gourmet food scene, covering all the different influences as well as the local cuisine.

For a Gonzo journalist or war correspondent, this might all sound boring, but believe me, it was a lot of fun. And it was a challenge. My nerves were frazzled. I was insecure, suffering from imposter syndrome, a feeling that you don't belong, that you're an intruder. The title of one of Bruce Chatwin's books, *What Am I Doing Here*, applied.

In preparation, I started reading as much as I could about Oz, and Sydney in particular. A few days before I was to leave, my phone rang. It was a nurse from Tygerberg Hospital, who informed me that my mother had been admitted for throat cancer. I hadn't seen her for a long time; her alcoholism had caused us to drift apart.

She had not wanted to leave Christie, even though Graham offered to help her with the divorce. She was suffering from Stockholm syndrome, a coping strategy for people who are abused or held captive. Perhaps trauma bonds people; emotional ties are formed with an individual as a result of a recurring, cyclical pattern of maltreatment that is sustained by intermittent reinforcement through rewards and punishments.

My last visit to Dassieshoek had ended in a nightmare. Graham had insisted on meeting my mother. I warned him, but no, he didn't want to listen. We drove all the way there, and on our arrival, my mother insisted that we take some wine and visit my grandmother's grave in Koekenaap. It was a sweltering day. The graveyard and graves were covered in a blanket of red sand.

My mother sat down on my granny's grave, proceeded to get drunk and started sobbing. We went back to the farm, where more action awaited us. Christie was drunk and told us to fuck-off off his farm. We must pack our bags and go, we were moffies and he didn't want us there. We ignored him, and he went to his room and passed out.

The farm was eerily quiet and dark, and my mother was in a strange mood. She told us to come to the spare room, where she ripped open her dress and threw her prosthetic breast onto the bed. She showed us her wound from the past mastectomy.

'Who wants to sleep with a woman like this? Who?' she asked. She turned around, went to the cupboard and took out a wooden hanger, with which she hit the prosthesis over and over. Crying. Then she stopped and walked over to the dressing table, where a candle was burning. She took the brush lying on the dressing table and said: 'Come, come to mamma, like the old days. Brush my hair,' which was long and wild. So, I brushed her hair as she stared into the mirror, a broken person, singing a lullaby to herself. The next morning, Graham and I left. There was nothing to say in the car on the way back.

That was the last time I saw her, about six years earlier. Now I had to decide whether I wanted to visit her in hospital, or just leave it. Her face in that mirror that night still haunted me. After thinking it through, I decided to go. When I saw her, though, I was horrified. She looked like a carcass. Alcohol, smoking, decades of abuse ... not much was left of her.

A doctor arrived and was surprised to find out she had a son. He knew so much about her, but not that part of her life. I was furious. Why would she hide that? Feelings of worthlessness, rejection and emptiness welled up in me. I fell into a deep depression, again.

The doctor asked if I could please follow him. We went into a room, where he showed me two X-rays. The one was of a normal woman's brain, the other was my mother's. He told me that he had never seen anything like it. Was she an alcoholic? I said yes. I went back to her room and saw that she was confused, even delirious. Despite having throat cancer, she had the audacity to ask me for cigarettes. Could I go and buy her a packet?

I was furious, but I pretended that I was going to buy her cigarettes. The neon lights, the long white passages ... it was all too much, so I just kept on walking. Down with the lift, into the car park, right to my old Volvo 144S,

1967 model, open the door, weep. Behind me, the brutalist architecture, like something out of East Germany.

That was the last time I saw my mother. I started the car and drove off at speed, back home. I realised that Graham wasn't only my lover and partner, but also my family. I had no one else left. I had lost touch with my cousins and had no siblings; my dad was dead, and I had to block out my mother. I was, to all intents and purposes, an orphan. Graham and the Sonnenbergs – his siblings and parents – were closest to me; they were my family.

I thought of how my parents had neglected me. They hadn't contributed either financially or emotionally since I was fifteen. I'd slept on the streets and had to be taken in by Shirley van Jaarsveld, Pieter Serfontein ... Various friends had to feed me at times. If they had been conscious parents who took an interest in my life, Coenie Slabber might not have happened; no, not might – it would *not* have happened.

They were just gone, lacking, missing in action. And my mother had the cheek to ask me for a packet of cigarettes? So, I placed her in a box, at the back of my brain, and closed the lid. She was dead. Gone. It was over.

I later heard that she'd returned to the farm.

68

M Y TRIP TO AUSTRALIA TOOK my mind off my mother. There was a time for being morbid and a time to celebrate. Graham took me to the airport. On my way there, I realised that it would be the first time since I'd met him that I would be away on my own. I was about twenty-eight. How would my life have turned out without him? I felt tremendous separation anxiety.

Once the plane took off, I pulled myself together. I was flying first class; in those days, journalists were treated like royalty. The wine was lovely, the seats were comfortable, I was in my element. In the gutter, I thought. From sleeping on the streets to flying high above the earth, in luxury. Someone has a sense of humour.

On arrival in Sydney, a driver collected me and took me to a five-star hotel right opposite the Royal Botanic Garden. I was dead tired, but I had to prepare myself for the first restaurant I had to review.

There were two other journalists, both from Tokyo, who could hardly speak a word of English, but we somehow managed to communicate. Our first gig was at the Bathers' Pavilion, which overlooks Balmoral Beach. Then, for the next ten days, we were treated at all the top restaurants in Sydney. I thought of the white bread dipped in black coffee that I'd had to eat as a child. Oh Tina, Tina, how shiny were these gutters.

I soon learnt that Sydneysiders didn't tolerate swearing or being loud. I had to tone down my personality.

In my spare time, I read all the newspapers I could lay my hands on and went in search of extra information that I could weave into my article. I made notes of everything, took plenty of photographs and absorbed as much of the atmosphere as possible.

69

ONE MORE LOCATION WAS PART of the deal – a stayover on Kangaroo Island. I realise that the tourism company meant well, but it was a ghastly place that felt so isolated, I wanted to swim over the ocean back to the mainland. I saw kangaroos and koala bears, all ridiculously cute, but once you'd seen one, you'd seen them all. Koala bears make a sound like an old Datsun bakkie trying to start up during winter in the Karoo. A choking noise, then a sudden rev.

Eating kangaroo steak in a restaurant while watching its brothers and sisters jumping around outside was creepy. Also, the wind howled on the island, and a feeling of loneliness hung over the place. The wind ripped the branches off the trees and into the air. It was the perfect setting for a horror movie; even the few inhabitants had that haunted, tired look in their eyes. Bless.

When I arrived back in Cape Town, I had to sing for my supper. A deadline was waiting, and I had to produce a well-researched and professionally written piece. My imposter syndrome returned, and I froze in front of my computer.

But once I started, it took on a direction of its own and I could eventually press the send button, feeling satisfied with the article. Or was I? Not really. Not ever, really.

70

I CONTACTED MY OLD SCHOOLFRIEND, GRANT Doidge, who had developed into a good artist in the interim. Sadly, he had also developed serious mental-health issues.

On one occasion, he arrived naked, in the rain, at a house in Noordhoek. He couldn't remember how he'd got there. Then he set alight the flat he was sharing in Vredehoek and burnt it to the ground after he'd spread his faeces on the walls. He told me that he'd faxed Oprah Winfrey to suggest that I appear on her programme and talk about the problems facing South Africa. He also faxed long letters to the United Nations.

Grant was arrested in Table View for driving under the influence of drugs. He told me afterwards that the interior of the police cells was worthy of a decor article, it was so chic and minimalist. Once, at a dinner party, he pulled out his erect penis in front of the shocked guests and told a guy that he wanted to have sex with him right there and then.

I didn't know how to help him.

One day, I returned from a movie and there was a message from his flatmate – please, could I phone? He told me that Grant had jumped from a building in Hillbrow and was dead. How he'd got to Hillbrow from Cape Town is still a mystery. Why he chose Hillbrow, of all places, was as overwhelming.

But Grant was dead. At his memorial, I bumped into another old schoolfriend, Veronique Malherbe, a beautiful woman who was also an artist. She was, let's say, not one for the conventional. On one occasion, we attended a party where she arrived in her mother's wedding dress. Her mom had died.

When I saw her at Grant's service, she was working on an art installation at a gallery in town. She asked me if I wanted to take part. Little did I know what it would entail. Her motto was that a clever idea that fails is still more interesting than a mediocre one perfectly executed. I could go along with that.

I was keen on new experiences. As part of Veronique's installation, a hundred men had to masturbate into a test tube. Separately, of course. I don't think an orgy was part of the plan. These test tubes formed part of a halo that hung from the roof of the gallery. Little lights lit up the installation.

We had to take our test tubes to the João Ferreira Fine Art Gallery in Cape Town, where the exhibition was held. He kept them safe for the big opening night. Donors were chosen based on their creativity.

We all had to go to Cape Town Station to have our photo taken in one of those old photo booths that were usually located at airports and train stations. The image had to accompany the test tube so that your photo could be stuck onto the tube.

I don't know if I remember all this correctly, as it was so way out. Cape Town had certainly never seen anything like it. Veronique also displayed chocolates, which she called Breastlay, made from her own breast milk, as she had just had a baby. Also on display were large photos of her posing as the Madonna, holding her baby and a Bible. Her son was clenching a crucifix with a badge symbolising female genitals.

It was a wonderful evening, complete with TV cameras, radio interviews and paparazzi taking photographs of this motley bunch of weirdos enjoying art mixed with madness. We were delirious; the Champagne never ran out; you could just keep drinking until you rolled down the stairs.

One of the attendees was a little man in a wheelchair dressed in drag. His toenails were painted red, and he wore a beehive wig made of flowers. Oh, and green lipstick, false eyelashes and lots of rouge. Later, he played the theme tune from the movie *Deliverance* on a banjo.

By the time we left, three people had fallen down the stairs and were lying at the bottom, not moving, passed out. We had to climb over them. It was a wild party, and the press wrote about it for weeks afterwards. South Africa was now open to innovative ideas, no matter how wacky they were. An exhibition like that would never have been allowed under the Nats; they would have closed it down. Verboten!

I remember when the artist Louis Jansen van Vuuren exhibited a painting at the Association for Visual Arts sometime in the mid-eighties. It was the peak of the police's assault on fellow South Africans, with dogs, sjamboks, teargas and rubber bullets. Louis painted a large pig's head wearing a South African Police cap. He was lecturing at Michaelis at that stage and was also the chairperson of the gallery.

The gallery phoned Louis and told him to please come in, it's urgent.

When he arrived there, he found a tiny man waiting for him. He was the head of police in the Western Cape. At first the cop was polite, even quite sweet, but when Louis told him that the painting was a tribute to Steve Biko, he exploded. He threw his cap onto the table and said in Afrikaans: 'Ek is trots op my kêps en waarvoor dit staan!' (I am proud of my cap and what it stands for.)

He demanded that the gallery remove the painting, but their committee decided unanimously that it would not do so. Of course, it was all over the press, and people who would never even consider going to a gallery flocked to see it. What lovely (free) publicity!

After years of censorship, suffocating narrow-mindedness, and the banning of books and plays, the arts bloomed after FW de Klerk unbanned all political organisations. You could feel it in the air: creativity was everywhere as pent-up innovation spouted forth.

One night, Graham and I were having dinner at Pieter-Dirk Uys's house in Maynard Street, Cape Town. That night, he told us about his plan to move to Darling, of all places. Frankly, we thought he'd lost it. It would never work. But how wrong we were! He moved to Darling in 1996 and thrived there for years, uplifting the community and opening a theatre, restaurant and bookshop.

Pieter once threw a wonderful soiree at his house, where Evita performed and Amanda Strydom sang. Here we met Pieter's sister, the pianist Tessa Uys, a dramatic woman with the most beautiful hands. They were so pretty, they were used in the Shirley MacLaine movie *Madame Sousatzka*, where the camera zoomed in on her hands playing the keys.

71

MY WORK ALLOWED ME ACCESS to people's lives, which is what journalism does. Another person who became a friend was the fashion designer Errol Arendz, who clothed the rich and famous, but he never bragged about it. He designed clothes for Joan Collins and the late Lisa Marie Presley, among others.

Errol started his fashion career working on an old Bernina sewing machine from his home in Elsies River, often toiling right through the night. His sister, Gloria, who looks like his twin, managed the business.

From Elsies River to Clifton, where he now lived, was quite an accomplishment; not that there's anything wrong with Elsies River, it's just that Clifton is probably one of the prime neighbourhoods in the world.

Errol never allowed fame and fortune to go to his head. What did go to *my* head, however, was when he took me for a spin in his white Porsche. Ugh, I was young and easily impressed; I'll forgive myself for behaving like the parvenu that I am.

Errol lived in a double-storey house overlooking the ocean. He got away with it during the apartheid years because he was designing dresses for many of the wives of the Afrikaner elite. As part of his job as couturier, Errol often had to entertain. He himself dressed casually, but always with style. He even had a butler. If Errol was ready to have dinner served, he would stamp his foot on the floor three times, which meant that the butler downstairs, in the kitchen, could instruct the waiters to serve the food prepared below.

Errol was quite the raconteur. He told us that one night he was relaxing with a drink when he nodded off in his chair. When he woke up, a group of men in red jerseys was dancing around him with twinkly Christmas lights flashing from each jersey. When he asked them what was going on, they danced down the stairs in a row and disappeared.

There was also the time he went on a romantic date to a restaurant. After he and his date had sat down and the waiter had poured the wine, the man raised his glass and said: 'Gloria [Errol's twin sister], I've always wanted to meet you. What a pleasure!'

72

PHILIPPE-JOSEPH SALAZAR WAS A FRIEND who lived in Melkbos-strand. An erudite man who lectured in the philosophy of rhetoric at the University of Cape Town, he studied under heavyweights like Roland Barthes but remained unassuming. He was very sharp, though.

I wrote about his bizarre house in Melkbos, which was painted in a variety of bright colours with a cubist feel to it. The house was conceived as an upturned ship, facing west, to the Big Blue, and in keeping with the legend-ary wrecks that dot the West Coast. So strange was this architecture in an otherwise dull suburb, people used to drive past on a Sunday just to stare at it. We laughed ourselves silly, as some of them would even park their cars and walk up to the house, their mouths hanging open.

Philippe was a gourmet chef who served exotic dishes from Casablanca, where he was born. One night stands out: he invited his friends Stuart and Anita Saunders for dinner. At that stage, Stuart was the vice-chancellor of UCT. You would have expected the couple to be quite serious, but they loved a good party, and both had a wonderful sense of humour.

One night, with them and a bunch of screaming queens in attendance, Philippe served a seven-course meal, accompanied by a different wine for each course. What we didn't expect was that he would dress up for each of them – in a dress with stilettos and make-up. Again, a touch of the Weimar Republic. The Saunders were unfazed. In the background, Maria Callas belted out some opera classics.

Years later, Philippe told us that he had briefly met Callas in his youth. He even wrote her obituary in 1977 for the French magazine *Libération*. On her death, the media made us believe that Callas had died of a broken heart because of Ari Onassis. But no, she actually died of something quite banal.

She was in the bath blow-drying her hair when the blow-dryer fell into the water, shocking her to death. Indeed, her heart did stop, but not because of Onassis.

73

I T ALL SOUNDS LIKE NAME-DROPPING again, but believe me, I can't help it if interesting people crossed my path. One night my friend Marianne Thamm and her partner, Glynis, came over for dinner. They brought along a young man who was frightfully introverted, but as soon as Graham started playing the piano, this young man began singing and turned into a different person. We had never seen anything like it.

Marianne suggested that he put on a little performance at the Coffee Lounge in the city centre, a new spot that gave up-and-coming artists a platform to test their skills. Marianne asked Graham if he would accompany this shy young man on the piano, so he started coming to our flat for rehearsals. He was brilliant, but Graham felt that his own approach to the music was too honky-tonk, more like a musical, and too little cabaret. Graham felt he wasn't up to it.

At the last moment, Marianne's friend got hold of someone who could play the piano for his show. We went to the opening night, and the evening was a major success.

After that, his whole life changed. His name was Marc Lottering.

74

I'D LIKE TO ACKNOWLEDGE SOMEONE who often helped me in life, until he died at the age of eighty: the radio broadcaster Leslie McKenzie. Leslie was a broadcaster for different stations, but he will be remembered for being one of the founding members and station manager of Fine Music Radio. He was also the last station manager of Springbok Radio, which, for some stupid managerial decisions higher up, was shut down.

Leslie's was the last voice to be heard as he announced the station's closure, saying good night to the listeners at 00:00. He showed me the video tape of those last moments; he was surrounded by people like Esmé Euvrard and all the others who had contributed to the station's success.

When Leslie was at Fine Music Radio, I had my own arts programme once a week, which later became once a fortnight, for ten years. I interviewed writers, actors, artists and dancers. It gave me a solid grounding in radio and the fine art of interviewing people live on air.

I owed Leslie money, which I was planning to pay back. One day, I met him for a drink at his flat in Sea Point, and he told me that I didn't have to pay him anything; I should consider it a gift.

A week later, he was dead.

75

OUR NEIGHBOURHOOD AND THE VARIOUS neighbours we've had over the years are worthy of a mention because you just can't make this stuff up. One cold, dark night, I smelt a braai, even though it was raining. I thought, 'How strange. Who wants to braai at 23:00 on a rainy night?' Inquisitive as I always am, I headed outside, only to discover that the cottage behind our neighbours' house was on fire. I could hear screaming. I saw a woman run out and jump into a car. Then the fire engines and an ambulance arrived. When the fire was put out, I watched as the ambulance crew carried someone out in a body bag. The smell of meat, like pork, hung in the air.

This is what happened: the young couple who lived there had had a fight. She had discovered that he was cheating on her. So, she waited for him to fall asleep and then poured petrol over him and set him alight. They never found her; she'd made a duck for Rio. Who would have thought? She was always so friendly.

Farther up the road, a block away, gangsters shot Advocate Pete Mihalik dead in front of his children. It rattled the whole neighbourhood.

One day, a car came speeding up the road. I heard sirens, then a bang. A car had driven through a wall and smashed into the courtyard of a house, where two retired and ever-so-gentle residents were enjoying a cup of morning tea. Two of the four passengers escaped by running through the house and jumping over a wall. The car had been hijacked. The two panicky inhabitants fled their house for two days.

On the other side of our road lived a woman who dyed her hair pitch-black and stared at you from under this bush. Sometimes she played the piano at night, but there were certain things I will never forget about her.

One night, during a blackout, I saw two sets of twinkly lights coming up the road. The streetlights were out, but these lights, flashing red, green and yellow, kept coming closer. I went out with a torch because I had to see what this was. It was the woman with the hair, taking her two dogs for a walk. Their collars were lit up so that passing cars could spot them. Bright idea, but Dadaistic, to say the least.

On another night, there was once again a knock on our back door. I found a strange man standing there, asking if I could please come upstairs. So, I went with him, and there was my young neighbour, dead, a packet of drugs on the table in front of him. His dog was at his shoulder, barking and licking his ear, but he did not move.

I held the man, who turned out to be the brother of our young neighbour. The neighbour was a DJ, always friendly and mad about his dog. The brother phoned their mother, then the police came, followed by the hearse. But the mother arrived first. I have seen sad scenes in my life, but this was traumatic, something that will never leave me.

She was a tall, proud woman, who slowly ascended the stairs. When she walked into the flat and saw her son, she turned around, held on to the wall, and screamed with sorrow and with such force, it echoed through the neighbourhood. Later, I looked out the window and saw the young man's lifeless body, now in a body bag, being carried down to the hearse. They slid him inside, closed the door and drove off.

On another occasion, about twenty years ago, I was reading the newspaper one Sunday morning when there was a knock at the front door. When I opened it, a man with a pipe stood outside. He introduced himself as Esmé. That's when I realised the 'man' was a woman.

'Are you Herman?' she asked. She said my upstairs neighbour was her cousin and she had a story to tell me. I let her in, and we sat down in the lounge.

Esmé van Zijl (she was forty-six at the time) then proceeded to tell me that her uncle, Imker Marais Hoogenhout, had raped her as a child. Her story gutted me. This had happened more than forty years ago. In his day, Hoogenhout was a diplomat and a big shot in the business world. He was someone who commanded respect in high circles.

Esmé told me how he had taken her virginity when she was six years old. He also sodomised and raped her more than one-hundred-and-fifty times over a period of eight years. She said that was why she looked like a man. 'So that I can be unattractive to men.'

The older Esmé got, the more her history with this man haunted her. Instead of forgetting, she knew the time had come to talk about it, even if it was decades later.

She told me about her poor self-esteem and self-hatred, the infinite sadness she'd had to fight over the years. Esmé had lodged a complaint with the police, but at that stage, such cases expired after a certain number of years. She was told that she should have filed it within three years of her twenty-first birthday.

Little did I know at the time that Esmé would be the first person to fight that legislation in court. She would win her case and pave the way for other people who had been sexually molested to expose paedophiles and rapists much later in their lives. Two other victims of Hoogenhout also came forward.

She had come to me to help her tell her story. 'I want to name and shame him,' she said. Little did we realise that paedophiles have no shame; they live in denial and quickly move on. Or die, like her uncle, before they can be punished.

At that point I was overwhelmed by my own deadlines, but I thought I could help her talk to other journalists to make her horror story public. I warned her that this was a big step; she would have to stand strong. People would not believe her. Blaming the victim is an old trick of people who have no idea what they're talking about.

Esmé said that she was going to stay in her cousin's (my neighbour's) apartment for a while: 'I will feel safe there.' My first call that evening was to the night office of *Die Burger*. I spoke to someone who had a nose for an important story.

The next morning, I went to Giovanni's Deli in Green Point for coffee and the newspaper. Esmé's story was on the front page. I still remember how shocked I was. After that, I went back home to give Esmé a copy. When I rang the front doorbell, she opened the door and slowly came out. She took the newspaper and looked at it.

Then she began to cry bitterly, repeating these words: 'Uncle, uncle, uncle, what have I done to you? What?' I was surprised by her reaction, because I didn't think she had anything to feel guilty about. She cried for a long time, and I stayed with her until she was calmer.

This story got huge coverage at the time.

Today, I thank that strange woman who appeared so unexpectedly on my doorstep for what she's managed to do for other victims. I also understand why she felt guilty, and why it took her so long to confront the past.

76

I T WAS 1994 AND I was turning thirty. Graham was so kind as to buy us tickets to London and New York for my birthday. To this day, it stands out as a tipping point and one of the best vacations of our lives. How kind and loving of him. This was the same year that Casper Schmidt died of AIDS-related illnesses. It was a pity; I had put our brouhaha behind me, and it would have been nice to see him.

Our accommodation was arranged: we were going to stay with friends in both London and New York. When we arrived in London, we went straight to our architect friend Brian's flat, which was in Grape Street, in the heart of London, near Covent Garden and Soho. We'd hardly put our bags down when Brian told us that we must get going, there was a gay pub he wanted to take us to.

Bar Rumba was a hot and happening pub and nightclub. Outside was a huge TV set, with the pop group D:Ream and Peter Cunnah singing 'Things Can Only Get Better'. Yes, little did I know – better and worse.

We went down the stairs into a room where beautiful people were dancing away; it was the start of the rave culture, which meant ecstasy. For the first time, Graham and I each took a club drug. Everybody was very loving, kisses everywhere; the lights whirled, the music thumped, hugs galore, the dance-floor shook. Outside, the sun was still shining, but inside the club it was a dark den of sin; time didn't exist.

It was the best time to be in London. We were young, bulletproof. Cynicism had not eroded our souls yet; everything was pretty in the garden.

A few years later, the front cover of *Vanity Fair* magazine would proclaim: 'London Swings! Again!' Inside, they wrote: 'As it was in the mid-sixties, the British Capitol is a cultural trailblazer, teeming with new and youthful icons of art, pop music, fashion, food and film. Even its politicians are cool. Or, well, coolish.'

Liam Gallagher from Oasis featured on the cover along with his partner, Patsy Kensit. A journalist wrote: 'Gallagher has been nonchalant about his frequent cocaine use, and he's not atypical. Young Londoners have a casual, positive attitude toward drugs that even Timothy Leary might not have countenanced; the American notion of drug taking as a sickness to be cured is utterly alien. "There's a heroin addict, a cocaine addict, and a marijuana addict on my staff," says James Brown, editor of *Loaded* magazine. "Sometimes it's difficult. Sometimes it's great fun.'"

We were part of that atmosphere. During the day we visited art galleries, discovered London on foot and ate at typical British pubs. At night, we went clubbing; there were so many to choose from.

One of London's oldest gay super-clubs, Heaven, was within walking distance of where we were staying. We had seen nothing like it in South Africa. It was huge, with thousands of people gyrating, entering, leaving, hanging over the balconies ... we danced until the sun came up.

We also went to the Fridge in Brixton, which had an industrial, hard-core, sexy feel to it. Pop groups like the Pet Shop Boys, Frankie Goes to Hollywood and Eurythmics performed there, as did world-renowned DJs like Armin van Buuren. The club showed pornography on one of its big screens, and lo and behold, we recognised a guy from Cape Town who had once been a drag queen and had pivoted to being a porn star and one of the most expensive rent boys in London. He was frolicking in an orgy. Goodbye Cape Town, hello big city, London. A boerseun from the platteland ... what a delightful contradiction.

But then I noticed that a *real* orgy was taking place in one of the rooms at the club, never mind on the big screen. Graham and I walked into the room, and the next moment my jeans were pulled down. London isn't Koekenaap, that's for sure. I noticed that medics were deployed on the scene, as they were at some other London clubs, which was very sensible. There was also an emergency room in case someone overdosed.

I spotted Grace Jones and Boy George, both huge stars at that point, in the crowd. I was certain that I saw Grace dancing naked, but because I was on LSD, it was probably a vision.

As an aside, did you know that Grace Jones has an indirect connection with South Africa? In her memoir, *I'll Never Write My Memoirs*, Grace refers to her modelling days in Paris in the early seventies. There, she stayed in a tiny hotel, where she met Esti Mellet, also a model, who was from Brakpan, of all places.

Two of their friends were Jerry Hall and Jessica Lange. They worked hard for little money, but Grace loved to go out and party at night. Before she went out, she would warm up by singing to herself, and her voice was big and loud, so people could hear her. Esti, who was in the room next door, thought that she had a great voice. She begged Grace to make use of it, but Grace hadn't made an impression at an earlier audition, so once bitten, twice shy, and she shooed Esti away.

But Esti did not give up. Her boyfriend worked as a talent scout for a small record company. His name was Stephan Tabakov and he was, according to Grace, charming and quite a looker. Esti told him: 'Oh, Grace knows how to sing!' Grace wasn't impressed. However, she changed her mind, and when Stephan invited her to his studio, she auditioned for him. Thanks to Grace's talent and Esti from Brakpan, everything came together like alchemy, and today Grace Jones is still one of the industry's big stars.

Our time in London was ending, but there was one big event that still had to take place. On 4 November 1994, I was turning thirty. Brian had organised a birthday party at his beautiful flat. The food was as if out of a gourmet magazine like *Bon Appétit*: caviar, crayfish, sushi, duck, foie gras. The Champagne flowed, and there were lines of cocaine on a silver platter. It was the first time I ever schnaffed it, and it took immediate effect. I went on and on about the wonders of Nelson Mandela, the ANC, South Africa ... soon, a little crowd formed around me; I was an orator.

The more cocaine I took, the more drama I pumped into my stories. At 03:00, we went to a club, where we partied till sunrise. The flight to New York was at 11:00. There was no time to sleep; we had to pack and get to the airport. The Big Apple was shiny and fresh, and waiting.

77

O N OUR ARRIVAL IN NEW York, we took a yellow cab to our friend
Irwin Weiner's apartment on the Upper East Side. At that stage of
his life, he was considered an architectural designer of note, so his
hard work had paid off; his flat had even been featured in a few magazines.

New York, like London, was pumping. At first, we did touristy stuff
like going up the Empire State Building and attending an art exhibition at
the Guggenheim, where there was a retro exhibition of Willem de Kooning's
work. We also popped in at the Algonquin Hotel, known for its Round Table
literary soirees with writers like Dorothy Parker.

We went to the Russian Tea Room, where they filmed scenes for famous
movies like *Manhattan*, *When Harry Met Sally* and *Tootsie*. While Graham
and I were resting at a coffee shop, taking a break from all the walking, Woody
Allen and his new wife, Soon-Yi Previn, walked past us. They were holding
hands and looked very much in love.

Yes, I was back in New York, where you bump into a celebrity on every
street corner.

78

IN NEW YORK, WE ATTENDED a different play or musical every night. What sticks with me was seeing Carole King in *Blood Brothers*. Her song 'You've Got a Friend' had made her an international star. Basia's concert was advertised on lampposts everywhere. The city was alive with shows and the theatres were packed every night.

After performances, the actors all came out on stage wearing a red ribbon, and a minute's silence was observed for all those in the entertainment industry who had died of AIDS-related illnesses. The disease was still having a devastating effect on the creative community.

A play about the pandemic, *Angels in America*, received excellent reviews and was rewarded with a ten-minute standing ovation the night we saw it. We also saw the musical *Show Boat*, starring Elaine Stritch. That night was also the opening night of *Sunset Boulevard* with Glenn Close. After our show, we walked past the Minskoff Theatre, where we were met with pandemonium. Glenn Close was standing on specially installed steps in a long, chic dress, waving at the crowd. A helicopter hovering above shone a bright light on her.

Glenn was beautiful and dripping with shiny jewels. People just loved her, and the atmosphere was contagious. I burst into tears. Next to me, a man smiled at me because I was crying, and I realised that it was none other than Clint Eastwood. Cowboys don't cry ... or do they?

Graham and I took the subway back to Irwin's apartment, overwhelmed by all the action and drama. The next morning, we heard the *New York Times*, usually thicker than the old *Yellow Pages*, drop at Irwin's front door. The front page featured a photo of Glenn Close, with the review inside – the morning after the previous night's opening!

The headline read: 'SUNSET BOULEVARD; Boulevard of Broken Dreams'. The first sentence: 'The mansion has landed.' That production received great praise, but also some criticism.

We also went to see the musical *Hello, Dolly!*, starring Carol Channing, in Boston. She'd first played the role of Dolly Levi in 1964, and then again in

1994, thirty years later. A revival that coincided with my birthday. It was important; Americans take their artists seriously.

Graham and I took the train to Boston to stay with an acquaintance overnight. We would drive back to New York the next morning. When we arrived in Boston, the freezing weather hit me like I had never experienced in my life. There was a chill in the air that drilled right through your head. Fortunately, the theatre was warm inside and the decor, with its balconies, red seats and golden chandeliers, majestic.

When Carol Channing appeared on stage, the crowd spontaneously jumped up, stamped their feet and clapped. After many minutes, she dramatically raised her hand and told us to sit down. We once saw Dame Maggie Smith do the same in London, in a play called *The Lady in the Van*. When she walked onto the stage, the huge audience stood up and gave her an ovation that went on and on. Eventually, she lifted her hand and said: 'Thank you, but the show must go on!'

Carol delivered a very professional performance, and it was a historic moment to see the original Dolly Levi perform on stage. We decided to wait outside in the cold for her and tracked down her limousine behind the theatre, where her chauffeur was waiting for her. The big black car was idling, with steam coming out of the exhaust pipe.

We waited and waited. Later, I started chatting with the driver, who told us how difficult Carol was. A drama queen deluxe. We were dying to meet her. After waiting an hour, we were done. We left with our tails between our legs, though we longed for an autograph.

The next morning, we returned to New York. I felt like enjoying a glass of wine in a bar, so we went into one and saw Carol being interviewed on TV about her role in *Hello, Dolly!* So, she had been giving interviews after the show while Graham and I were waiting for her outside the theatre, nearly passing out from the cold.

Oh well, we have the memories. At least we spoke to her chauffeur.

79

To IGNORE NEW YORK'S NIGHTLIFE would have been a sin. The old 'bookshop', Les Hommes, was still there; I remembered it from my days when I'd lived in New York as a youngster. Les Hommes sold pornographic material in the foyer, and in the back was a small cinema where pornographic films were shown. A curtain separated the shop from the theatre. Then there was another curtain, which took you into the cruising area.

If you don't know what cruising is, let me explain: you flirt with a stranger, and if you like what you see, you have anonymous rumpy-pumpy. I was amazed that Les Hommes still existed.

Farther down the street was a bar that broadcast an episode of *Dynasty* on a big TV screen every night. As soon as Joan Collins made her appearance, the queens practically squealed like cats, and some of the drag queens dressed up specially as the female characters.

We visited a club called Splash almost every night. We asked for ecstasy, as was the custom in London, but no, the general mood was against it. Drugs were not as popular in New York as they were in London, so Absolut Vodka shots had to do. And how!

At Splash, go-go boys walked naked on glass counters while the showers installed above splashed water all over them. The go-go boys danced lustfully and suggestively with one another, and you could leave tips for them in a big box.

There were erections galore; it was one massive orgy with loud music and a mass of dancing bodies. I noticed a man in a black coat, with big sunglasses and a walking stick, standing in one corner. It was none other than the fashion designer Karl Lagerfeld. He looked sour.

Another club we frequented was Limelight, which was in a big old church with a pulpit, from where the DJ played his music. Above the DJ's head was a cloth that said: 'God is a DJ'. The confession booths in which the Catholics confessed their sins were still there, but no confessions were heard behind those curtains. Instead, they had glory holes through which you could push your bazooka while someone on the other side polished it for you – if you get my drift.

A trapeze artist, dressed as the devil, swung through the air holding a red pitchfork. Flashing red lights, fastened around his head, accentuated his two horns. In front of the pulpit was the figure of Christ on the cross, and his crown of thorns also had flashing lights.

Topless, often completely naked men wearing angel wings writhed around on the dancefloor, and they would call you hither to one of the booths to beg for forgiveness. If my grandmother could have seen that 'church', she would surely have thought it was the end of the world.

After two weeks, our time in New York drew to a close. It was time to face our lives in Cape Town.

80

I N SOUTH AFRICA, IT WAS back to the grind. After London and New
York, it took us months to get used to small-town Cape Town, but change
was imminent. The mood in London would sweep through Cape Town,
too. In Green Point, a gay ghetto appeared seemingly overnight. New clubs
came on the scene with excellent resident DJs who played international hits.
Restaurants flourished and a new one opened almost every week.

The gay clubs included Club 55, Bronx, Angels, Detour (BAD) and Blah
Bar. The latter would be destroyed by a bomb, with a bartender losing one
of his feet. Café Manhattan opened in De Waterkant and, farther down, a
theatre, On Broadway, saw the light of day. You could start the evening with
dinner at Manhattan's, go on to On Broadway to see a drag show, and then
dance the night away at one of the many clubs that stayed open until the sun
came up.

During this time, I acquired a new cellphone, a Nokia, which was as big
as a brick. You had to pull out an aerial to speak. One day, it rang. A friend
of my mother's asked me if I didn't want to come to her deathbed; the throat
cancer had returned. She was dying alone in her bed on the farm, as Christie
was in hospital, also with throat cancer. After I ended the call, I thought again
about what my mother meant to me.

I had golden years with her when we lived in Kloof Street in the boarding
houses filled with interesting people. We had happy years in Sea Point. Yet
there was the year in the orphanage, and the time at Braam Lategan's with his
wife, Tina, who made me feel unwelcome. After that, I was sent to my father,
who was a total alcoholic and neglected me.

My mother went to live on a farm, under the impression that she was
marrying a wonderful saviour. Instead of divorcing him when he turned
out to be anything but, she stayed on and became an alcoholic. Neither she
nor my father ever contacted me when I achieved something successful in
my life. There was always a resounding silence. I had had no financial or
emotional support from either of them since the age of fifteen.

I called my mom's friend back and told her to mention all these things to my mother, and then to ask her why, after all that, I should come to greet her on her deathbed. After that call, several people came to me, begging me to go. Sheila Cussons heard about this through my trusted friend Amanda Botha and asked me to please go and see my mother. I refused.

The day that my aunt called with news of my mother's death, I was sitting with my friend Petra Mason from Associated Magazines in the Perseverance Tavern in Gardens. Maria had wanted me to remember that she'd always loved me. They were meaningless words because her actions had disproved it. I continued hanging out with Petra in the bar and then went home.

The next morning, I sat in the bath and cried loudly. Just as I had with my dad. My mother was only fifty-two. Again, I was crying about what could have been: missed chances, years, lives, potential, all lost. Both her and my father's lives were half-lived. I thought of the beautiful young woman in Sea Point by the pool, her beautiful skin, the sun hat on her head. Connie Mulder's signature, which had changed so much. Fritz deported.

A great sadness hung heavy over my shoulders. Only later would I learn the necessity of forgiveness and that I could love both my parents unconditionally.

81

O<small>NE DAY, THE EDITOR OF</small> *Cape Style* magazine approached me and asked if I wanted to come and work for them as a features writer. In those days, *Cape Style* was like a local version of *Vanity Fair*; they published articles on a wide variety of subjects. I would get my own office downtown.

It was difficult for me to make the decision because I had grown to love everyone at *House and Leisure*. But in 1996, after about five years in the same job, I thought I might be ready to take a leap. There was a big farewell, but for months afterwards I wondered if I had made the right decision.

Cape Style threw me in at the deep end, as the cliché goes. My column on the back page, 'Spilling the Beans', was about people and the scandals they got involved in. I also wrote other columns, like 'Nightlife', 'Where to Eat Now', 'Gay & Lesbian News' and 'Theatre', plus I had to write two or three features a month.

I can't believe how hard I worked. Almost every night I had to go to a new restaurant, an art gallery, a nightclub or a function. I had to read widely about everything under the sun because my features covered so many diverse topics.

I learnt a lot by rereading the articles of the journalist Andrew Donaldson and my editor, Hilary Prendini Toffoli. Their writing style was different from that of the gentler, kinder *House and Leisure*. At *Cape Style*, they followed the British style of critical journalism. You had to write honestly, and with irony, about people and places. This led to a lot of trouble.

There was the time when I had to conduct an interview with Jeanette Harksen, wife of the German fugitive Jürgen Harksen. They were glamorous personalities on the Cape social scene and lived in a palazzo in Constantia.

I couldn't get an interview with Jürgen himself, so I got hold of Jeanette. We had to pretend we were terribly interested in her house, in her and her garden. In this way, we would be able to extract information that might relate to her husband. I went to the mansion with a photographer and arrived in front of imposing gates that looked like they belonged at Buckingham Palace.

A security guard let us in, and we drove along a long driveway to the front door. Jeanette, beautifully dressed, opened the door and took us through her palace of a house. She guided us to a spacious room full of dresses, then to another room full of shoes; everything was only the best.

The luxury in the house was breath-taking. Where the money came from was unclear, but Jürgen later went to prison for fraud. Jeanette also later divorced him. But at that stage, they were the couple of the moment. I conducted the interview, but Jeanette was reluctant to talk about her husband and mostly just discussed the decor and her clothes.

I wrote the article and added additional information about all her husband's shenanigans in a sidebar to the story. In juxtaposition with the photos and the story about their opulent lifestyle, it did not make them look good.

Jeanette was deeply hurt when the article appeared; she called me and cried on the phone. Jürgen was furious and called and threatened me. I must admit I was scared because he had contacts in the underworld. I had to watch my back, but I'd managed something that no other journalist could, and that was to show readers how the Harksens lived.

Then there was the time when I decided to visit some of the top restaurants in Cape Town to check out how clean their toilets were. I would give them points out of five for cleanliness, access to toilet paper and general appearance.

I visited ten high-end venues on a busy Friday evening along with Jackie Meiring, who took the photographs. We had to move quickly because we didn't want to attract attention, but I also had to spend enough time in each location to make informed decisions. Very few of the establishments scored four out of five; most scored two, and one even zero, so shocking was the state of their toilets. Jackie assessed the women's loos.

When the magazine hit the shelves, pandemonium broke loose. Some of the restaurateurs were furious and turned up at *Cape Style*'s offices to lash out at me. We had to ask the security guard downstairs not to allow anyone in.

When Princess Diana came to Cape Town and stayed with her brother, Charles Spencer, I wanted to track her down, but it was obviously top secret that she was here. One of my contacts informed me that she was considering moving to Cape Town permanently. Another person let me know that the princess was going to eat at Blues in Camps Bay on a certain night. A photographer and I waited there but didn't notice anything. I then abandoned the story because I didn't feel like following her around like a paparazzo.

A few days later, as I walked past Sotheby's, I saw her. What a beautiful woman. She was surrounded by security guards, and I didn't have my camera with me either. You win some, you lose some, and, as I've said, the whole paparazzi vibe wasn't for me. In the end, those vultures would chase her into the tunnel of death.

At this time, I also wrote profiles on Richard Branson and the international representatives of Boss Models. These were exciting times at *Cape Style*, but after almost five years at *House and Leisure* and the same number of years at *Cape Style*, I was keen to go freelance.

82

WHILE I WAS STILL AT *House and Leisure*, I befriended an older journalist, Lin Sampson. She was an established name in the media industry and known for her brilliant features. I learnt from Lin how to make a story come alive, something she could do much better than me. Other, lesser journalists were jealous of her, something I couldn't fathom. Lin didn't write press releases about people – she wrote the truth. This made her a target.

Celebrities, thugs ... many people hated her. On this point: the problem with certain Afrikaans publications is their sanguine approach to celebrities. In interviews, everything about the person is fantastic and wonderful. If they've just discovered a new love, it becomes a story; if a baby is born, it warrants a major article. Of course, there is a place for lighter stories, as you can't only read overly serious ones, but bring in some irony, dish a bit of dirt ... don't let an interview or obituary sound like a CV or press release.

Most Afrikaans publications are obsessed with religion, and if a celebrity's career begins to wane, there is always help: you have suddenly found the Lord. After becoming a drug addict, or being gay, you find Jesus. Come on! Get real. And readers fall for it. This is banal journalism; it dishes out candyfloss to readers who simply accept it as good journalism. Okay, one should not generalise; not all Afrikaans publications are the same, and you must take your readers' interests into account. Lose your readers, and you're toast. But it does say a lot about your average Afrikaans reader, I'm afraid. Bless.

What I enjoy about the English press is their honesty and willingness to experiment with different topics and critical writing, even if it offends readers. When I started out as a freelancer, I wrote for numerous publications and sent stories to the *Sunday Times*, *Mail & Guardian*, *Weekend Argus*, *Cape Times* and a whole lot of other newspapers. I also wrote for magazines, and my columns featured in *Fairlady*, *Cape Etc*, *Sawubona*, *SA Citylife* and *Cape Style*.

Some of the overseas publications in which I was published were *Vogue Entertaining & Travel*, *Men's Health* and *Time Out*, to name but a few. My freelance life was productive, but I also started drinking more.

Vernon Adams from Cape Talk radio station asked me to appear on his Friday-night show to talk about what was happening in the city. Here, I sometimes went too far. I don't know how I got away with it. Times were different. I did absurd things, like ask listeners to call James Small at home to tell him what they thought of him. I gave them his cell number.

James had infuriated me because he'd refused to pose for a magazine cover. I thought, 'When you need the media, you know when to use us. To hell with you.' The dashboard started lighting up as people called in. One man threatened me with death; another told me I did the right thing, James Small should be put in his place. What place this was, I don't know. The radio station was just starting out then; I don't think anyone had had to deal with such anarchy before. The next moment the producer showed up, arms waving; there was an important call. James Small was on the line.

I let rip and criticised him for refusing to appear on the magazine cover. I said he owed his fame not only to his talent, but to the media as well. The conversation went back and forth, but he was so charming that we made friends at the end, and I apologised on air. Yes, James had a soft heart and could wrap you around his little finger.

Later, he and I spent time together at the Vasco da Gama Taverna in Green Point, and I was really ashamed of my unprofessional behaviour. My nasty side, or my Jungian shadow, was slowly starting to self-sabotage.

Fine Music Radio was another radio station just starting out then. Leslie McKenzie was the station manager and he asked me and Marianne Thamm if we could invite a guest every second Sunday evening and chat about any topic.

Later, as I've mentioned before, I also had an arts programme, which aired for almost ten years. All great fun, while it lasted.

83

ON WEEKENDS, I STARTED TAKING drugs like LSD, cocaine, crack, khat, GHB, ecstasy; basically, anything I could lay my hands on. We had riotous parties at our flat and at the clubs in Green Point every weekend.

I was fit, in my thirties, drove a 1967 Volvo 144S, dressed like a cool dude and felt on top of my game. My weekend usually started around lunchtime on a Friday when I went out to eat. Mostly, it was about drinking, though. The food was an afterthought. One of my big drinking buddies was David Bullard, who had a popular column in the *Sunday Times*. He was good company and had a defiant attitude towards everything he saw as hypocrisy. In later years, he was fired as a columnist with great fanfare, and he subsequently became the darling of the conservatives; I don't think out of choice. I never experienced him as racist or homophobic, and he was a great raconteur.

One day, after a liquid lunch with him and the late *Sunday Times* food writer Lannice Snyman at Café Paradiso in Kloof Street, I was so drunk that I couldn't find my car. I took a taxi to our flat where, when I opened the car door, I rolled out onto the pavement. A bit like *Absolutely Fabulous*. These were my Friday afternoons.

Speaking of Café Paradiso... Another drinking friend was Madeleine van Biljon, a journalist who certainly was a legend in her own lifetime. She read widely, knew about food – in fact, about anything under the sun – had a large network of friends and could be quite rude if she felt like it.

Once she invited me and Marianne Thamm to her flat in Parliament Chambers for some soup. Then she turned to me and said I could leave, as it was now time for the *real* writers to have a discussion. I left, taking no notice, as I was used to her oddball behaviour.

One Sunday, we went to Café Paradiso to have lunch outdoors in the sun. The restaurant belonged to Madeleine's daughter, Mapula Swanepoel. David Bullard, Graham, and Lien Botha and her husband, Raymond Smith, were also there. The drink was flowing; Madeleine and I, in particular, had a fun time. At one point, Madeleine got up to go to the bathroom. She walked up the stairs, where she fell over. The place was packed inside and out. She was on the floor, rolling around like a sea lion, screaming and moaning. She couldn't get up. It took four of us to lift her and load her onto the back of Raymond's bakkie. There she lay, her rotund body neatly fitting into the small space.

We decided to take her to her flat in a convoy. When we got there, Madeleine jumped off the bakkie by herself. 'Come on, people! Let the party begin!' We then went upstairs where we continued to drink until past midnight. Madeleine and I took the lead. It was Monday morning.

Later, I couldn't any more, and I had to go and dry out at the Cape Mediclinic. When I checked in, I saw someone lying in the corridor, complaining. Madeleine! I could not believe it. I greeted her, but she looked befuddled. She was also there to dry out. Later, the psychiatrist, whom we shared, told me that Madeleine had asked him if she was going crazy. Was it Herman Lategan she saw? Was I a chimera? Was I part of her delirium tremens?

One day, after the detox episode, Madeleine and I decided that we would go to Alcoholics Anonymous together. We would turn over a new leaf, start a new life; we'd be sober and upright citizens of the world.

We first drank a few fixers and then went to a church near the Gardens Centre. There, we got rowdy and were asked to leave. She kept telling people to shut up and stop moaning. That was the end of that plan. Don't get the wrong idea, Madeleine wasn't a lush; she was a fine, intelligent woman with a kind heart, and one of our top journalists. I will always admire her.

Another time, when I was at Cape Mediclinic, drying out again, I pretended I was going to an AA meeting, but instead I went to a bar where I could drink alcohol and swallow some of the pills they give you to calm you down. I arrived back at the hospital high as a kite, where I somehow ended up in a ward full of elderly women. I had baby wet wipes with me. I don't know where I got them. I started wiping the women's faces. It was cool and they loved it. Except for one woman, who raised the alarm and chased me away.

The next morning, the psychiatrist called me in and asked me to leave the hospital.

84

M Y WEEKENDS BECAME REPETITIVE: A cycle of drugs, drink and shame. A cliché of a junkie's life, really. A garden-variety alkie and druggie. No weekend special. Fridays would start with a so-called 'networking lunch'. Just to get oiled, really. I started feeling disconnected and unable to communicate effectively with others. On Friday evenings, I ordered drugs and drank some more before going to a club until the morning. After that, I went home to pass out, wake up and eat vodka jelly. It's a bottle of vodka that you pour into jelly, mix, and then leave in the fridge overnight.

On Saturdays, we would have lunch with a group of elderly Sea Point queens at Posticino in Sea Point. A motley bunch who spoke like Noël Coward but loved to talk about their sex lives, always wildly exaggerated, and mostly set in Rome at midnight around a fountain.

The honorary queen who joined us was a woman called Catriona de Morgan, the newsreader Michael de Morgan's widow. She was frightfully well-mannered. We named her the Widow de Morgan. She had been a flight attendant in her day and wore Versace sunglasses, and always a blue blazer, with epaulettes, as if she was a ship's captain. Also, white slacks, gold sandals and a long cigarette. She drank heavily but never got drunk.

When Timothy Cursons, one of our Saturday lunch friends, died, the Widow de Morgan hired a vintage limousine and arrived at the church dressed in a red Chanel suit and her trademark Versace sunglasses. What an entrance!

Saturday nights I would do drugs again and go clubbing until Sunday morning. On Sundays we chilled, and people from the club came to listen to music. I would order more drugs and would snort and drink until late.

Men would pop in for shtupping and horizontal refreshment. It was like a bordello. We had a friend who specialised in pubic trimmings. Dressed in a sarong, he would invite you into the room, with his scissors. Oy, so wrong, but also so right. He'd tie a shoelace around your balls, which doubled as a makeshift cock ring. Then he would blindfold you and give you a temple rub.

On Mondays I would be so depressed and guilt-ridden because of all the drugs that I often wanted to end it all. On Tuesdays I felt better, on Wednesdays I was fine again, and on Thursdays my mouth started watering for Friday and the weekend.

When the fancy took us, Graham and I would get on a plane and go to Johannesburg, where we'd go dancing for the weekend.

Money just went down the drain. Graham was tame compared to me; I was the wild one. It seemed like my future had arrived, but it was not a good one. I felt like I was experiencing numerous realities and that I was stuck in the wrong one. Was I trapped in an alternate universe?

My drinking and drug abuse increasingly made me behave like an insane person. One evening we accompanied some friends to the Labia in Cape Town to watch the film *Pleasantville*. Well, there was nothing pleasant about that night. I was tiddly and the man behind me was eating popcorn. Loud, from a brown paper bag. I asked him nicely to eat quietly because the movie had started. He taunted me and ate even louder. I asked him again to eat quietly. He turned to a woman next to him and asked if I was a psychopath. I got furious and asked him if he wanted to see how a psychopath behaves.

I took pepper spray from my bag, turned around and emptied the can on him. He was so startled, he fell backwards and rolled onto the seats behind him. The theatre was permeated with what smelt like teargas. People started coughing and stumbled to the door to get out. I started running.

There was a crowd outside the entrance, and I heard a blonde woman behind me say that someone had pointed a gun at Herman Lategan. Back home, I waited for the police to come and arrest me. Afterwards I felt bad, of course, and whenever I could, I gave the Labia good publicity.

But my behaviour was getting more unpredictable as the drugs and alcohol took hold of my psyche. Evita Bezuidenhout performed to a packed opening night at the Theatre on the Bay. I'd had about two bottles of wine, mixed with Alzam, a toxic mix that takes away all your inhibitions. When Evita sat down and asked the audience if we had any questions, I screamed: 'Show us your poes!' Pieter-Dirk Uys, an absolute professional, simply ignored me.

One day, Esmaré Weideman, then the deputy editor of *Fairlady*, called me, as I wrote a column for the magazine at the time. On behalf of the editor, Alice Bell, Esmaré was letting me know that a piece I'd written about Breyten

Breytenbach would not resonate with their readers. Being at the height of my lunacy, I yelled at her and said that I was on my way, *now*.

I jumped into my car and rushed to the Naspers building. But not before first having three double whiskies at a Portuguese restaurant just around the corner. Then I stormed into the building, took the lift up to *Fairlady* and ran into the open-plan office. I rushed towards a shocked Esmaré and asked her where the hard copy of the column was, then grabbed it from her hands and tore it up. Alice Bell jumped up from her chair and shouted that I had to get out.

The next day, of course, I felt guilty again, as I should have, and wrote an apology. The column kept running. I was even invited to two of their Christmas parties, but after I resigned the tenth time, they accepted.

It didn't stop there. I had a column in *Cape Style*, too. One day, the editor told me that Dullah Omar, the then Minister of Justice, had bought a house in Constantia and was moving there. I assumed the story was true. What any 'normal' journalist would have done was to get three different sources to confirm it or look it up in the Deeds Office.

Not me. I wrote that it was a sad day when the Minister of Justice had to flee his home in Athlone because Constantia was safer. The *Weekend Argus* picked up the story and repeated it.

Soon afterwards, a lawyer's letter arrived at *Cape Style*, informing us that Minister Omar had simply been in Constantia to attend a property auction. He had not bought anything and still lived in Athlone. The magazine must issue an apology. I was furious with my editor and told her that she was the one who had to apologise; the apology would not appear on my page.

By that time, I was already drinking at 11:00 in the morning. When the new issue came out, I saw a big apology on my page at the back of the magazine. I was enraged and called the *Cape Style* editor, who was actually a good friend of mine, and told her to lock her child in her room and call the police – I was on my way with a bread knife and TV cameras.

With a knife in my hand, I ran to my car and started it, but Graham came running after me and grabbed the keys. That was the end of the column. Luckily the editor and I are still good friends to this day, and we often refer to that fracas.

I had the insight that I was destroying myself and behaving like a monster; I was in the jaws of addiction. But I didn't stop.

My friend Suzaan Steyn, who lived just opposite me, once flew to Johannesburg to audition as a TV newsreader with Riaan Cruywagen. When she came back, she asked if I could pick her up at the airport. Her plane was due to land at 17:00. I was there at 15:00 to have drinks while waiting for her. When she landed, I told her we should quickly have a 'sip' so that I could hear how the audition went.

She could drink moderately, but I had one whisky after another. Later, at 21:00, we left. When we arrived at the flat, I rolled out of the car into the road, slammed the car door, crawled to the front door and passed out.

85

ESPITE MY INCREASING BOUTS OF stupidity, there were more overseas trips. Graham and I went to Sydney, twice to attend Mardi Gras. The second time (my third and last visit) was to see our good friends Deon Schoonbee and Colin Polwarth. They were an important part of our lives, and we were devastated when they emigrated. This is a common South African story, the diaspora of people we love. Deon was the superintendent of Tygerberg Hospital and Colin was an architect.

In Australia, their careers made a rapid upward trajectory, and they were soon at home in Sydney. It made us feel broken, because when we went to visit, we realised that they were there to stay. Our plan had been to grow old together. The drive to the airport on our return was terrible, something I will never forget. We said a long goodbye. When the plane took off, I looked over the city for the last time.

I also flew to Germany, Nigeria, the Philippines, the US, the UK and Mozambique on press trips. My trip to Antarctica was certainly one of the great highlights of my life, but that's also a book all on its own.

At least I behaved myself during these visits, considering that my addiction was turning me into a walking cliché of an addict. Whenever I returned to South Africa, I would have that sinking feeling; I was powerless, unmanageable.

I became suicidal and fell out with more people. My friend Lin Sampson had to listen to my troubles and suggested that I go to Dignitas in Switzerland. There was no money for that; I had to think of another way.

86

ONE DAY, AFTER A TRIP to New York, I went to the garage and threw all the articles I had written over the years, including the prizes I had won, into the rubbish. The garbage truck picked it up and left with it. It was a Friday morning; I stood watching as it all went.

My life was a void. I drank more and my drug use was no longer limited to weekends. Tranquillisers left me in a haze. Just writing about it now makes me feel nauseous. I started walking or driving for days, just to get away from myself. I ended up in strange bars in Salt River, Maitland, Paarden Island. I was a classic barfly, a loser, finished.

During one of my aimless long walks, I passed a house in Gardens. There, I saw a sign with the name Dr Pieter Cilliers, psychiatrist. I remembered him from my schooldays, when he was the doctor who looked after many of the scholars. For me, it was a sign that I should make an appointment. When I first saw him, he could tell that I had been drinking. He explained therapy wasn't going to work if I arrived drunk.

That was at 07:00 in the morning. The next time, I arrived drunk again. Pieter said that this wouldn't work. He would only see me if I went to a rehabilitation centre. I was devastated. Me? An alcoholic and a drug addict? My denial was strong, but I knew that if I wanted to survive, I had to see Pieter. So, I had to go to rehab.

First, I went to Stepping Stones in Kommetjie, but I only lasted one night. Next to the rehab was a pumping bar, the music fantastic, a laughing crowd. The lure of the underworld was too strong.

Again, Tina Lategan's words haunted me as I lay alone in my room. Gutter, this child will land up in the gutter. But I wanted out. The next morning, I called a friend to fetch me. The rehab people begged and pleaded with me to stay, but I wanted none of it.

Back in Green Point, I at once went to the nearest bar, where I drank a bottle of vodka. Then I called my drug dealer. On the phone, I heard people singing in the background. No, he told me, he was practising in the church choir. Oh, the irony ...

I saw Pieter again, and he warned me that I would die if I continued to drink and take drugs. He diagnosed me with bipolar disorder and gave me a prescription for the condition. This time I booked myself into the Kenilworth Rehabilitation Centre, where I stayed for twenty-eight days. It was a wonderful place.

As part of the programme, we attended Alcoholics Anonymous and Narcotics Anonymous meetings. These gatherings irritated me no end because they mostly resulted in whining and complaining. And, oh, the self-pity and endless 'poor me, poor me'. Many people's addictions shifted, as they do. If you get rid of one, it moves on to another, like sex or food addiction. I started eating non-stop. Then, after hating the meetings at first, I became addicted to them.

I went to every meeting possible – for alcoholics, drug addicts, food addicts and sex addicts. Every day and in every imaginable suburb, from Melkbosstrand to Hout Bay and Sea Point. Some of the people, whose names I prefer not to mention, who attended these meetings were famous. From all over the world, mostly actors and writers. Cape Town was a popular place for them to dry out; there's the pretty scenery, plus the rehabs are world-class and celebrity junkies are left alone; nobody makes a fuss of them.

I thought that when I lived a clean life, I would start to write productively and finish a novel in no time. However, I could not write a single word. It reminded me of the time in the orphanage when I couldn't talk. It was obviously my primal wound, the lonely boy, wordless, abandoned by his mother. The one I tried to drown out with alcohol and drugs. Now he was back, in full force. Every Monday morning at exactly 07:00, I went to Pieter Cilliers for therapy sessions. I had no confidence and simply could not write.

I became drastically impoverished and had to rely on Graham financially, which put a strain on our relationship. Let me just mention here: his family is like my family; they always accepted me as one of them. They were and are the relatives I never had: Graham's father, Dr John Sonnenberg, his wife, Jerry, Graham and his sisters, Penny Sonnenberg and Pamela Blomefield, and Pamela's husband, Tom Blomefield, and their children, Jessica and Stephen, as well as their spouses.

I continued with therapy, but I sat in front of my laptop for hours and not one, not *one* word would appear on that screen. But something even more dreadful was about to happen; change was in the air.

87

O NE COLD AND WET FRIDAY night I went to bed early. Graham had gone out to a party. I often stayed away from such things because I didn't want to start drinking again. I fell asleep. When I woke up, a young man was sitting on top of me, with his knife against my throat. Another was standing next to the bed; he, too, had a knife. They wanted to know where the safe was.

Both were aggressive and didn't believe me when I said there was no safe. I slept naked, so I felt even more vulnerable. They opened all the drawers and cupboards and dumped everything on the floor. When I pressed the panic button, the one stabbed me in my hand and arm with the knife. The other guy pushed my other hand against the wall and, with the handle of the knife, smashed my thumb. They then began pulling all the wires from the walls, throwing paintings on the floor and overturning the furniture ... pandemonium erupted.

It then occurred to me that it was Nelson Mandela's birthday. It was July the eighteenth. I asked the men if they were not ashamed of their behaviour on Madiba's birthday. My question changed the atmosphere and saved me from certain death. They hadn't just come to steal; they'd come to kill.

Just then I heard someone at the front door; it was the security men with torches and all. The burglars were startled, as was I, and they pushed me back into the bedroom. At least by this time I was dressed. They instructed me to say that I was fine, all was perfect, it was a false alarm. They showed me their knives. I walked to the front door and opened it. It was scary.

A torch shone on me, and the security man asked me if everything was all right. I answered loudly, so that the other two could hear, that everything was fine. But with my mouth I mimicked the word 'help', and I rolled my eyes in the direction of the two intruders.

The security man nodded his head and left. The two attackers were exuberant and laughed loudly, jumping up and down. I couldn't believe it; it was like something out of a Quentin Tarantino movie.

Amid the jollification, men in uniforms kicked open the front door, and a horde of police and security guards entered. The two housebreakers wanted to escape through the back door in the kitchen, but the security men caught them. They were handcuffed and taken to a van outside. Flashing blue lights, rain falling. I called Graham to come right back from the party; something terrible had happened.

The police questioned me late into the night. Months later, during the court case, I felt sorry for the two guys. They were young, with their lives ahead of them. But my sympathy was short-lived when they told the magistrate that I had stood outside the apartment and invited them in for a 'job'. This 'job' being a 'blow job'!

I couldn't believe what I was hearing. First, I burst out laughing. Then I got angry and said that if I were heterosexual, they and their lawyer would never have come up with such a ridiculous fib. They should be ashamed; it was homophobic.

The magistrate agreed and sent them to prison for twelve years. When I heard this, I felt sorry for them again.

88

WHEN I TOLD MY PSYCHIATRIST about the attack, he said I should write about it. Immediately. As in, go home now and start. At that stage, I was reading books where the action started at once. There were no long introductions to the narrative; you were pulled into the scene from the first sentence.

I sat down and wrote: 'When I awoke, I could smell his warm, moist breath against my face. A man with a bloodstained knife was sitting on top of me; the blade held against my throat. I was alone in bed, naked.'

The *Cape Times* published the story, and after that, the words flowed. A combination of therapy and a terrible incident had turned out to be a tipping point, spurring me on to unblock the sewage.

I started writing frantically. Sometimes two of my stories were published in different publications on the same day. Then everything changed again.

Graham had had enough of our relationship, which was eighteen years old. I admit I was hard to live with, especially during my wild drinking and drug days. And when I stopped drinking, I became a 'dry drunk', as they say in rehabilitation centres. This is a person who has stopped drinking but has not yet been psychologically detoxified. They are like a drunk person: moody, even aggressive, and I humiliated Graham in front of other people.

Obviously, I was devastated and decided to move out and then take my own life. As chance would have it, there was a furnished apartment available on the very top floor of the Gardens Centre. I moved in. The views were right to the end of the horizon – the perfect place from which to jump.

My first night there, I looked down towards the street. A car came around the corner at high speed and crashed straight into the bridge underneath. I heard screams, then the car burst into flames. Soon after, the fire brigade and ambulances arrived.

I thought it was a sign: Don't jump, look how precious life is. I was only forty at the time. What a comedown. I was twenty-one in New York, thirty in London and alone at forty in the Gardens Shopping Centre, one of the ugliest buildings in Africa, with suicidal thoughts.

Meanwhile, I applied for a job as a writer at e.tv. Amid the pain of a broken relationship, life had to go on. There, I started by writing copy for newspapers and magazines about the films and programmes they broadcasted. I learnt how a TV station works, what goes on behind the scenes, the importance of viewership numbers; also about production, documentary programmes, news and marketing.

It was a cosmopolitan and dynamic place, and the station performed well. I liked my colleagues and the vibe. Viewer figures soared.

But I was lonely without Graham. I missed the cats. The flat in the Gardens Centre had become boring. There were interesting people who lived there, though. One man lived with his snake; I even wrote a story about him. The editor asked for a picture of the man with his snake outside the place where he worked, which was the fashionable Long Street Café. Then something terrible happened. Once the photographer had taken the photo, the snake escaped, never to be seen again. The man never spoke to me after that.

There was also a man with a dog who often took the lift with me. The dog's name was Koos. He also looked like a Koos and could understand only Afrikaans.

Other interesting people included an odd, poor-looking couple who mostly walked barefoot. They looked malnourished. I felt sorry for them. We regularly took the lift together and they had a tiny baby, called Sixteen. I suspected it was because the mother was sixteen when Sixteen was born.

Later, I moved from the Gardens Centre to an apartment in Sea Point just behind the SABC, next to my friend Leslie McKenzie from Fine Music Radio. One night I watched TV and, lo and behold, who do I see performing in a wacky and wild music video? My poor neighbours with their bare feet and the beautiful baby, Sixteen.

They had just been 'discovered', and they were Die Antwoord.

89

E VERYTHING WENT SMOOTHLY AT E.TV, and I was even nominated twice as employee of the year. Then I made the mistake of stopping my medication and starting to drink at the odd social occasion.

One night, I was on my scooter and the traffic police pulled me over. I was used to the licence disc being stolen by tik addicts and kept a copy of it under the seat. When they asked me where my licence was, I showed them the paper. The police officer looked at it and said that he couldn't read it.

I snatched it from his hands and started eating it, spitting it onto the pavement. He was so shocked that he called for help. A van arrived with sirens blaring. Secretly, I longed for a night in the Sea Point police cells so that I could write an article about it. Just for the experience.

The next moment, I was handcuffed and thrown into the back of the van. To punish me, they drove at high speed around and around the Green Point traffic circle.

At the station, a bevy of sexy policemen was waiting for me. I was told that if I was over the limit, I would sit until Monday.

It was a Thursday night; I didn't expect to sit for four days. That night, I'd had more than one tipple, believe me. I had to blow into the breathalyser; my heart was beating. But I passed the test, and the cops were very disappointed. I could go. Looking back, I realise how juvenile my behaviour was. But that was not the end.

I was still off my pills. At night, I couldn't sleep, so I just went into the office at 03:00 to work. By 15:00, I was completely exhausted. A new manager started, and he asked me why I was working such strange hours. My work was always up to date, I thought, so what was the problem?

But he didn't want me to come to work at night; no, I had to check in at 08:30 and leave at 17:30. For me, things didn't work that way; I hated such corporate twaddle. But this guy loved rules and regulations.

I had permission from my previous manager to write freelance articles. One day I read that Paris Hilton had had her anus bleached; it was then high fashion in America. What a blast ... I had to write about it. I got hold of a few local plastic surgeons, who told me that it had also become a fad in South Africa. Ferial Haffajee was still the editor of the *Mail & Guardian* at the time, and I wrote a tongue-in-cheek (no pun intended) piece about it for her.

That Friday, when the paper appeared, I almost rolled my car when I saw the posters on the lampposts: 'Bleach Your Way to a Pretty Little Pucker'.

My manager heard about the piece, which was just a bit of satire, but he told me I couldn't write stuff like that. I began making plans to leave; I didn't want to work with such an old curmudgeon.

I'd been at e.tv for five years at that stage, but it was time to move on, and I wanted to write more articles. I found out from someone that if I resigned, I couldn't claim from the unemployment insurance fund (UIF). Depending on the circumstances, they would pay for six months, and that's what I needed to kickstart my freelancing. I needed to be fired or retrenched.

While thinking about all this, I hung out at the Corner Bar in Sea Point, drinking whisky and taking Alzam again. It was a rough crowd; every week someone would drop dead because of alcohol.

There was a man who owned a shiny, gold Mercedes. He later lost his home and job because the drinking devil destroyed him. He'd park his car right in front of the bar and sleep there. People who wanted to spend the night in his car had to pay him fifty rand. Every night, that car was packed until the sun came up. Virginia Springett, nearly eighty years old and the oldest sex worker in Sea Point, told me she was sleeping on the beach, as it was cleaner than the car. She'd slept in it for a while, but some bugs bit her. The car stank.

I sat aimlessly at the Corner Bar, thinking that the best way to get away from e.tv was to get fired. I'd tell them to fire me. I asked my boss to sack me or let me go. He said no. This meant I couldn't get my money from the UIF.

Then I spoke to someone who told me that if I threatened to strangle my boss, I would be fired at once. I would never, ever kill him, but if that was the only way I would lose my job, then I would do it.

One day, my boss made me angry again. I knew the time had come; time to pretend that I would strangle him. I walked into his office and shouted: 'I want to strangle you!' Well, there and then I had to leave the building. The childishness! I'm ashamed when I think back.

What I forgot to mention was that sometime during my stint at e.tv, I attended another rehab. I went back to Stepping Stones for twenty-eight days. It worked for a while, but I soon fell off the wagon again.

They were a good bunch of people; the problem, I'm afraid, was me.

90

BECAUSE I WAS ABLE TO start freelancing, I thought it might be time to dry out again. This addiction saga was becoming both predictable and boring. First, I went to Stikland, with its clean green floors and everything nice, tidy and professional. I was there with a mix of grape harvesters, people living on the streets and businesspeople who had lost it all. It was fascinating.

After a week, however, I wanted to leave. Again, I tried to stay clean, but I started hanging out with druggies and sex workers at Café Erté in Sea Point. There were drag queens galore and the music was loud; the place went on for twenty-four hours a day. So would I.

But I had to change, I had to change … This time I booked in at Harmony Clinic in Hout Bay, which belonged to a friend of mine. Twenty-eight days later, I was out of there, clean and sober. My friend asked me if I would like to manage their website and create content for it. It was fun, because there were many animals on the premises to help with the therapy, among them piglets, chickens, two emus, geese, ducks, turkeys and two goats. My office's front door was always open, and the goats and chickens came to visit me daily; also, a few piglets.

If I was on the phone to someone, the person would ask me what the noises in the background were. I decided to ignore that question because nobody would have believed me. One day, an emu got sick, as did one of the piglets and a turkey, and I had to take them to the vet. A heroin addict, a pale woman, accompanied me. All the way to the vet, the emu bit the back of my head, the pig squealed, and the turkey shat all over the car.

So, I had to drive fast, and I wondered what we looked like to passers-by. The pale woman said nothing, but I was worried that she would jump out and make a run for it. She'd once complained about the food – she didn't like aubergine. The owner said: 'You've sucked every cock on the Main Road of Woodstock, but you won't eat eggplant!'

In the meantime, Graham had met someone, Athan Glover, with whom I got on very well. Athan was a chef and could cook incredibly well. I was invited to eat at my old flat every night, and Graham's father, Dr Sonnenberg, as I always called him, also came. Athan made the food, and soon every meal felt like a family gathering.

Somehow, I landed up subbing for *Die Burger* in the night office for a year, which was exciting and challenging. Another job that I can add to my list of experiences is that of writer and translator at the tabloid the *Daily Voice*, which lasted for three days. Nothing wrong with the paper; it just wasn't 'me'.

During this time, I got an unexpected call from the University of Cape Town's Centre for Film & Media Studies. Could I teach a six-month seminar on creative non-fiction? I really enjoyed those six months, as I took my head tablets and began to feel as if I had a purpose in life again. My freelancing was also going well, and I was being published in all sorts of publications. Also in Afrikaans, which I had neglected for twenty years. It thrilled me to taste the language in my mouth again, and I started playing with old Afrikaans words on Facebook, where I would choose a word and then make up a story around it. *Rapport* called and asked if I would consider writing a column in which I did the same. Later, I also started writing obituaries for them.

Then I developed this overwhelming longing for my parents. I understood so much more about addiction, so it was time to make peace with them. I had to forgive them. Graham drove me to my mother's burial place outside Koekenaap, where I sat beside the grave and could think for a long time about the woman I'd known when she was young, beautiful and poised. She was the woman I wanted to remember.

The day was hot, and the red sand was blowing everywhere over the graves. The train no longer stopped in Lutzville; it felt sad, but my bond with her was restored, right there in the cemetery.

But making peace with my father would require something else. Something I never thought I would consider in my life. The healing had to begin.

91

IN 2013, I MOVED INTO the Salvation Army, a tall, lean, red-brick building just outside the Waterfront in Cape Town. I had my own room, for which I paid R3 000 a month, and which included three meals a day.

I'd decided to follow in my father's footsteps to form a better understanding of his past. I also saw a story in any experience. I could write about it. The last time I'd seen him he was begging barefoot in the city, and he mentioned he was staying at the Salvation Army on the Foreshore. I still thought how pathetic that was. How humiliating. Thus, I had to get off my pedestal and see what it felt like for him.

It was strange when I first sat down for a meal there. Is this the dining hall where my father sat? I wondered. It had to be. How must he have felt after losing everything in his middle age?

Next to me at the table was Jervis Pennington, former pop star of the band The Soft Shoes. He'd ended up there via life's detours and would later write a play about his experiences. The play did well, and he was brilliant in it.

The smell of cabbage permeated the dining hall. My room, with a view of the Waterfront, nogal, was on the seventh floor. I was lucky to have my own room because most people had to share, up to six in a dormitory at a time.

The toilets and showers were communal. The passages were grim and dark.

I could have stayed in my own flat, but I had to come and find Sammy. No, I was not in the gutter as Tina Lategan had once predicted; I was on the road to forgiveness.

The Salvation Army taught me about poverty. Yes, as a child I was poor and even slept on park benches later in my life. I knew about hardship. Yet this revisiting of my father's past was essential.

Besides the singer Jervis Pennington, from whom I learnt humility, the theatre designer Keith Anderson was also a resident. He was well-known in circus circles and for his marionettes. It was sad to see that a respected man from the theatre world had ended up there in his old age.

The building was blazing hot in the summer and freezing cold in the winter; people kept coughing, and the smell of food and tired bodies permeated everything. One day, people noticed that Keith was no longer sitting at his table. When they went to his room, they discovered his decomposing body. The smell was bad, but no one on his floor had paid attention to it because they thought that was just how the place smelt. No one missed him in those three days, no one came to visit him, no one called him.

Many of the people at the Salvation Army no longer had any contact with family or friends. The man a few rooms away from me had Alzheimer's and just sat on his bed all day with the bedroom door open, staring out in front of him. Later they took him to a home. He looked so young.

We ate food that was donated by supermarkets but was already past its expiry date. Sometimes, it tasted like that, too – old. One day, a lorry transporting Vienna sausages overturned and the tins were dented in the process. We ate those sausages for weeks afterwards. In the evenings, I drove with my scooter to Graham and Athan, to have a nice dinner. Dr Sonnenberg was often there; they all thought I was cuckoo to live at the Salvation Army.

For breakfast, I usually got something from the local supermarket, but I ate lunch in the Salvation Army dining room. In the evenings, I was at Melrose Mansions. During the day I sat in my room and worked. It was like sitting and writing in a monastery with a stripped atmosphere. I enjoyed it.

The perpetual siren, however, that announced breakfast and lunch reminded me of the army. Insufferable. I was at my most productive in that little room. It was there that I heard on the radio that Nelson Mandela had died. It was 5 December 2013.

One afternoon, on a ridiculously sweltering day, a woman arrived with a lot of furniture, which she wanted to donate. The man who would normally receive it was sick, and I was asked if I could help the woman. She was there in a fancy car, but the crap she unloaded that day was beyond sad. Broken toys and plastic chairs. When she saw me, she gave me a look as if I stank or was infected with a virus. My hygiene was and is always impeccable; she was just a snob who looked down on me. Just like I'd looked down on my father because he'd also lived there.

Here, among the church mice, the outies, I learnt to forgive my father. Some precious moments were when I befriended the homeless people under the bridge next to the Salvation Army building. They were mostly farmworkers who had come to Cape Town from various parts of the countryside in search of greener pastures. Unfortunately, as with my mother and father, things did not work out for them as they should have.

I bought them food and then just stayed for a chat. One Sunday, it was somewhat chilly, I walked past my homeless friends, and they had erected an old wooden door on some stones. The 'table' was covered with a weathered tablecloth, and old knives and forks marked each place setting. The plates were cracked.

The menu offered bread and bully beef. I was asked to join them. The wine was pale and the 'glasses' were old cans that had been washed clean.

We sat down, held hands and Gertjie said grace, thanking the Lord for the food. After that, I ate one of the best lunches I'd had in a long time. We laughed and talked a lot.

92

THERE WERE RIVETING STORIES AT the Salvation Army. I asked one of the men how he'd ended up there. He told me that he could never really work, but he gave no reason for this. His mother had looked after him; they'd lived in a small flat in Green Point. He was an only child, and his mother was everything to him. They had loved each other so much, but she grew old and weakened. He held her one night and begged her to never leave him. She mustn't die. Her last words to him were: 'No, my child, Mamma will never leave you alone.' Then she died.

A man with a ducktail told me that every man who had ever lived in a night shelter knew one thing for sure: 'You must always have your own spoon. Always!'

Someone named Fanie sat and listened to opera in his room all day. Loudly. One day, when I walked past his open door, he said to me: 'I was in La Scala in my day, my dear. Yes, La Scala!'

A man in a pink suit and pink shoes, who spoke with a posh English accent, whispered to me: 'They're all negative in here. That's the problem with this place – you wake up one day and suddenly you've been here for three years.'

I realised that it was time for me to move on. It had been a year. Never again would I romanticise or look down on poverty in any way.

While living there, I read George Orwell's *Down and Out in Paris and London*. This paragraph struck me: 'And there is another feeling that is a great consolation in poverty. I believe anyone who has been hard up has experienced it. It's a feeling of relief, of pleasure, at knowing yourself at last genuinely down and out. You have talked so often of going to the dogs – and well, here are the dogs, and you have reached them, and you can stand it. It takes off a lot of anxiety.'

One afternoon, I started shaking and felt as if I were dying. My foot and leg were swollen. I was in severe pain. I called Graham and asked him to take me to his father, quickly – I was dying. I said I'd wait outside. We rushed to his father's surgery, and he looked at my leg and said I had chronic tissue inflammation, also called cellulitis. I was on the verge of organ failure.

He gave me an injection and a prescription for medicine that I had to take as soon as possible. I couldn't recover on my own; I had to go and stay with Graham and Athan so that they could keep an eye on me.

After a few days, I started to feel better. Then Graham suggested that I leave the Salvation Army. I could move in with them.

93

IN THE MEANTIME, INGEBORG PELSER from Jonathan Ball Publishers asked me if I would be interested in having my *Rapport* columns, 'Woorde wat wip', published. She approached the journalist and my friend Amanda Botha, who would select the best ones.

This was unfamiliar territory for me, and I felt nervous because it meant talking about the book, called *Binnekring van spookasems*, in public. My first talk was at the Book Lounge in Cape Town. I asked my friend Pierre de Vos to lead the conversation. The place was packed, and I was finished; my nerves were frayed. Would I swear too much? Would I talk too much kak? But the conversation with Pierre went well, and afterwards the audience could ask questions.

Dr Sonnenberg, my surrogate father, spoke in perfect Afrikaans about the book. It was an honour to have the man who had delivered me speaking with such authority.

Then a woman stood up and sang a line from the song 'You Can Call Me Al' by Paul Simon. There was a bemused silence. Then it came to me. After more than four decades, I realised who it was – Tannie Prins from the Durbanville children's home. The kind woman who had held my hand as I sat on the bench and waved goodbye to my mother. I jumped up and gave her a hug, and we both cried. Not only us, but most people in the audience shed a tear. What a special launch for my first book.

After my first collection of columns, a second volume appeared at Penguin, *Opstokers, fopdossers en tweegatjakkalse*. I stopped driving because I became too neurotic on the roads, and poor Athan had to drive me from reading circle to reading circle. I became very fond of Athan; he was like the brother I never had.

I've mentioned that apart from my fortnightly columns in *Rapport*, I also wrote obituaries for them. Over the years, this put me in touch with many interesting people. With so many South Africans having already emigrated, I had to contact family members in Paris, Sydney, New York and many other places. Also, on remote farms and villages, people who grieved and would cry over the phone. This was and is a challenge, and as an empath I am prone to absorbing their pain, which can be emotionally draining.

Often, you come across rude people, but among the most decent ones, for example, is Anneline Kriel, who gets back to me at once when somebody she knows has died. One bad-mannered person I had to talk to was Pallo Jordan, when his mother, Phyllis Ntantala-Jordan, died. I called him on his cellphone, and he started scolding me for phoning him in the middle of the night.

Huh? It was 10:00. He then shouted at me in Afrikaans: he was in America, what was wrong with me? As far as I knew, he lived in Oranjezicht. How should I have known that he was in America? He was furious and wrote me an email the next day in which he admonished me again. I would have been nice to people if I had lied for decades about having a so-called PhD, as he did.

I find many spokespeople in the ANC rude, abrasive, aggressive and arrogant. I have dealt with all political parties in South Africa, and not one other person has been as grumpy as the ANC's spokespeople. The Nats were the same, always abrupt and shouting, and look where that got them. I always remind myself that one day you're the cock on the catwalk and the next day you're a feather duster.

One day I asked Thabo Mbeki's gatekeeper for a quote on someone Mbeki had met in Dakar back in the day and who'd died. This guy told me that the 'president' was at the African Union and very busy, but he would try to track him down later that evening. I was on a deadline, and by the next morning, I still had not heard a word. I sent another message, only to be told: 'The "president" is busy, he's not sitting at the unemployed (sic).'

'Sitting at the unemployed'? Is that what the former president thought of the 30 per cent of his countryfolk who had no work? That they were loafing at social welfare, waiting for handouts? Unlike him, who was so busy and important? There was nauseating hubris in that statement. The more dealings I had with the ANC, the more I realised that they were not terribly fond of poor people.

94

DR SONNENBERG'S WIFE, JERRY, FELL ill and died, and he moved into the Berghof Retirement Village in Oranjezicht. He worked as a doctor right up to the age of eighty-seven, still doing house calls.

When he had been there for a while, the writer of *The Long Journey of Poppie Nongena*, Elsa Joubert, asked if I wanted to visit her over a cup of tea. She was elegantly dressed in white slacks, and was already in her nineties, but still fit at that stage. Elsa wanted to talk to me about my book *Binnekring van spookasems*. It was kind of her, as she was an established author and had made herself available to talk to a newcomer.

I asked her how she'd tackled her own writing when she was younger, and she told me she'd had to write when she could; there were no set times. She was a mother, raising children, so there was no fixed routine to her writing.

Elsa looked out of the window; downstairs, an ambulance had come to collect someone. 'Once they fetch you, you never come back,' she said. Elsa later died of a Covid-related illness at the age of ninety-seven. She was pushed across the road in a wheelchair, to the Cape Mediclinic; she never returned.

95

WHEN DR SONNENBERG CAME FOR dinner one evening, he arrived with a stranger. He introduced us to Mona Timlin, who was eighty-five. She was vibrant, charming and perfectly dressed in a long kaftan, with jingling bracelets on her wrists and red lipstick on her lips.

Dr Sonnenberg asked Graham if he would be okay with it if she was his companion. Obviously, we were all happy for him; he was lonely. After retiring, he had more time at his disposal. Mona made a fuss over him and cooked all his favourite meals for lunch; they even went to the Victoria Falls together.

One day, Graham, Athan and I were sitting in the noisy Vasco da Gama Taverna in Green Point when Graham's cellphone rang. It was his father. Mona had been admitted to hospital and had just died.

We went to scatter Mona's ashes on Signal Hill, where a short service, led by pastor Gordon Oliver, former mayor of Cape Town and friend of Dr Sonnenberg, was conducted. Graham's father looked sombre; he was on his own again. As we stood there, children were playing soccer and laughing in the background. New life, old life; a contradiction.

Three months later, Graham, Athan and I decided to go and eat at Damhuis in Melkbosstrand. It was a Saturday morning, and Graham and I went shopping quickly beforehand. We often went out for lunch on a Saturday.

At 09:30, we were back at the flat, and I asked Graham to wake Athan up so that we could get ready for the drive. Athan usually slept late on a Saturday. Graham called me: Come to the room, quickly. Athan lay on the bed, unmoving. We stood there looking at him.

'Is he dead?' Graham asked.

'Yes,' I said.

Only forty-two. Graham and I couldn't believe it. He tried massaging Athan's heart and giving mouth-to-mouth resuscitation. Nothing. Athan's body was still warm. We were devastated.

I hugged Athan, Graham too, and we told him how much we loved him.

I called all the neighbours and asked if they could come over. Graham called his father. We sat next to Athan and stroked him. I felt his short hair, which Graham had cut the previous day. Next to him on the bedside table lay the last book he'd read, the Grace Jones autobiography. He had still told me how much he'd loved it.

We then called all our friends, and many people showed up. Graham's father arrived with his partner, Dr Solly Lison, and a friend, Dr David Eedes. All three pronounced him dead and Dr Lison wrote out the death certificate: heart failure.

David pulled a sheet over Athan, then took a rose and laid it on him. Time felt thick and sticky, and Graham and I were crying. A vital part of our family had died.

Graham called one of Athan's sisters in Johannesburg to let his mother, Rene, know. The three sisters went to their mother with a pizza and pretended they were coming to visit her for a picnic. When they sat down, they told her the news. She needed to be sedated.

What was strange was that a week before Athan's death, I had asked him what he would like to have done with his ashes if he died. He mentioned that he wanted his ashes to be sprinkled on the Melville Koppies in Johannesburg, where he grew up.

In the meantime, we waited for the hearse to arrive; it took hours. Athan lay lifeless. One moment someone is still alive, and the next, that person will never speak to you again.

When they finally came to fetch him and put him on a stretcher, we just stood there and touched him for the last time. The two cats, Bingo and Daisy, followed the stretcher; they knew. As the hearse pulled away, they stared after it. We watched Athan drive away forever, down the hill, gone.

As the full impact of what had happened sunk in, Graham cried loudly on their bed, and I cried along. My heart went out to him. Athan had been his partner for thirteen years, and now he was gone. We cried at night for months and months.

We flew to Johannesburg with Athan's ashes. Graham's father came along. First, there was a short service in a building at his mother's retirement home. Johannesburg was hot that day.

Dr Sonnenberg and Rene hooked arms and walked up the steep hill of the Melville Koppies. When we got to the top, everyone stood still for a while.

We looked down and saw the house in which Athan grew up. As a child, he played on these koppies.

Graham took his ashes, looked out over the neighbourhood, and scattered them in the breeze. Away. Forever. We walked down the hill slowly. That afternoon, we flew back. Graham and I had to keep working. We had to continue living.

Mona and Athan were gone. At the dinner table, where there had been five of us, only three remained.

96

I T WAS THREE MONTHS LATER. Graham and I were again in the Vasco da Gama Taverna, when his phone rang. It was his sister, Pamela Blomefield. It was her husband, Tom. She'd got home and found him on the bed; she couldn't wake him. Now, he was on his way to hospital, where he would be diagnosed with an aneurysm.

There was no chance of survival. They would keep him alive until his children could come to say goodbye. For us, it was the end yet again; the end of another era, clichéd as it sounds.

Tom had an open mind and profound sense of humour. He and his family often invited us for lunches and braais. For decades, we visited them in the same house in Somerset West. The children grew up before our eyes. Three gone in nine months.

Then Dr Sonnenberg turned ninety and we held a big party for him at the Winchester Mansions Hotel in Sea Point. He bloomed, but Mona, Athan and Tom were not there. We felt the loss.

Afterwards, he arrived for dinner one night and had difficulty breathing. A few weeks later, he was diagnosed with lung cancer. When I went to visit him for the last time, we both knew why I was there. By that time, he was already weak, and a carer looked after him. I caressed his hands when I said goodbye. The very hands that had delivered me.

During this time, his daughter Penny came to stay with him over weekends. It was a Sunday morning when Graham and I were having breakfast in a small restaurant in the back streets of Green Point. His phone rang. Penny said he had to come. I stayed behind. Half an hour later Graham called me; his father had died.

The man who had been one of Sea Point's most beloved doctors for decades, someone who had saved thousands of people's lives and caught countless babies, was dead.

It was the year 2018: four deaths in one year. At a dinner table where five people had sat for many days a week, for years, two remained. Only two.

97

H OW DOES ONE END AN autobiography? With a clumsy metaphor relating to a real-life experience. That's why I've left this event for last, even though it happened in my early thirties.

I was thirty-three and happy. One morning, at *Cape Style* magazine, my editor came into my office and asked if I had a lot of work that day. I always had too much work, and she could tell that I was exhausted. She said she had a surprise for me. A new mineral water was being launched in the Karoo.

The rugby player Mannetjies Roux's son Pieter (now deceased) had discovered an underground water source on their farm near Victoria West. A group of journalists was invited to fly there in a small jet. We would spend the day on the farm and fly back the same evening. It wasn't a feature or an investigative piece, just something soft. I could do an interview, which would feature in the food pages.

I went to the airport, where the other journalists were waiting. The plane was small but spacious; we drank Champagne. Below us, the landscape looked beautiful; we flew over mountains and valleys. In Victoria West, we got into shiny 4 x 4s. Pieter and Mannetjies welcomed us warmly when we got to the farm.

Pieter took us to the source of the water, and we asked questions, after which they entertained us outside with tender and fatty Karoo lamb chops, which Mannetjies braaied.

We had a lovely afternoon, talking about the water, the food, all kinds of things. By 15:00, we had to get ready to go to the airport before the sun set. I climbed into the back of one of the 4 x 4s; there were four of us in the car. The rest of the guests were already on their way to the airport.

We were driving on a dirt road. I was sitting in the back, talking, when the car overturned and rolled a few times. The 4 x 4 landed on its roof. In the middle of nowhere. Delirious with shock, the driver ran aimlessly around the vehicle. I thought that the car was going to catch fire and wanted to get out of there as soon as possible. I opened the door, but when I lifted my leg, my foot was hanging by a thread: an open fracture.

I was bleeding to death. The driver was still running around, so I shouted at him to quickly take off his T-shirt and wrap it around my leg. I had to stop the bleeding.

I thought my leg would have to be amputated. That was if I survived. A car came past and our driver signalled for it to stop, but it just drove on. The sun was setting. Finally, another car came by, and this one pulled over. It was Pieter. He loaded me onto the backseat and rushed me through to the clinic in the village, where a doctor immediately stitched and attached the veins so that the blood circulation could normalise.

I was in so much pain, they gave me morphine. I drifted away.

When I woke up an hour later, I was outside on a stretcher, being loaded onto an emergency evacuation plane with medical personnel checking my condition. An oxygen mask was put on my face. Later, I found out that the runway at Victoria West's tiny airport had no lights. All the farmers in the area had parked their bakkies and cars so that their headlights could shine on the runway and the aircraft could land and take off safely.

In the belly of the plane, I began to fall asleep, with the engines whirring. I only woke up when we landed in Cape Town. I was loaded directly from the plane into an ambulance. It was a fight against time to save my leg and foot.

When I arrived at the old Chris Barnard Hospital in downtown Cape Town, the orthopaedic surgeon was waiting for me. 'My leg, just save my leg,' I begged. The look in his eyes was one of uncertainty.

I went into the operating room at midnight. When I regained consciousness, a nurse was standing next to my bed. 'My leg. My leg?' I asked.

Thank God, they could save it. But that was just the beginning. When the car rolled, I also broke my collarbone. Furthermore, there were lacerations on my skin, arms, hands and back.

I was confined to bed; my muscles ached. Morphine kept me sane. There were pipes everywhere. I couldn't go to the toilet by myself, and the embarrassment of having someone wipe and clean me was indescribable.

The days went by and when my wounds were better, I had to undergo the next operation. A piece of bone had to be cut from my hip and implanted into my leg. Then, we had to keep our fingers crossed that the bone would knit.

During this operation, a plastic surgeon had to close the open wound with a flap of skin that he harvested from my leg.

Right after the operation, I had to try to step on my foot, as it would help with the growth and knitting of the bones. A physiotherapist had to help me with this.

One day, the surgeon examined my leg and I could see that he looked worried. An infection had developed in the wound, and I had to be operated on immediately.

Although the infection cleared, I had to go in again for another procedure. This time, they drilled external fixators into my leg so that it could fully heal. After a while, I couldn't stand it in the hospital any more. I begged Graham to take me home, but the doctors opposed this. I kept nagging. Eventually, I was taken home by ambulance and carried up the stairs to my bed.

It was a mistake. I had to lie alone all day while Graham was at work. I could not read; I had to take too many pills to relieve the pain. I couldn't concentrate. And I couldn't get to the toilet myself; Graham had to help me. Everything was still sore from the accident, including my muscles. Then, one day, the leg started to hurt again. I went to the hospital in an ambulance. I had another infection.

Back to theatre, where they had to pump antibiotics into the infected area. Again, I lay in the hospital, again I complained and whined to go home, and again it was a mistake. Graham had to rush back to the flat during his lunch hour to feed me. He sometimes had to come home up to three times a day. I had to crawl to the toilet.

Dr Sonnenberg came every day for a month to clean my wound. By the fourth month, I could sit in a wheelchair. Being confined to a wheelchair changed my view of everything I had taken for granted. People glared at me. Entering most restaurants was an ordeal. The city is neither designed nor equipped for people in wheelchairs. After three months, I was able to upgrade to crutches. I had to learn to walk with them and often fell over.

During this time, the time of the crutches, I had to start working again, and it was difficult. I was simply too confused to concentrate properly. However, the chief editor in Johannesburg of both *Highveld* and *Cape Style* magazines was unapproachable and she forced me to work just as hard as before the accident. If the work wasn't up to standard, she summarily returned it. I got little sympathy from her. I was a burden, and they wanted their pound of flesh. I had to toil.

After three months on crutches, I could start walking on my own again. It wasn't easy; I had to learn to balance. My injured leg was thinner than the other one, and I limped.

After all that, I had to go back to the operating theatre so that the external fixators could be removed. The scars on my left leg, even after plastic surgery, were terrifying. But, today, I have full use of both my foot and leg. I can walk, though the injured leg is one centimetre shorter than the other.

The star during this tragedy was Graham, who had to take care of me, listen to my moans and groans, feed me and carry me around. Without him, everything would have been impossible.

So, I look back on my life with sadness and pride. Yes, as mentioned, the car accident is a clumsy metaphor to describe my trajectory. I was once bedridden, then I could move forward in a wheelchair, then I had to continue on crutches, fall a lot, get up again, and later I walked with a limp, even though it hurt.

What remains is a man with many scars on his leg, but he moves forward. He can walk. So much has happened. The days in Kloof Street, with my mother in the boarding house. Our poverty – bread and coffee when there was no money. Later, the orphanage, Oom Braam, who tried to help me, his wife Tannie Tina, who condemned me to the gutter.

Then there were the happy days in Sea Point with my mother, where I learnt to love fringe figures, poor people, and also how to enjoy life. Then my father's alcoholism and absence.

The first days of school, when I went to Sub A on my own, to Standard 6 on my own, and was expelled from matric. Important rites of passage that I had to go through without someone holding my hand.

The school from where I was expelled honoured me years later for my contribution to Afrikaans. It was a satisfying feeling that brought closure. Afrikaans, the language I didn't want to write in ... the irony.

The deputy head of the school during my time there, Barry Volschenk, met up with me after the publication of *Hoerkind* and unconditionally apologised for my expulsion. It takes a big person to do that.

Then, looking back at the army, the suicide attempt, the detention barracks and New York. Sleeping on benches in the Company's Garden. Yet, I fought back.

I finished my drama studies, earned extra money as a waiter, became a journalist, published short stories and poems, and four books.

There was the drug addiction that I was able to put behind me. Graham Sonnenberg was sent my way, because without him I don't know what direction my life would have taken. I can look back and think, jirre, I survived a lot.

Had all these things not happened, I wonder what type of person I would have been. Would I have had as much empathy for the underdog? Would I have been able to write with compassion? Would I have been less angry?

When I die, I will be able to look back on one hell of a life that wasn't boring. But there is still more to come: new experiences, more setbacks and, perhaps, successes. More deaths, but, as they say, we are all just walking each other home, hand in hand.

Finally, my friend Lien Botha had this dream about me: I'm riding a huge penny-farthing through the streets of Sea Point, my hair is thick and silver-grey, I lift my hand and I wave in the wind, I laugh, triumphantly.

Or do I?

Acknowledgements

Thank you to all those people who made my life hell. Bless the bastards, without you there wouldn't have been a book. To those who enriched my life, you know who you are.

Books by the same author

Binnekring van spookasems: Stories oor die lewe (Jonathan Ball)
Opstokers, fopdossers en tweegatjakkalse (Penguin Random House)
Hoerkind: Die memoires van 'n randeier (Penguin Random House)